THE
BEAR HUNTER'S
CENTURY

Books by Paul Schullery

THE
BEAR HUNTER'S
CENTURY

Paul Schullery

Dodd, Mead & Company
New York

America's sporting past is not all glory and adventure. As the text of this book suggests, some of our greatest hunters, being no more than men of their times, had attitudes about race and sex that we now deplore. Thus, the publisher and author of this book must specifically assert that though the book is a celebration of American sport, it should in no way be construed as a celebration of all the attitudes and beliefs held by past sportsmen. In the interest of historical accuracy, the sometimes racist remarks of early sportsmen have been presented in their originally published form. It would be dishonest, and a disservice to the sometimes troubling legacy of these men, to portray them otherwise than as they actually were.

Brief portions of Chapter One first appeared in *Safari*

Published by Dodd, Mead & Company, Inc.
71 Fifth Avenue, New York, N.Y. 10003
Manufactured in the United States of America

Designed by Laura Stover

First Edition

1 2 3 4 5 6 7 8 9 10

Library of Congress Cataloging-in-Publication Data

Schullery, Paul.
    The bear hunter's century.

    Bibliography: p.
    Includes index.
    1. Bear hunting—North America. I. Title.
SK295.S37 1988   799.2′774446   88-11811
ISBN 0-396-08923-2

To the memory of
A. Starker Leopold
(1913–1983),
sportsman, ecologist, conservationist, and friend

How infinitely small is the span of the written word as compared with the thousands of years in which man has fought the bear.

—Mikhail Prishvin,
Nature's Diary (1958)

The black bear is a timid, cowardly animal, and usually a vegetarian, though it sometimes preys on the sheep, hogs, and even cattle of the settler, and is very fond of raiding his corn and melons. Its meat is good and its fur often valuable; and in its chase there is much excitement, and occasionally a slight spice of danger, just enough to render it attractive; so it has always been eagerly followed.

—Theodore Roosevelt,
The Wilderness Hunter
(1893)

Whatever you do, save the dogs.

—Wade Hampton III,
c. 1857

Contents

Acknowledgments

I must thank many people for their help with this book. My agent, Richard Balkin, and my editor at Dodd, Mead & Company, Cynthia Vartan, had faith in an unusual idea; their enthusiasm was very important to me. My wife, Dianne Russell, helped with the project in many ways, especially with her careful reading and editing of the material.

I've been studying the history and lore of bears for more than fifteen years, during which time I've produced a couple of other books on the subject and gathered files that are much too heavy to lift comfortably. Though I have dealt with many libraries by mail and have done occasional research at others, I would like especially to thank the staffs at The Bancroft Library, University of California at Berkeley; The American Antiquarian Society, Worcester, Massachusetts; The Yellowstone Park Reference Library; the State Library, Harrisburg, Pennsylvania; the Hershey Public Library, Hershey, Pennsylvania; the Ohio State University Library, Columbus, Ohio; The American Museum of Fly Fishing, Manchester, Vermont; and the Montana State University Library, Bozeman, Montana.

I was given several useful leads in my study of David Crockett by James C. Kelly of the Tennessee State Museum, Nashville.

For my research on Wilburn Waters, I was given help by the following: Todd Estes, McClung Historical Collection, Knoxville Public Library, Knoxville, Tennessee; L. C. Angle, Historical Society of Washington County, Virginia; Margaret Davis, Abingdon, Virginia; Charlotte Lewis, County of Washington Public Library, Abingdon, Virginia; Alice Cotten, North Carolina Collection, The University of North Carolina at Chapel Hill; Jane Sumpter, Virginia State Library and Archives, Richmond, Virginia; Larry B. Keesee, State Library, North Carolina Department of Cultural Resources, Raleigh, North Carolina; Chaddra Moore, Tennessee State Library and Archives, Nashville, Tennessee; and Robert Jones, *Tennessee Historical Quarterly*, Murfreesboro, Tennessee.

Wade Hampton's bear-hunting adventures were made intelligible to me largely through the efforts of Paul Begley, an archivist with the South Carolina Department of Archives and History, Columbia, South Carolina. I suggest the magnitude of Paul's assistance in the text, but must thank him more formally here. His special interest in an unfortunately obscure aspect of Hampton's life made this chapter possible, and his reading of the manuscript improved it substantially. Elbert Hilliard and Madel Morgan of the State of Mississippi Department of Archives and History responded to my repeated inquiries, not only regarding Hampton, but also Collier and Bobo. Others who helped with my search for information about Hampton's bear hunting were: Maurice Cockerham, State of Louisiana Department of Wildlife and Fisheries, Baton Rouge, Louisiana; Patricia Bennett, Charleston Library Society, Charleston, South Carolina; David Hahn, The Museum of the Confederacy, Richmond, Virginia; Rose Lambert, Louisiana Historical Center, Louisiana State Museum, New Orleans, Louisiana; John Stanchak and Jim Kushlan of *Civil War Times Illustrated*, Harrisburg, Pennsylvania; Wallace Finley Dailey, Theodore Roosevelt Collection, Harvard College Library, Cambridge, Massachusetts; Herbert Hartsook, South Caroliniana Library, University of South Carolina, Columbia, South Carolina; and Dotsy Boineau, South Carolina Confederate Relic Room and Museum, Columbia, South Carolina.

William Pickett: Ellen Waggoner, Park County Historical Center, Cody, Wyoming; Ann Nelson, Wyoming State Archives, Museums & Historical Department, Cheyenne, Wyoming; Wanda Bond,

Greybull Museum, Greybull, Wyoming; and William C. Davis, the National Historical Society, Harrisburg, Pennsylvania.

Robert Bobo, Jr., of Clarksdale, provided me with copies of the family clippings and manuscripts relating to Col. Bobo, and read the manuscript of the Bobo chapter. Others in Clarksdale who helped were Linda White, Carnegie Public Library; Judith Flowers, Farm Press Publications; and Harry B. Abernathy, the *Clarksdale Press Register.*

William Wright: Dale Johnson, Maureen and Mike Mansfield Library, the University of Montana, Missoula, Montana; Dave Walter, Montana Historical Society, Helena, Montana; and Lee Silliman, Deer Lodge, Montana.

I was studying the outdoor adventures of Theodore Roosevelt for years before I began this book, and, as always, I must thank John Gable of the Theodore Roosevelt Association, Oyster Bay, New York, and Wallace Finley Dailey, Theodore Roosevelt Collection, Harvard College Library, Cambridge, Massachusetts, for their continued enthusiasm for what must seem to them a singularly narrow field of historical endeavor.

Ben Lilly: David Brown, Phoenix, Arizona: Amy Ouchley, Tallulah, Louisiana; Frederick R. Rinehart, Boulder, Colorado; William Richter, Eugene C. Barker Texas History Center, The University of Texas at Austin; and Catherine T. Engel, Colorado Historical Society, Denver, Colorado.

Holt Collier has found an able champion in Sandra Dahl Desmond, now of Long Beach, California. Through her efforts to preserve the history of Roosevelt's southern hunts, and her independent research into the life of Collier, she has performed a great service to sporting history. She provided me with many clippings and documents I might not otherwise have found, and filled in many gaps in my knowledge of the history of Collier's career and home country. Her reading of the manuscript of the Collier chapter was so thoroughly annotated that I wished there was room for two chapters on Collier. Others who helped with Collier: Mamie Younger, Baton Rouge Genealogical and Historical Society, Baton Rouge, Louisiana; Harley Metcalfe III, Greenville, Mississippi; Joseph T. Reilly, Washington County Historical Society, Greenville, Mississippi;

Georgie Cooper, La Habra, California; Gretchen Fairbanks, Louisiana State Library, Baton Rouge, Louisiana; Donald Finn, Natchez, Mississippi; and Kelby Ouchley, Tensas River National Wildlife Refuge.

Others who helped in some way were Lance Olsen of the Great Bear Foundation, Missoula, Montana; Jim Casada of *Sporting Classics;* Dr. Mary Meagher of Yellowstone National Park; and Charles Fergus of Port Matilda, Pennsylvania.

Introduction

HE historians we grew up with—the people who wrote all those deadly high school textbooks we lugged around—were fond of assigning names to various periods of time: the Roaring Twenties, the Age of Enlightenment, the Middle Ages, and so on. Sporting historians have been inclined to do the same thing. In organized sport, for example, there are similarly recognized periods—the "bareknuckle era" of boxing, the 1950s Yankee dynasty. But "outdoor" sports have their ages, too. In my book *American Fly Fishing: A History* (1987), for example, I point out that the Victorian era was a time of great innovation and growth in American angling, and that the years since 1970 have seen a remarkable acceleration in fishing's technological and theoretical development. Sports are just like most other human activities. They go through times that, when we look back on them, seem to have been unusually lively or dynamic, just as they go through times when it seems little is happening. Sometimes interest in a sport lags; at other times it surges. (It's also true that sporting historians, like other historians, often disagree about just what causes these changes.)

But it's always a little arbitrary, this process of picking a slice of time out of history and calling it an age. When I refer to the hunters in this book as having lived in a golden age, or in a bear hunter's century, (roughly 1820–1920) I know that I am creating an artificial boundary of time that is not perfect. But it is an instructive boundary nonetheless. These men lived in a special time, and under special circumstances, and now earn our attention not only for what they did but for what their lives tell us about our own age.

I don't mean to suggest, for example, that there was no bear hunting before Crockett; hunting was a popular sport in the New World even in the 1600s. Nor do I propose that bear hunting was past its prime when Holt Collier died in the 1930s; there are states where bear hunting is better now than it has been for a century, and modern science and management techniques are doing wonders for some bear populations.

What I do propose is that the century or so bracketed by the hunting careers of Crockett and Collier, including Waters, Hampton, Roosevelt, and the others I've written about here, was different, and was different in a very exciting way. Any good conservationist knows that it was an era of extraordinary waste. But it was also an era of extraordinary plenty. There were fewer hunters, and more game. There was the opportunity for one man to accumulate a life experience and firsthand knowledge of bear hunting that no hunter (and only a few guides) could even imagine today. There also was (as there had not been before Crockett's time) an enthusiasm not only for having these experiences, but also for chronicling them. The result of that enthusiasm is the exciting documentary legacy of books, letters, articles, and other evidence that makes books like this possible.

I was attracted to the study of these men because in the history of American sport, bear hunting has a peculiar magic. It is not as dangerous as hunting the big African animals, but danger isn't really at the heart of the magic.

It has to do with the near-humanness of bears, I suppose. I can't say for sure, never having shot a bear, but it appears to me (and to others who have studied the subject), that the animal's bipedal habit has as much to do with its mystique as game as does its occasional capacity for eating someone. African lions are much more dangerous, woodcock are much harder to hit, wild turkeys are probably more wary. The bear has something else going for it. It *can* be dangerous, which separates it from most other North American game, but rarely is; many thousands of bears are no doubt killed for every one hunter hurt in return. It must have to do with the image—the strange, primatelike form rearing up to investigate, trying to decide whether to flee or attack, trying to sense what is wrong, trying just as we would to figure out what's going on—that reminds us a great deal of ourselves. Add to that image all we've absorbed in nursery rhymes, outdoor magazines, movies, and conversation, and you've got an animal that could not avoid becoming the subject of some pretty wild yarns.

That wild, unruly lore is why I'm drawn to the lives of these long-dead hunters. In my many years of reading and writing about bears, I've become intrigued with many things, but with nothing more than the men who hunt them. They are a diverse lot, ranging from a governor and a president to paupers and social misfits. They hunted on horseback and on foot, from stands and on the trail. They hunted with rifles, shotguns, and even knives, with and without dogs. They hunted for a remarkable number of reasons, some not even applicable to today's bear hunters. They killed bears for the bounties, they killed bears to rid the forest of "vermin," they killed bears because killing bears upheld family tradition, they killed bears in what amounted to manhood rites, they killed bears as practice for war. They killed bears because they were hired to do so by men with reasons of their own. But most of all, and at the same time as they held all the other reasons, they killed bears for sport.

Sport. It is a term abused almost beyond recognition, misunderstood almost beyond recovery. If bear hunting, or hunting in general, is new to you, I can't hope to fully acquaint you with the term's historical complexity and cultural richness in this brief introduction. In its way, sport is as involved and challenging a concept as is art; both are products of human culture, both are subject to a thousand subtle influences as the society that created them evolves. But I do have sympathy for the newcomer, the person who has had no opportunity to become acquainted with such matters as the evolution of sporting ethics. And so I offer this word of warning: do not equate the word *sport* too directly with the word *fun*. There is much fun in sport, but there is much more as well. Sport is a difficult notion, one involving self-imposed trial, tightly defined codes, competitions both subtle and direct, and a host of subjective, emotion-based judgments that few good sportsmen have even tried to articulate. The gleeful child thrilling to her first catch of a sunfish is having a world of fun. The hunters in Faulkner's powerful tale "The Bear" are a grim, unlaughing crowd participating in something that only they, in a moment of fond reminiscence, might call fun, but that all of them in that story reveal to be sport in its deepest and richest form.[1] One of the things that makes these bear hunters so interesting to me is the variety of ways in which they define—either through their actions or through their words—just what sport means to them. This is a book of hunting stories rather than a study of social attitudes, but here and there I may interrupt myself to consider the attitudes and philosophies of the hunters; the way they thought is as important a part of their story as is the way they hunted.

Which leaves me with only an invitation to offer before we meet the hunters. There were many others besides these. There are many more today. In my search through the literature of bear hunting, I ran across dozens of them whose stories might be dug out by the interested, and I've used both the notes and the bibliography of this book to get you started if you want to read more. I've spent many a happy, distracted hour in files of ancient sporting periodicals getting to know the fishermen and hunters of previous generations. I certainly don't claim that the few men I've featured here are the only ones worth our attention.

What of Boone, the great trailmaker himself? We know he earned his place as one of our first great hunters, and there is a substantial documentary trail already laid out by historical scholars. Or Johannes Plott, who came to America in 1750 and brought with him the ancestors—he called them "cur dogs"—of the great Plott hounds, still known today as terrific bear dogs.[2] Or Allen Hasselborg, who early in this century lived alone for many years with the great bears of Admiralty Island, Alaska, and who was immortalized in John Holzworth's fascinating book *The Wild Grizzlies of Alaska* (1930). Or "Bear Howard," an enormous, mysterious man who killed bears obsessively in Arizona in the years after the Civil War.[3] Or Edwin Grimes, a rafting pilot on Pennsylvania's Allegheny River in the late 1800s, who shot his two hundredth black bear on his eightieth birthday.[4] Or Don José Ramón Carillo, a Spanish Califor-

nian who fought and killed grizzlies with a light sword. Or Ramón
Ortega, who *lassoed* two hundred grizzlies in southern California in
the mid-1800s.[5]

I've run into many of these people, some almost completely forgotten now, all of whom participated in the grand tradition of bear
hunting. Some were game butchers and market hunters; some were
not only good sportsmen, but were also exemplary students of bear
natural history. Some contributed to the decline of bears; others saw
to it that bears flourished. But all left us tales of their exciting, peril-
ous, amusing, and even silly encounters with bears, and all left us an
opportunity to share, at least vicariously, a bit of the outdoor life of
another age. I think you'll agree with me that theirs was a good time
to be a bear hunter.

Chapter 1

David Crockett

ONE reason that bear stories are so attractive is that bears, like very few wild animals, reach us from clear across the emotional spectrum. From the slapstick comedy of cubs to the tragedy and horror of a mauling incident to the spiritual force of encountering a grizzly bear in its remote wilderness home, we respond to bears in many ways, often in more than one way at once.

Consider the proportions of stories in outdoor writing. For every book of deer hunting stories, there seem to be ten or so instructional books that concentrate on teaching the hunting of deer. But for every book on how to hunt bear, there are many that just tell stories about bears and bear hunting. This may be partly because a lot more of us will someday actually shoot a deer than will ever have a chance to shoot a bear; there are a lot more people *needing* instruction in deer hunting. But these strange proportions are surely a lot more complicated than that.

They're more complicated because the bear is more complicated, or, more precisely, its image is more complicated. It's the only truly dangerous North American big game. Yes, it's true that if, when, and where walrus and alligators are game, they can kill people, and it's true that moose, elk, and even white-tailed deer have the physical equipment to kill people. But the former are too rare, and the latter too rarely lethal in their actions, to stir the peculiar mixture of fear and exhilaration that

1

bears do. And, of course, that bear stories do. It takes a good bear-mauling story to curdle the blood of your average urbanite.

A famous woodcut of Crockett, published in *Davy Crockett's Almanack* for 1837; ironically, this woodcut was based on an engraving portrait of an actor, James Hackett, who portrayed a character named Nimrod Wildfire in the popular play *The Lion of the West*, a play about a Crockett-type frontiersman. Inventions like Wildfire added to the Crockett legend just as Crockett himself did, with tall tales soon becoming entangled with historical realities.

And yet bear lore is also a rich source of humor. How can it be that we find bear stories so amusing, given the reality of the bear's talents for violence?

I think this seeming contradiction is possible because the stories so rarely contain the tragedy. For example, there's the tale of two fishermen who hiked into a backcountry lake. Just as they arrived and were getting their waders out of their backpacks and putting them on, a huge grizzly bear rushed from the forest across the lake and circled the lake toward them. Both men took off, but after running a few yards one of them stopped and began digging around in his pack. The other stopped, puzzled, until he saw the man pull a pair of running shoes out, take off his waders, and put the shoes on.

His companion screamed at him, "What are you doing? You can't outrun a grizzly bear!"

And his friend, just finished tying the laces, jumped up and answered, "No, but I can outrun *you*."

And there it ends, before anything ugly takes away the fun. But even when something awful does happen, it still doesn't intrude if the story is intended to be funny. Consider the three scientists, one each from England, France, and Czechoslovakia, who were invited to America to study grizzly bears. Before leaving for the high country in western Montana, they left word that they would be back in two weeks. After three weeks went by without their return, their hosts, American scientists, went looking for them. They found their camp, utterly destroyed by bears, but no sign of the foreign scientists. Two of the Americans wandered off down the trail, looking for sign of the foreigners. Suddenly a pair of grizzlies, a male and a female, charged from the brush. The scientists, heavily armed, shot the female, at which point the male turned and ran away. The rest of the scientists rushed to the spot, and quickly performed an autopsy on the dead female bear. Sure enough, both the British and the French scientists were in her stomach. After a moment's thought, one of the Americans said, "I guess that means that the Czech's in the male." A good joke can make almost anything laughable, even death by grizzly bear.

But we are rarely occupied with dark thoughts of tragedy when we read bear stories. It is true that we are attracted to good bear stories as often because they are thrilling, adventurous, or scary as because they are funny, but whether the story is funny or frightening we are reacting to the tension and suspense in the events. Laughter comes from nervous release, or fictional misfortune, as well as from a simply funny situation. That tension between humor and danger is a key element of traditional American bear stories, and is exemplified in this fragment of dialogue from the folklore of the bear:

"I have caught a bear."

"Bring it here."

"It won't come."

"Then come yourself."

"It won't let me."[1]

"Fatal Bear Fight on the Banks of the Arkansaw," from *Davy Crockett's Almanack*, 1837.

But, of course, there is even more to the best bear stories than humor and adventure. There is a mythical quality about bears, a quality only rarely applied to a great old buck deer or bull elk. These animals are seen to take on personalities, and not necessarily personalities we can understand. Bears inspire storytellers today much as they inspired native Americans, who invested the bear with near- or superhuman attributes, so that many bear stories also have an element of the supernatural in them, of a bear that is a little more than a bear.

Our modern tradition of bear stories might best be said to have sprung from the outdoor humorists and journalists of the early years of the nineteenth century, from what scholars now refer to as "the big bear school of humor." The centerpiece of this rich and vastly entertaining literary tradition is a story called "The Big Bear of Arkansas," by Thomas Bangs Thorpe, first published in *The Spirit of the Times* in 1841. Thorpe's story contained many if not all of the important elements of the modern bear story, including a bear of human traits, abundant exaggeration, an almost epic hunt, and humor. Thorpe also well understood the spiritual potential of the bear; his bear "loomed up like a black mist, he seemed so large." The hunter in the story does finally kill the bear, but he realizes with humility that he only killed it because it allowed him to: ". . . that bear was an unhuntable bear, and died when his time had come."[2]

"A Desperate Fight Between Two Women, One Man, and Two Bears," from *Davy Crockett's Almanack*, 1838.

And it is with Thorpe and his big bear school—that is, with the great flowering of sporting writing that occurred in this country before the Civil War—that we arrive, suitably prepared if by roundabout means, at the subject of this chapter. For no other man has come more to represent the outrageous, marvelous, and enduring qualities of bear stories in the American mind than David Crockett. A remarkable combination of backwoodsman, self-promoter, and raconteur, Davy Crockett personifies the best and the worst of the bear story. The best, in that he lived some great bear adventures; the worst, in that his tales of bears form part of the foundation of unreliability upon which the modern bear-lore tradition uneasily rests.

This isn't simply a matter of Crockett's bear stories' being doubted. The man himself was almost totally dismissed from historical reality until recent years. A string of serious, even distinguished, historians and students of American culture gradually developed the view that Crockett was mostly a legend, unknowable through the haze of adulation and mythologizing that had surrounded him and his adventures.

That all changed in 1956, when James Shackford's *David Crockett, the Man and the Legend* was published.[3] Shackford (who died before publication) sorted out the tremendous amount of spurious material attributed at various times to Crockett and identified the one authentic work, *A Narrative of the Life of David Crockett of the State of Tennessee*, which Crockett had written in collaboration with Kentucky congressman Thomas Chilton. An assortment of other supposed autobiographies, as well as the many short-lived "almanacs" that used Crockett's name, were a part of the greater Crockett legend but had only occasional relevance to the actual events of his life.

It was—and is—this larger body of material, however, that gave us much of the modern public idea of Crockett as a bear hunter. Most of us know, thanks to the theme song of the Walt Disney movie, that Crockett "kilt him a bar when he was only three," and that he could grin down a bear. I don't know where the story of his infantile hunting originated, but reports of his grinning skills date at least from the 1830s. An account of them appeared in one of the biographies of which Crockett did not approve (though apparently he helped the author prepare the book and then later had a falling-out with him), Mathew St. Clair Clarke's *Life and Adventures of Colonel David Crockett of West Tennessee* (1833).[4] Clarke had Crockett making the following speech in one of his political campaigns.

Though it is about coon hunting rather than bear hunting, and though its authenticity is now uncertain, it is a perfect example of the sort of yarn then most fashionable in the Old Southwest of America before the Civil War, and it is good evidence of why Crockett—the real person—became so difficult for later historians to identify. He and his admirers wrapped him so thoroughly in this manner of tale that he almost became the person of his stories, a figment of his own imagination. Here is Crockett, speaking of his opponent:

Yes, gentlemen, he may get some votes by *grinning*, for he can *outgrin* me, and you know I ain't slow—and to prove to you that I am not, I will tell you an anecdote. I was concerned myself—and I was fooled a little of the wickedest. You all know that I love hunting. Well, I discovered a long time ago that a 'coon couldn't stand my grin. I could bring one tumbling down from the highest tree. I never wasted powder and lead, when I wanted one of the creatures. Well, as I was walking out one night, a few hundred yards from my house, looking carelessly about me, I saw a 'coon planted upon one of the highest limbs of an old tree. The night was very *moony* and clear, and old Ratler was with me; but Ratler won't bark at a 'coon—he's a queer dog in that way. So, I thought I'd bring the lark down, in the usual way, *by a grin*. I set myself—and, after grinning at the 'coon a reasonable time, found that he didn't come down. I wondered what was the reason—and I took another steady grin at him. Still he was *there*. It made me a little mad; so I felt round and got an old limb about five feet long—and planting one end upon the ground, I placed my chin upon the other, and took a *rest*. I then grinned my best for about five minutes—but the cursed 'coon hung on. So, finding I could not bring him down by grinning, I determined to have him—for I thought he must be a droll chap. I went over to the house, got my axe, returned to the tree, saw the 'coon still there, and began to cut away. Down it come, and

I run forward, but d—n the 'coon was not there to be seen. I found that what I had taken for one, was a large knot upon a branch of the tree—and, upon looking at it closely, I saw that *I had grinned all the bark off, and left the knot perfectly smooth.*

Now, fellow citizens, you must be convinced that, in the *grinning line*, I myself am not slow—yet, when I look upon my opponent's countenance, I must admit that he is my superior. You must all admit it. Therefore, be wide awake—look sharp, and do not let him grin you out of your votes.

Crockett the hunter was often placed by his exploiters and admirers in the context of preexisting tales. One good example involving bear hunting is a story that appeared in *The Crockett Almanac* of 1840. These almanacs, like many others of the day, were small, cheaply produced compendiums of information on many subjects especially of interest to rural people, farming and related topics being often most important.[5] Crockett's almanacs (which were

Two engravings from *Harper's New Monthly* magazine, October 1855, suggest the degree to which the public and even respectable periodicals "humanized" and misunderstood bears.

produced with no benefit to or involvement by him) were distinguished from most others by their stories of wild animals and hunting, often casting Crockett in the lead role. Plots were lifted from any convenient source, whether it be local lore, ancient literature, or even the editor's own imagination. Thus did Crockett appear in the story of the bear and the swallows.

According to this tale, Crockett found a flock of swallows that had wintered in a hollow sycamore, or at least he suspected they had spent the whole winter there. In order to investigate their nest, he climbed the tree, lowered himself into it, and found himself immersed in a winter's worth of swallow manure. Before he could figure out how to escape from this predicament, a bear appeared at the opening and, for reasons only the bear knew, proceeded to descend into the tree, rear first. Crockett, finding the sunlight suddenly blocked by this great bruin bottom, bit down hard on the bear's tail, at the same time giving it a poke in the "posterities" with his knife to encourage it to climb. The frightened bear climbed out, hauling Crockett with it to freedom. Out of kindly feeling for the favor it had done him, Crockett then let the bear go.

There is much more to David Crockett than these tall tales, however entertaining they may have been to generations of readers; the very existence of such a body of myth and lore around one man must be some kind of proof that the real person, whoever he might have been, was really something. It's true: he was. Though not the Paul Bunyanesque figure of legend, and though not the nationally famous success story portrayed in the movies, David Crockett deserved to become an American institution simply for what he was, rather than for what we have made him. Richard Hauck's recent biography summed up the meaning of Crockett's life for us:

> . . . its unheroic details are fascinating in their own right, since they show so clearly that life on the frontier was often nasty and ridiculous rather than glorious, and because, taken together, the details reveal how a tough, honest, and intelligent backwoodsman could be shredded in the machinery of politics and enmeshed in the absurd complexities of history. . . The biography of Crockett is not the history of an institution builder, conqueror, king, or president. Instead, it is a story of a common man who fought with uncommon style.[6]

David Crockett was born in eastern Tennessee, along the Nolichucky River, on August 17, 1786. It was a raw country for settlers; only nine years before his birth, his paternal grandparents had been killed by a Creek raiding party. One of nine children, son of a tavern owner, Crockett ran away from home at age thirteen, went to Baltimore, dreamed briefly of going to sea, and eventually returned home after a three-year absence; his family had long given up on him, and were thrilled to have him back. His adult life, from the time of his first marriage in 1806 to his death thirty years later at the Alamo, is a classic saga of frontier hardship, drudgery, romance, and adventure. A man who in thirty years was a justice of the peace, a militia officer and participant in some arduous and gruesome Indian wars, a state legislator, twice married, three times elected to Congress from Tennessee, lionized by the press and exploited by savvier politicians, "talked about" for the presidency, and at most times engaged in the fatiguing process of surviving in a rough country would seem to have little time left for hunting. But he was as much a hunter as he was anything else; perhaps he was more a hunter than he was anything else. It is certain that his fame as a homey philosopher, patriotic American, and politician was built on his frontiersman's image. Again, to quote Hauck, ". . . at the center of the various portraits of America's frontier heroes is the dynamic picture of the bear and the hunter locked in mortal combat, tooth against knife."[7] It was, indeed, a dynamic picture, and, whatever else may or may not have been true about Crockett, there is no question that he is the man in that picture.

We don't know when Crockett killed his first bear. We do know that he was admired widely among his friends and neighbors for his skill as a hunter; numerous stories of his shooting prowess have come down in the Crockett tradition, including one involving his fighting at the Alamo. (It is said that he very nearly picked off Santa Anna one day when that hotheaded general, knowing he was out of range of the Texan's rifles, wandered unknowingly within Crockett's range, and the Tennessean almost made an incredibly long shot that would certainly have changed the course of the movies, to say nothing of history.)

We do know that, by the time Crockett served in the Creek Wars between 1813 and 1815, he was an excellent and ardent hunter. He often helped feed his troops, perpetually short of food, with wild game, and in one episode described in his *Narrative*, he expressed frustration on not being able to shoot a bear he got a glimpse of, "for of all the hunting I ever did, I have always delighted most in bear hunting." He had been hunting bear for some time by then; in 1811 and 1812, while living in Lincoln County in south central Tennessee, he had done a great deal of hunting, though he was disappointed that "the bear had been much hunted in those parts before, and were not so plenty as I could have wished."

No tales of Crockett's bear hunts have survived from the years immediately following the war, but it is clear that by then he was a famous hunter. In his early political campaigns, he often feigned the sort of simplistic forthrightness he knew his constituents would approve of by casting himself as merely "an ignorant back-woods bear hunter." In 1821, high water on Shoal Creek wiped out his mill and distillery there, and Crockett, his oldest son, and a friend "cut out for the Obion," even wilder country in northwestern Tennessee. This was across not only the Tennessee River, but nearly to the Mississippi, some of the wildest country left east of the great river. In 1822, Crockett returned home, gathered up his family (including his second wife, Elizabeth), and took them to a homestead on the south fork of the Obion River, where among other things he at last found bear hunting that measured up to his hopes.

In the spring, prior to bringing out his family, Crockett found time to kill "a great abundance of deer" and ten bears, though he left no account of any of them beyond their numbers. (We can't always trust his stories of hunting, but there is no special reason to doubt numbers like these, about which he had no reason to lie and which seem perfectly believable now.) After his family arrived, Crockett fed them mostly with wild meat and his first corn crop, but in midwinter found himself short of both powder and food. After a harrowing trip through the snowy forest for powder—falling in icy streams, numbed to the bone by a sudden arctic cold—Crockett set out early in the new year for meat.

Two companions set out the same day for turkey, but Crockett allowed that "I was for larger game." He confided to them that he had "dreamed the night before of having a hard fight with a big black nigger, and I knowed it was a sign that I was to have a battle with a bear; for in a bear country, I never know'd such a dream to fail." (Alas, Crockett was a man of his time, and no doubt as bigoted as many other whites; blacks were often compared to "lower" life forms, including both bears and primates.)

His trip grew harder as the first day wore on; heavy sleet covered the brush and the ground, making going difficult for him and his dogs. He shot a couple of turkeys, making the day less than a waste, but was taking a rest in dejection when his lead hound suddenly scented a trail and vanished in full cry, leading the rest of the pack off with him. Crockett trudged hopefully along behind, hauling two turkeys besides his flintlock (one of his rifles was reported to weigh twenty-seven pounds, so the carrying of a long-barreled weapon of this sort was no easy part of hunting).[8] Several times he came up on his dogs, only to find them barking up empty trees. Under the circumstances, Crockett found this a less than fulfilling kind of sport:

> They served me in this way three or four times, until I was so infernal mad, that I determined, if I could get near enough, to shoot the old hound at least.

He held off, though, and, catching up with the pack one more time, he spotted them across a meadow, hot on the heels of a huge bear, the largest he had ever seen in his years in bear country. It was such an imposing animal that these seasoned dogs would not risk closing with it. Instead, they merely tagged along behind, noisily pestering it. Crockett suspected that they were so frightened by the size of the bear that it was that fear, not stupidity, that caused them to stop with no bear in sight until he caught up with them each time. They wanted some help with this one.

Crockett quickly deposited his gobblers in a tree and, in a hot rush of adrenaline at the sight of the bear, tried to catch up with it, a task made difficult by the dense, icy tangle of cane bordering the meadow. But soon the dogs treed the bear in an old oak. Crockett made his way through the thicket to within eighty yards of the tree, waited until the bear was facing him, and put two balls into the bear's chest. The second shot dislodged the animal, which tumbled heavily into the midst of the pack, probably not quite what the pack had in mind. Crockett rushed in, knife in one hand, tomahawk in the other, hoping to rescue the dogs, but at the sight of him the bear dropped the dog it had caught when it landed and came for the hunter. Crockett retreated "in all sorts of a hurry," retrieved his flintlock, and with a third shot "killed him good."

Crockett had to recruit his friends to skin the bear and carry the meat home; he estimated the bear at six hundred pounds, the second largest he ever killed (the largest being 617 pounds, apparently an actual measured weight). Again, I see no reason to doubt him in this; as many bears as he killed in his life, he certainly had the odds in his favor to come across one this large.

Crockett's bear was the black bear, *Ursus americanus*, one of the most widely distributed of American game animals. In the Old South, they were the delight of sportsmen and an enormous nuisance to settlers. There were as yet no laws whatever regarding their hunting; the concept of "harvesting" them as a game animal was utterly foreign. Bears were something to be killed, sometimes out of necessity, sometimes out of sport, sometimes for both reasons. Even in parts of the country that had long been settled, the bear did not have the sporting status already, even in the early 1800s, assigned to trout, or grouse, or deer. There were ample stirrings among outdoorsmen by then, stirrings that would eventually become a powerful game-conservation movement. Those stirrings would protect many other animals long before they would do the black bear any good. The bear was a varmint, and it was not only necessary, it was almost good citizenship, to go out and kill a few. That alone must have made David Crockett, in the eyes of his neighbors at least, one extremely good citizen.

And yet I think that historians and biographers have overstated the necessity of bear hunting in Crockett's life. There is a tendency among scholars, perhaps because they want to make sure readers understand Crockett and don't write him off as a mere game slaughterer, to overexcuse Crockett's hunting.[9] He did it to feed his family, to feed his neighbors, to rid the woods of pork killers and corn thieves, they tell us, and that's all true. But this was a man who said, plainly and proudly, that he loved to hunt bear. Whatever his domestic circumstances, however much or little he needed meat or skins (which he sold), he was out there having a big time.

In the fall of 1825, for example, when Crockett had a break from his business (at that time he was making pipe staves), he set out to get enough bear meat for the winter. His own needs were met quickly, but soon a neighbor stopped by to ask his help. The bears were too thick over where he lived, the man complained, and they were also very fat. Crockett couldn't pass it up; in two weeks they killed fifteen bears, salting down the meat for winter, and Crockett went back to work on building boats to take his staves down the river to market. But, and here Crockett reveals his sportsman's sense of priorities, he was soon restless, and "at length couldn't stand it any longer without another hunt."

Crockett took his youngest son, then about nine, and returned to the area of the fat bears. The first day they got three, which they salted down. They built a scaffold to keep the meat out of reach of wolves, then set out on another day's hunt, the sort of day that reveals not only what extraordinary action a hunter could expect back then, but also what a robust ecological setting it must have been to support bears in such numbers. First, his dogs chased a large male bear right into camp, where some other hunters were resting at the time, and took the bear. Then Crockett and his son followed their dogs into a canebrake, where the pack split. Crockett and his son each followed one group of dogs, Crockett finding his group swarming over a young bear that was quickly dispatched with the butcher knife. He heard his son fire, and soon found that he, too, had taken a bear (this is a nine-year-old boy, remember). There was no time for skinning it, as one of their dogs had hit another hot trail. Soon a third bear was located, treed by one dog, and shot.

Father and son skinned the bears and began looking for a campsite for the night when the dogs scented another trail and the chase was on again. Night came on too soon, however, and the hunters had to let the dogs go, make camp, and wait until morning. The dogs, he found out later, did tree a bear some five miles away near a farmhouse, and they kept the farmer up all night with their baying. Crockett found it more amusing than the farmer did, no doubt:

> In the morning, as soon as it was light enough to see, the man took his gun and went to them, and shot the bear, and killed it. My dogs, however, wouldn't have anything to say to this stranger; so they left him, and came early in the morning back to me.

John Gadsby Chapman's oil portrait, "The Backwoodsman Davy Crockett," painted in 1834. (Courtesy of the Harry Ransom Humanities Research Center, the University of Texas at Austin.)

By the end of the week, Crockett and his son had taken seventeen bears, and stocked up the larders of a local settler whom Crockett happened upon while trailing a bear one day. The hunt was finished about New Year's Day, 1826, before bad weather set in. But as soon as he got home, Crockett was invited on another hunt. Again, he found himself unable to say no, though there was now plenty of meat stored away, and though he was afraid the bears would be holing up soon, which, as he said, they did by going into "their holes, in large hollow trees, or into hollow logs, or their cane-houses, or the harricanes; and lie there till spring, like frozen snakes."

Bear habitat in the South is different in important ways than it is in other parts of the country or, better put, than we imagine it to be when we think of the storybook bears we all grew to know as children. Terms like "canebrake" and "harricane" are exotic, but are not especially meaningful to the modern reader, especially those who think of bears as spending their winters in neat little caves (which is not always true in other parts of the country, by the way). Crockett's use of these terms— canebrake and harricane—is wonderfully complicated.

The Obion country, near what is now called Reelfoot Lake in northwestern Tennessee, had been hit by massively destructive earthquakes only a few years before Crockett got there, and the quakes were followed by powerful storms. The whole region must have had the appearance of a jackstraw maze, with open crevices and downed timber everywhere. When Crockett used the term "harricane," suggests historian Hauck, he might have been referring to the "hurricanes" that swept the region, or he might have been combining meanings—hurricane, harried cane, or some other combination—to make his own term. The common southern wild grass called cane grew in dense thickets, often appearing in openings in the forest canopy that had been created by the storms. The effect of this joining of natural catastrophes and faunal abundance was an almost impenetrable tangle that was as full of good cover for bears as a place could be.

Crockett was right that they sometimes denned in logs, sometimes climbing up dead trees to hollows several yards off the ground. They also would dig out a little hole under a downed tree, or just bed down in a good thick brake. Black bears are known for the informality of their winter arrangements, and it seems no surprise to me that Crockett's dogs were able to stir up so many bears even in winter. Unhunted and unafraid, they would be fairly easy to find by the first hunters in an area.

Some of Crockett's bear lore involving bear denning has been challenged by historians, incidentally. In his *Narrative*, Crockett maintained that when the bears came out of their dens, after being there from January to April, "they are not an ounce lighter than when they went to house." Shackford, in his annotations to the excellent University of Tennessee Press edition of the *Narrative* (1973), casts Crockett's remark aside as "simply a good story, contrary to known fact." This hardly does justice to Crockett's observation.

In fact, many other hunters over the years have made similar statements. No doubt the belief that bears don't lose weight during denning has become a part of bear folklore, but it isn't really suitable for a historian to presume too much expertise on this point; Crockett saw a lot more bears than Shackford did.

First, some of the old sporting writers said that though newly emerging bears *appeared* as fat as when they went in the den, their fat was spongy and not solid, so that the appearance was not reliable. Even today, scientists are still learning about the physiology of denning and hibernation, and though they have shown beyond question, with captive bears, that bears do lose weight during denning, there are still questions to be answered about how the process works.

Second, Crockett's observations may have had another sort of basis. A recent study of black bears in the Great Smoky Mountains National Park, not far south of Crockett's birthplace, revealed that following emergence in the spring, these bears lost weight for several weeks.[10] Crockett, not having any systematic way to measure the weight of a bear when it denned and when it emerged, may have actually seen one newly emerged bear over a period of a few weeks after it emerged and noticed that it did indeed get smaller then. From that he may have erroneously assumed that it did not get smaller during the winter. It is not hard to imagine someone making such an assumption. In any event, Crockett's observations should not have been so offhandedly rejected.

On the other hand, I think we can safely say that some of his bear-hunting stories—that is, some of the stories that we can pretty much count on being from the pen of him or his chosen coauthor—are less than reliable. Or, to be kinder to Crockett, some of his stories are wild enough that even he would be surprised to know that we believed them without suspicion.

Such is the case with one bear Crockett tangled with that winter of 1825–1826, though at least one early Crockett researcher claims to have located a reliable person who knew Crockett and corroborated the important elements of the tale.[11] There's nothing impossible about it, so I'll leave it up to you to accept or reject.

In this one, Crockett heard his dogs pick up a trail late one afternoon. He followed them on foot, through the heavy downfall as best he could in the gloaming that quickly became night. His progress was now impeded by both the thick timber and the darkness, which caused him to fall in "cracks made by the earthquakes." (I wonder about those cracks, because most earthquakes don't produce great numbers of fissures, but rather cause slumps and faults; there seems no question he found some kind of holes, so I'll just give him the benefit of the doubt and call them cracks, too.)

After three miles of this, Crockett waded an icy creek, but was so overheated from his struggles that it caused him "no great inconvenience." At that point, he could hear his hounds bark treed, and knew the bear was held at least for a while. But his way was blocked, first by a steep hillside and then by the absolute blackness of the night, which caused him to misjudge his direction and climb a ridge far past the baying dogs.

When at last Crockett reached the pack, he found they had a large bear well up a poplar. His attempt to find some wood for a fire was described in the sort of understated humor that occasionally appears in his book:

> . . . I set in to hunting for some dry brush to make me a light; but I could find none, though I could find that the ground was mightily torn to pieces by the cracks.

Which was to say, of course, that he stumbled around in the dark some more, occasionally stepping off into these accursed holes that pocked the forest floor.

Giving up on the light, Crockett took aim at what he thought was the form of the bear high in the tree. The first two shots only seemed to move the dark blob a little higher up the tree. But as he was reloading to try again, the bear changed direction and was suddenly next to him, involved in serious discussion with the dogs. Crockett drew his big butcher knife, fearing immediate attack, but the dogs kept the bear busy while Crockett, squinting frantically into the roaring, squealing, thrashing darkness, could only make out the shape of one white dog ghosting here and there in the midst of the fray. It might have gone badly for the dogs had the bear not slipped into one of the cracks, a narrow slot about four feet deep. There it was better able to hold off the dogs, and there Crockett was able to get close enough to it with his (finally) loaded gun and put a shot into it, though in the darkness he only hit a foreleg.

At the shot, the bear jumped briefly from the crack, but the dogs forced it back down. Crockett, still stumbling around in the thick darkness, could sometimes "tell the biting end of him by the hollering of my dogs," but seemed able to do little else. He had for some reason put his gun down, and now, the shrill bear-and-dog fight ringing around him, was groping on the forest floor in search of it. He found instead a long "pole," presumably a tree branch, and, writing with a detachment that he couldn't have felt at the time, "concluded that I would punch him awhile with that. I did so, and when I would punch him, the dogs would jump in on him, when he would bite them badly, and they would jump out again." In the heat of this exercise, it occurred to him that the bear just might stand for a little company in the crack, so as his dogs distracted the biting end of the bear, Crockett got in behind it, crept up on it, and gave him "a dig with my butcher," luckily finding the heart almost right away.

It was now the middle of the night, and what makes this story most suspect is Crockett's conclusion that, in order to keep from freezing to death—soaked, exhausted, without fire or shelter—he spent most of the night climbing a tree again and again in order to wrap his arms and legs around it and slide down so that the friction would warm him. A hundred times or more, he claimed to have done it.

By the end of the hunt, Crockett's total for the winter was fifty-eight bears, either killed by him or killed by other members of his party at his guidance. By the end of the year, his total was 105. It is the only year for which he gives us such a total, so we have no way of knowing his lifetime totals.

Nor do we have any way of knowing just what other adventures were involved in all those "bear fights." Most he did not describe at all, and some are mentioned only briefly, as in the story of one bear shot in cane so thick that visibility was limited to a few feet. The excitement of such hunting, with a bear likely to burst upon the hunters from somewhere closer than the end of their flintlocks, must have been one of the reasons Crockett kept at it as he did; there was surely nothing in farming to compare with *this*.

And that may be the best place to leave him. Crockett would go on to political success followed by comprehensive defeat, then to historical immortality at the Alamo, where, according to the most recent scholarship, he was captured by the Mexicans and executed shortly after the battle. But that was another Crockett, a public hero rather than a private sportsman. So let's leave him, instead, there in Tennessee wilderness, in frozen buckskins and sucking mud, wrestling his way through a soft wall of twelve-foot-high cane, his wildly barking dogs surrounding some stout old boar bear in a walking bay only yards away, yet completely obscured by the "harricane." Leave him there, before the inevitable political disappointments of his later years and the tragic glory of Texas, when he was still more man than myth, still more a simple bear hunter than an American institution.

Chapter 2

John Adams

ONE summer morning about 150 years ago, up in the rugged mountains near what would become the border between Canada and Washington state, an adult grizzly bear—for the sake of narrative, let's say it was a male, and for the sake of the picture, let's say it weighed, oh, about six hundred pounds—was working its way through a dense thicket, feeding where it might. Bears are wandering feeders much of the time, except when they find some unusually good concentration of food such as at a salmon stream or a berry patch, so it's probably safe to say that this bear was out shopping. There was lots to eat. The bear may or may not have scented the deer that were grazing nearby, but it almost certainly hadn't scented another pair of travelers until they nearly collided with him.

The other travelers were as unlikely a pair as that forest had seen. One was itself a bear, a yearling sow, which would have made her something less than 150 pounds, maybe much smaller. Her companion was a man of forty-some years, in the worn, stained garb of the mountain man, with long, flowing gray hair and an equally gray beard. The two had just taken some moments crawling through the brush, sneaking up on the grazing deer. The man, whose name was John, had only a pistol and a knife with him; he'd left his rifle with his companions earlier in the day. The bear, whose name was Lady

Washington, was held on a short chain and collar. She was following—quietly, obediently, almost devotedly—behind John as he crept through the bushes toward the deer.

Just as John got close enough to risk a shot with his revolver, it occurred to him—why then and not before I can't imagine—that this was grizzly bear country and he should not be out wandering around without his rifle. At that, John made "Lady" understand that he wanted to reverse field, and the two of them began backing, ever so quietly, away from the deer. This seemed to work well until he heard Lady, behind him, nervously snapping her teeth and snorting. Turning, he looked over her and up—and up—into the face of the big bear, towering over them as it stood on its hind legs only a few yards off.

"The Frightened Grizzly," running from Adams and his tame bear.

The hunter assumed the worst: that this bear was looming over them about to attack. Actually, standing on hind legs is not an attacking position for a bear; it is not able to move quickly on two legs. Bears generally stand on hind legs in order to see better, or in order to appear more imposing to an enemy (the latter, I assure you, works well for them). Truth is, this bear had just been surprised by the sudden appearance and odd behavior of this pair of strangers. It was probably trying to figure out what to do next.

So was John. Even had he been sure the big bear was not aggressive, no one wants to be this close to a grizzly bear in the wild. He grabbed the loose chain from around Lady's neck and picked out a nearby tree to which he could run, but he was not at all sure how to protect his bear companion even if he were able to save himself. He suspected that his pistol probably wasn't up to dealing with a bear of this magnitude.

As he stood there, the big bear came down on all fours, stepped even closer, and rose again. Getting a better look, I'd guess, but hardly what the hunter hoped for.

Finally, the waiting was too much for John, whatever the bear felt about it. Firing the pistol into the air, rattling the chain with his other arm, and giving an inspired whoop, he instantly replaced the bear's curiosity with fright. It turned and bolted for cover.

There we see the last of them for the moment, the massive grizzly crashing panicked through the undergrowth, with the little bear and her companion charging along behind in a chorus of bellows, growls, and clanks, as if there was nothing they would rather do than catch that bear.

One of my favorite stretches of highway on the interstate system is Route 80, as it goes west out of Sparks and Reno, Nevada. The road climbs quickly up and over Donner Pass, and then descends almost as quickly to the great inland valley of California, on into Sacramento, and then to the Bay Area. It's a ride I never make without excitement about the setting: not the ski chalets, gas stations, and endless developments, but the obvious glory of the land itself. Within a few hours, I pass through a full range of life zones, a kaleidoscope of ecological opportunities, and I see, not the crowded housing of today, but the wonder that this place must have been 150 years ago.

Then, when steelhead and salmon ran into every little coastal stream all the way down to Ensenada, when elk and deer ranged over vast, unbroken tracts of wilderness, when native Americans and Spanish settlers lived with relatively little impact on the whole scene, and when the state's now-extinct symbol, the grizzly bear, roamed both the valleys and the high ranges, California would have been worth the walk. If I could choose to be a sportsman any place and time in the modern history of North America, I would surely choose California a few years before Sutter's Mill.

The most famous of all California bear hunters did not beat the great gold rush of the late 1840s and early 1850s; in fact, he was part of it. But he soon removed himself to remote parts of the state, and wandered out of the state to equally remote wildernesses elsewhere in the "far West," so that his experience wasn't far off from what it would have been in those same areas thirty years earlier. For his purposes as a sportsman and businessman, John "Grizzly" Adams, "The Wild Yankee," got there in time.

What he found was, by the standards of anyone interested in bears for sport, study, or simple admiration, a paradise. Even the towns of California had a tiny population. In 1848, the settlements contained fewer than twenty thousand people, including all Spanish Californians, native Americans, and "foreigners."[1] No accurate records exist of the numbers of grizzly bears in the state at that time, but the number was unusually high because of the introduction of Spanish livestock, including cattle, sheep, and horses. Great numbers of free-roaming stock eventually became more or less wild, and, as they replaced the more wary native grazers on parts of the range, they also provided bears in the low country near the coastal settlements with an enormous new source of food. Storer and Tevis, in their superb book *California Grizzly* (1955), estimated that by the 1830s there were upwards of ten thousand of the bears in what is now California. They lived well and they occasionally provided Californians with wild sport. But within a century they would be completely gone, victims of an appalling surge of development that still pretty much continues.

But it was really something there for a while. Spanish ranchers found in the grizzly the strongest sort of sport. They hunted on foot and horseback, with swords, lances, and firearms. They developed skills at lassoing the bears with their *reatas,* capturing and hauling them back to the towns and ranches. There the bears were pitted against almost equally wild bulls in events that would not meet with the approval of most modern sportsmen (including me, I must say), but that must have been spectacles of almost Roman proportions. Many things changed when Americans began pouring into California in the decade before the Civil War, but the California grizzly bear's role as the center of spectacle did not. No one took better advantage of that role than Grizzly Adams.

I find Adams both more frustrating and more intriguing than Davy Crockett. He is more frustrating because although his stories of bears, being mostly of a now-extinct subspecies, are potentially of greater value to modern students of bears than Crockett's tales of eastern black bears, his reliability as a storyteller is frequently questionable and occasionally poor. He is intriguing because he sometimes revealed a knowledge of bears that was nothing short of amazing, and because, however much or little we may trust him, he, more than any other hunter in this book, brought evidence of his special skills to town.

The trouble was that Adams, rather like Crockett, saw no real harm in spinning tales. To him, his real achievements as a hunter were impressive enough to make him confident, and his reputation was solid enough that he saw no harm in embroidering it a little, adding a few percent to the total here and there.

There is no question Adams did this. Here is the recollection of that great huckster P.T. Barnum, who hired Adams after the hunter had left California and gone to New York for his last hurrah:

> "Old Grizzly Adams" was quite candid when, in his last hours, he confessed to the clergyman that he had "told some pretty large stories about his bears." In fact, these "large stories" were Adams's "besetting sin." To hear him talk, one would suppose that he had seen and handled

everything ever read or heard of. In fact, according to his story, California contained specimens of all things, animate and inanimate, to be found in any part of the globe. He talked glibly about California lions, California tigers, California leopards, California hyenas, California camels, and California hippopotami. He further declared he had on one occasion, seen a California elephant, "at a great distance," but it was "very shy," and he would not permit himself to doubt that California giraffes existed somewhere in the neighborhood of the "tall trees."[2]

Or course, Adams knew he had a gullible audience in New York, where so few people could challenge him on the basis of their own experiences, so he was more at ease with wild yarns there. But even while in California, he showed himself to be unreliable. When he related his life story to the San Francisco journalist Theodore Hittell, he left a trail of confusing, contradictory details. *The Adventures of James Capen Adams, Mountaineer and Grizzly Bear Hunter of California* (1860) is a wonderful, exciting book, but it is also frustrating. Richard Dillon, a modern Adams scholar and author of a very helpful (if often adulatory) biography of Adams, defined the essence of the problem faced by historians trying to unravel Adams's story. Dillon, in discussing the difficulty of locating the sites of Adams's various Sierra camps, put Adams in a tradition as famous for prevarication as that of the Old South hunters like Crockett: the western mountain men.

> Pinning down the exact whereabouts of Adams's camps and cabins is not always easy because the old codger was, to say the least, "careless" with fact. It is not that Adams was a liar, *per se*. He simply saw little point in distinguishing hard, cold, facts from wishful thinking. Like Jim Bridger or the Negro mountain man Jim Beckwourth, or, for that matter, like almost any mountain man worth his salt, Grizzly Adams simply could not resist making a good story better. He apparently did not keep a diary but trusted to memory and his mind played tricks on him, too.

This led him in one instance to give a single hunting companion three different names—Drury, Browne and
Carroll—at three different points in his memoirs. This
kind of reminiscing can give regional historians and biographers the very vapors.[3]

Even more vapors were to be had when historians looked beyond
Adams's own story (which was told to other journalists in other versions inconsistent with what he told Hittell[4]) to external evidence.
There they found, for example, that though Adams frequently mentions his brother William, and occasionally even referred to himself
as William, there was no William in his family. Worse, they found—
though the public has not really absorbed this yet, forty years after
the scholarship establishing it was published—that his name was not
James Capen Adams.[5] For reasons that have never become entirely
clear, he chose to use the name of a brother that did exist, rather than
his own name, which was John Adams.

But for all of that, Adams showed, at many points in his dictated
narrative, a remarkable knowledge of some wild animals. It seems to
me that, although too many things happened too fast on some of his
trips—rather like modern television nature programs in which
every two minutes some other rare species is shown passing the
camera: "Oh look over there, Marlin, it's a herd of cougars . . ."—
every now and then he offered a judgment or an observation of
singular wisdom. For example, Adams anticipated modern behav-
iorists by a century in his comments on the facial expressiveness of
his captive bears. In commenting on one named Jackson, he suggested that he could read his bears' attitudes on their faces:

Certain philosophers have taught a science, called
physiognomy, in which they profess to find an index to
character in the form of the face. If character were an at-
tribute of the face, there might be some plausibility in the
science; but hardly otherwise. It is certain, however, that
the face is frequently an index of the emotions; there seem
to be certain muscles called into action by certain feel-
ings; and an experienced eye will seldom misinterpret this

language of the features. The repeated exercise of these muscles may give a cast to the face, indicative of the general character, and thus partially sustain the claims of physiognomy; and, so far, the science applies as well to beasts as men. When, therefore, I say Jackson had a pleasant countenance, I mean that his face expressed a good and submissive spirit.

Recent research has shown that bears do have quite a range of facial and other "signals" (just as domestic animals do, of course), but Adams seemed to have worked out a good bit of it on his own.[6]

Another instance of his wisdom, one I find amazing, is an observation Adams made about bear teeth:

> ... in this connection, it may be stated that the grizzly bear generally cuts its teeth at about two months. It does not have full teeth till its maturity, at about two years of age, though it has a dangerous mouth at six months. Every year a ring is added to its tusks,—the first ring being for the second year; and as the animal sometimes reaches the age of fifteen or sixteen years, a corresponding number of rings are found.

This is a fascinating statement for several reasons, including Adams's observation that California grizzly bears bred (assuming that's what he meant by "maturity," and other statements in the book support this assumption) at age two (which I take to mean during their third summer). That is much younger than most present grizzly bear populations, which may not successfully mate until five, six, or seven years of age, but it is not impossible that in the food-rich California valleys, grizzly bears came of age much sooner. Adams claimed that Lady Washington was successfully mated during her third summer, and he had a cub named Fremont that he said was the product of that mating.

But the greater wonder of this statement is Adams's comment about bear teeth. A century later, scientists, using microscopic-examination techniques, would show that bears can be aged accurately by counting the number of layers of cementum over their teeth, just as trees can be aged by counting the rings.[7] Adams knew this, but I can't imagine how.

And, as if all that isn't enough to get from one paragraph, have you ever heard a more useful and powerful phrase than "a dangerous mouth"?

Adams's entire life story is thick with such stuff: great yarns, entertaining language, fascinating lore. It is as dismaying as it is intriguing. Just as we wonder at the strange things he somehow knew, we are made suspicious by the things he seemed ignorant of.

But we have no choice but to accept the historical reality of his achievement; the proof is incontrovertible. If someone tells you he caught a nine-pound bass and let it go, you may say, "Gee, that's great, right, good for you," and feel comfortable not believing a word of it. But if he says he captured a thousand-pound grizzly bear and maybe you don't want to stand quite so close to the cage, then you have to think twice about writing him off as a phony. Adams was many things, but he was not a phony.

Research by the great California historian Francis Farquhar shows that John Adams was born in Medway, Massachusetts, on October 22, 1812.[8] He was taught shoemaking, but gave it up as a young man (he said he gave it up when he attained his "majority," which may have meant at age twenty-one) to hunt and trap in New England. It was there he developed many of his skills at capturing animals—cougars, wolves, foxes, and others—while working for wild-animal shows or zoos. He had not been at this too many years when, according to the story he told Hittell, he was terribly mauled by a tiger in one zoo and forced by the resulting health problems to return to shoemaking. Adams spent fifteen years at it in Boston, then lost all his money in a risky investment. Just as this disaster struck, he learned of the discovery of gold in California, so, leaving a wife and three children, he joined the crowd of equally irresponsible hopefuls heading west.

Adams's life from 1849 to 1852, while traveling to California and working there, is only a blur in his narrative; he claimed to have been rich at times, and to have suffered mightily at others. He did some bear hunting, enough to earn a reputation as a hunter, but we know little more than that. We do know that in the autumn of 1852, he abandoned his hopes of civilized success, loaded a wagon with his few belongings, and went back to the life he had loved most, that of a hunter. He built a cabin on land he would eventually buy, in the then-wilderness foothills of the Sierras just about where the town of Long Barn now sits.

Adams was quite a sight. Hittell, who would see him only four years later, when Adams's great Sierra adventures were concluded, described him:

> He was a man a little over medium size, muscular and wiry, with sharp features and penetrating eyes. He was apparently about fifty years of age [actually, he was only forty-four]; but his hair was very gray and his beard very white. He was dressed in coat and pantaloons of buckskin, fringed at the edges and along the seams of arms and legs. On his head he wore a cap of deerskin, ornamented with a fox-tail, and on his feet buckskin moccasins.

As near as can be told, Adams held to that outfit the rest of his days, even after moving east in 1860.

We've heard so much about Adams and his many wilderness adventures, and about his amazing skills. He has come to epitomize the mountain man almost as much as has Jim Bridger. And yet he did what he did, and earned his strange immortality, in only four years of actual adventures.

Four years. But then, they were really full years. Not only did he hunt the Sierra extensively, he made several arduous trips—to what is now Washington, Idaho, and western Montana in the summer of 1853, to the Great Basin in 1854, to hunt the Russian River near the coast in 1855—to other parts of the West. And everywhere he went, he seemed to find bears.

Adams's first winter in the Sierra was a fairly quiet one, but the following spring he determined to become a trapper and hunter of commercial proportions, selling live animals, hides, and meat as he could. It was this decision that started him on his way to Washington Territory, by wagon and muleback, for his first summer's hunting. He traveled steadily along the foothills with his companion/ assistants, a young Texan named William Sykesey and two young Indians, twenty-year-olds that Adams referred to as Tuolumne (pronounced "*twa*-lum-nee") and Stanislaus, after their respective tribes. Up through the Klamath Basin they moved, into what is now Oregon, keeping east of the main Cascade range, then east up the Columbia to the mouth of what is now the Snake (and what he called "Lewis's River"). Then on into the border country of eastern Washington, Idaho, and western Montana they went, where Adams found friendly Indians and lots of bears.

It was here Adams made his first important capture, one that would serve him well throughout his career. He was camping near a wide, open valley where he had seen ample bear sign, and on a slope he found a den occupied by a sow with two yearlings, which he decided to capture. Locating a trail the bear family used on its way to and from their feeding grounds, Adams had little trouble ambushing the bears and putting a ball from his Kentucky rifle (a large rifle, about .54 caliber) into the sow, causing a charge that he then answered with his "Tennessee" rifle, a lighter weapon (probably in the neighborhood of .42 caliber). The second shot, fortunately for Adams, hit the sow's brain and killed her instantly.

The yearlings, which he assumed he would simply round up, proved much more troublesome than their mother had. After chasing them with his lasso for a while, Adams suddenly found himself under attack by these two "truly formidable" little bears. Between them they certainly outweighed him (Wyoming grizzly bears today average over 150 pounds by late fall of their second summer), and they had those dangerous mouths, as well as powerful, raking claws. The hunter found himself in what to him was a "ludicrous situation": so fiercely attacked by the young bears that he climbed a tree to escape. When the bears tried to join him in the tree, he had to beat on their paws to force them to retreat, and it was only because they were young and impatient that they soon deserted him, returning to their mother's body and giving him time to escape.

It took several days, and more embarrassments, before Adams finally lassoed one of the cubs after a long chase on horseback. In only a few weeks, what with some stern discipline and complete control over the cub's food, he had a companion for life, one who would stand by him in such awful circumstances as the encounter described at the opening of this chapter, one who would eventually learn to carry a pack for him, one who would provide him a backrest and warmth on long nights in open camps when he lay facing his small fire.

Most of Adams's scrapes with bears, whether grizzly or black, were not so amusing, and certainly not so rewarding for both bear and man. He seemed to have a knack for stumbling onto grizzlies at close quarters, and an equal knack for getting out of such altercations with a good part of his skin.

Adams certainly didn't lack courage. One black bear, first shot from ambush by Sykesey, received only a minor wound that "seemed rather to madden than disable," causing the bear to rush around a hillside tearing up the vegetation and looking for the cause of its pain. Getting few opportunities for a clear shot at the racing bear, Adams put a ball from his rifle into its chest, only stunning it momentarily; it fled for heavy cover. Without hesitation, Adams was after it, dropping his rifle and pulling out his Colt revolver and knife as he ran.

But the bear, perhaps hearing pursuit, wheeled and faced Adams just as he closed with it, and for an instant the man and the bear stared at each other in the heat of fear, pain, and anger. Then the bear rushed him, and Adams's hasty pistol shot hit the bear square in the face, his only hope at such short range.

It often wasn't that easy. While in Washington Territory, Adams and his party fell in with three hunters from Texas, one of whom, Kimball by name, Adams had met during his crossing to California. They persuaded Adams to help them hunt, and together they found much game. But one night the camp was invaded by a large grizzly bear that took flight when Adams awoke, saw it, and tossed a hasty shot in its direction. Another of the Texans, a man named William Foster, became agitated about hunting it, almost to the point of rushing after it in the dark. But Adams wouldn't let him. In the morning, however, Adams did lead the three of them in search of the bear. In short order, it was sighted some distance off in company with two cubs.

Adams stationed Foster in a good position to shoot, insisting he not fire until the others reached a nearby hillock, from which they could provide supporting fire. As Adams feared, Foster was too impatient to wait, and took his shot while the others were still climbing the hill. The shot was followed by a tremendous roar that, as Adams said, he recognized as the roar a bear makes as it attacks.

By the time Adams had rushed to Foster's aid, it was too late. The poor man had panicked in the face of the charge and attempted to climb a tree, but the bear grabbed a foot and pulled him down, jumped astride him, and disemboweled him with one swipe of its claws.

Adams took the opportunity of this episode in his narrative to offer yet more enduring wisdom about bears, saying that he had lectured Foster and the others repeatedly about what to do if caught by a bear. Playing dead, he maintained, was the best course of action, the most likely way to get the bear to let you alone. Again, he was right. Modern researchers have established that in statistical terms, at least, playing dead is the least likely way to get mauled by a bear that's got you.[9]

Anyway, the cubs and the sow began to sniff at the dead man, perhaps showing some appetite, so Adams found a tree to steady his rifle against and shot the sow high in the chest. A second shot, in the head, finished her. By then the others had joined him, and five or so of them fired together to kill the cubs, finishing one of them with knives after it did some damage to Tuolumne. Foster was buried on the spot.

It's easy to underestimate the drama of trying to shoot a grizzly bear with the rifles that Adams carried. At least it was easy for me, until I fired such a rifle and read some more detailed accounts of what was involved in such shooting. First, there was the smoke. You took your shot, trying to hold the big thing still as you touched it off and waited through the little delay before the shot. Then, as the smoke and sparks flew from both ends of the barrel, your view of the grizzly bear just then charging you was at least partially, and probably totally, obscured, just when you'd most like to be able to see it. At that point, with your eyes smarting and bear-charge sorts of noises getting louder, you tried to peek around the cloud that hung there in front of you, so that you could tell if it was time to dodge, run, or climb a tree.

I am struck, as I read Adams's accounts of his "bear fights," with the extent to which they really were fights—that is, by the number of times killing a bear required what could only be called close work. I'm sure this was partly a function of the less powerful firearms of the day. His larger rifle should have had little trouble killing a bear at a couple hundred yards or more, provided it hit the right spot. But a slightly wounded bear can cover a couple hundred yards in a matter of seconds, while the hunter needs that much time and more to reload. A tree seems to have been almost as essential a piece of gear as a rifle in this kind of hunting. As well, Adams spent a lot of his time in tight places—heavy cover, narrow ravines, and so on—and only rarely had a clear shot at a bear from a long distance. So it was quite often that it came down to getting right up against the bear and shooting or stabbing it.

That sort of thing happened on another hunt with the Texans. Shocked by the death of Foster, the others were properly cautious. But caution will only help so much. Adams, Sykesey, and Kimball located another sow with two cubs in a wild oat field on the edge of the forest, and Adams sent the two others to surround the animals, so that all three hunters could fire from cover more or less at once. Adams was creeping through the oats for a clear shot when he heard Sykesey's rifle fire. Getting to his feet, he saw the sow rushing across the field toward the frantically reloading Sykesey. As Adams yelled for Sykesey to find a tree, Kimball reached his position and fired into the rear of the bear, which then turned and charged in *his* direction. Adams, at first not sure Kimball could reach a tree, ran toward him and the bear, but as soon as he saw Kimball make it to a nearby oak, he again hid in the oats.

Kimball had dropped his rifle, and had only his pistol and knife. In Adams's accounts, revolvers were often of no real worth against bears (they remind me of the advice given the sheriff in the cowboy movie spoof *Blazing Saddles*, when he was trying to arrest a brutish bad guy played by Alex Karras: "Don't shoot him—that'll just make him mad"). So the man was essentially helpless, and the bear seemed about to try to climb the tree. Grizzlies, despite popular mythology to the contrary, do sometimes seem able to climb a tree, especially if the tree has ladderlike branches and the bear of the moment is angry enough.

Adams, seeing his friend in peril, rose up and fired his rifle, hitting the bear in the neck but, sure enough, only making her mad. She renewed her attempts to climb, even as Kimball unloaded his revolver in her direction (though he was so frightened his aim might have been poor). Adams, yelling encouragement to the treed man, ran to the tree, got *under* the climbing bear, and fired a fatal shot that stretched her out on a low limb for a moment before she slipped loose and fell heavily to the ground.

The other thing that strikes me about so many of these accounts is that they involve sows with cubs. Sows with young are among the most secretive of bears, the least easy to see in the wild most of the time because they are so cautious and protective. It doesn't surprise me that Adams saw so many, considering the wildness of these bears and the relative shortage of mortal enemies in their range. But it is disappointing, now, when the animal is so thoroughly exterminated, to hear of the most fruitful part of the bear population being run through like this. I know that development and human population growth, as well as agriculture and industry, also helped to wipe out the bear. But in today's world of isolated, threatened little remnant populations of grizzly bears here and there in the Lower Forty-Eight, it's hard to see this luxurious abundance of breeding sows—the most critical element of the population—being blasted away.

The late A. Starker Leopold, one of the leading California naturalists of recent decades, made the following comments in his last book, *Wild California* (1985):

> One of the people that contributed most to the extermination of the grizzly bear was Grizzly Adams. I was amused to watch the television series about him where he was set up as a sort of St. Francis in buckskins. In point of

fact he was one of the deadliest of hunters in California history. He spent all his time shooting grizzly bears for the tallow, which was sold at very high prices, and for the meat.

"Adams and Ben Franklin," an engraving from the original edition of Hittell's biography of Adams.

Starker could have added that Adams also hunted them for their hides, and to capture them for sale; an animal trapped and carried away live is removed from the breeding population as effectively as if it were killed.

At the same time, Adams loved bears themselves, and, when he gave them a chance, they got pretty fond of him. Lady Washington wasn't the only bear to stick by him in a fight; in fact, it was another of his captive bears, Ben Franklin, that became most noted for helping the hunter.

Adams caught Ben in the summer of 1854, near the famous Yosemite Valley in the heart of the Sierra. Ben became his favorite, the most responsive to his training, described by Adams as "the flower of his race, my firmest friend, the boon companion of my after-years." He had good reason to admire the bear that much.

In the spring of 1855, when Ben was only a little more than a year old, Adams moved his camp and his now-large collection of animals to Corral Hollow, in eastern Alameda County, not more than thirty miles from present-day Oakland. But he needed to make a quick trip to his old camp in the Sierra, so he set out with Ben, now thoroughly trained, and a greyhound named Rambler.[10]

Traveling by wagon, they soon reached his camp, where Adams enjoyed some hunting before deciding to return to Corral Hollow. As Adams and the two animals were walking back to his wagon one day, just about to leave the area, they passed through a dense stand of brush, Adams in the lead. At arm's length, Adams heard a branch snap, turned, and was smashed to the ground by a great old sow grizzly. (He said she had three cubs, and so I assume he surprised her, causing her to react with the grizzly's typically offensive defense.)

At the sound of the bear, Adams had swung his rifle toward her, but the same blow that knocked him down knocked the rifle from his grasp. He hit the ground unarmed and partially scalped by her claws. He seemed to have no chance of escape, but before the bear could cover him she was herself covered, as Rambler launched himself at a hind leg and Ben went for her throat. While the surprised sow dealt with these two new adversaries, neither of which had much hope of lasting long against her, Adams slipped from underneath the fight, grabbed his rifle, and, seeing Ben being bitten and mauled, gave a desperate yell. As the big bear turned toward the noise, he put a ball in her heart, then jumped in and followed the bullet with his knife, repeatedly stabbing her to make sure she was dead.

"The Dead Grizzly and Her Cubs," the former killed and the latter captured by Adams.

Finding Rambler okay, and wiping the blood from his own eyes, Adams turned in time to see Ben disappear down the trail to camp, where he found the bleeding, frightened yearling huddled under the wagon. Adams, overcome with gratitude, treated the bear's wounds before attending to his own.

His own were probably more serious. Over the years of his hunting and training of bears, he received numerous head injuries, some even more serious than this one. These injuries eventually killed him while he was still fairly young, though no doubt all the other knocks he got—clawings, buttings, bites, and even one case of near-fatal poisoning—contributed to his gradual decline in health, too.

But it wasn't so much his skill at killing bears that made Grizzly Adams famous as his skill at capturing and taming them. The big bears known variously as grizzly and brown bears have long been known for their adjustment to training by humans; various Europeans had been training brown bears for centuries. Adams was very good at it, and though he didn't teach his bears the sort of circus tricks common among captive European bears, he did teach them more practical things. Visitors to his famous "museum" in San Francisco, established in late 1856, noticed that the fur was thin on the backs of his bears; when asked why, he explained that they were used for pack animals. They not only carried his blankets and gear, they were docile enough to carry freshly killed game, or pull logs for the building of his traps. He could even ride them.

The quality of this discipline seemed at times unsurpassed by even the best-trained modern hunting dog. Ben's devotion and obedience were best illustrated by Adams in telling of the killing of a pronghorn antelope. Ben was with him, and was hungry. Adams had just shot one antelope, and both Rambler and Ben had run after the rest of the herd.

> The grizzly Ben started with the greatest courage and the most resolute determination; but, after loping four or five hundred yards over the sand, he wheeled around to see whether I was doing my part. Seeing I was not following, he at once decided that such treatment was not justice; and, returning, sat himself down on his haunches in front of me, as I began to skin the antelope. The noble fellow was already so well trained, that he never presumed to touch anything till I gave it to him; but he had a way of grumbling for food, when hungry, that was irresistible. I shall never forget how he sat there, wistfully eyeing my carving, looking into my face, and remonstrating about my strictness with him. His perquisites were generally the entrails of game, of which he was remarkably fond; but as

he now had to wait until they were removed, his impatience at last assumed such a pitch, that he got excited, and grumbled more than ordinarily. I resolved to try him a little, and placed food in such a way as to tempt him; but the faithful fellow continued true to his training, and the meat remained inviolate. Seeing this, I threw his portion to him, and he ate until I almost thought he would burst—devouring the entrails, and lapping up the liquid of the antelope's stomach, which to his palate seemed as sweet as honey.

"Samson," Adams's greatest triumph as a capturer of wild animals, never became reliably tame the way his other bears did.

That sort of devotion to Adams was characteristic of Ben, who on several occasions pitched in to help fight other bears with Adams, and who followed the man with an almost puppyish affection.

Adams caught many animals, but his greatest achievement is now seen as the capture of an immense boar grizzly named Samson, taken near his Sierra camp in the winter of 1854–1855. Seeing the tracks of a bear of unimagined size, Adams hid along the trail until he saw the bear itself, "like a moving mountain" it was, walking by. Even Adams, an exceptional braggart by any standards, admitted fear in the neighborhood of this one, but he was more determined than ever to catch the animal.

Gathering up his Indian helpers, he built the largest, sturdiest trap he'd ever made. The trap, similar to those built by the Spanish and other American Californians for similar purposes, was made of large pine logs shaped into a secure, sturdy cabin. It was mounted on buried logs two feet in diameter, and had sliding doors on each end that were triggered by a rope attached to bait in the middle of the trap.

Depending upon which account you read, it took either a few days or four months for the bear to enter the trap. Adams and Tuolumne moved to a small tent near the trap, so as to be available quickly if they got lucky. On the night they did get lucky, Adams said he was awakened by the "awfullest roaring and echoing in the mountains I ever heard, with the single exception of an appalling thunderstorm in the Humboldt Mountains . . . " They had the bear.

But it wasn't clear they could keep him. As Adams ran to the trap, he saw that the bear was biting chunks from the trap wall faster than Adams could have cut through it with an ax. Quickly reinforcing the trap with more timbers, Adams and the Indians spent a week-long vigil watching over the bear, beating him back from his attempts to break loose, bringing him water, and generally trying to wear him down in this first stage of adjustment to captivity.

Adams left the bear in the trap for a couple of months at least. Then, facing the prospect of several months more of winter, with game scarce, he moved his camp down to the Merced River, leaving Samson behind in the care of some woodcutters, who saw to it that the now-quiet bear was fed regularly.

Adams finally arranged to find a big enough iron cage, and to haul it up to the camp, where he placed it up against the wooden trap. His experience had taught him that bears become active and even enraged when moved from one cage to another, and Samson was no exception. He didn't want to budge. Adams had to hire a teamster with a pair of oxen to pull the big bear into his new home. It was done by pushing the cage up against the trap, opening the two doors that separated them, lowering a heavy chain over Samson's neck (imagine doing this), then running the chain out through the far end of the cage, where it was hooked to the oxen (who couldn't have been too happy about all of this themselves). A foot at a time, the giant bear (fifteen hundred pounds, Adams claimed) was hauled toward the cage, until he "suddenly bounded into the cage, and commenced tearing around, as if he were going to demolish it." The door was dropped behind him, and he was home.

Then, with the cage perched on a groaning wagon, came the laborious trip to a nearby ranch, where Adams put the bear in safe storage while he set out for his final summer of adventure in the Sierras.

It was Adams's final summer of adventure because all the hard living and tough fights were catching up with him; he suffered miserably from fevers and the wear and tear of so many injuries. It occurred to him to take advantage of his many adventures, and, rather than sell off his beloved animals, to put them on display himself.

That's another story, of course, not having to do with his adventures, but a marvelous, engaging, and sad part of the saga of this strange man nevertheless, so I ought to tell you a little about it.

Late in 1855, Adams took his little menagerie to San Jose, on the south end of San Francisco Bay, apparently his first showing of the whole group. But it wasn't until September of the following year that he set up permanent shop in San Francisco, opening his "Mountaineer Museum" on Clay Street, with Samson ("The largest Grizzly Bear ever caught, weighing 1,510 pounds," read the first advertisement; the ten pounds was a nice touch, I think), Lady Washington, Ben Franklin ("King of the Forest"), and "Two young

WHITE BEARS from the Rocky Mountains. ELK, LION, TIGER [jaguar, which Adams hunted in southern California], PANTHER, DEER—and numberless small animals." It was a great show, promoted by Adams's habit of wandering around town with Ben and the other bears at heel, and it was regularly featured in the local papers, especially by an enterprising young reporter named Theodore Hittell.

Hittell was the one who eventually took the time to interview Adams at length, getting the material for the book published in San Francisco and Boston in 1860. Adams, who slept in his museum among his animals friends, was delighted at the attention, and though he would later cooperate with other ghostwriters, none would treat his story as respectfully, or produce a book as durable, as Hittell did.

Though Adams achieved great local fame in his few years in San Francisco, and though his museum was popular, he was unable to save any money. He was never good at business; by late 1859, he was still more or less broke, and lost his zoo in a suit filed by his landlord to collect back rent. In January 1860, he loaded his remaining animals on a ship for the three-and-a-half-month trip to New York. (Ben had died in 1858. The bear was the subject of a famous and touching obituary in the San Francisco *Evening Bulletin* entitled "Death of a Distinguished Native Californian," so dear had he become to the press and the people.) Once there, Adams signed himself and his bears on with the showman P.T. Barnum, made enough money to give his long-suffering wife a little financial cushion, and continued to deteriorate in health. Barnum, in describing his first meeting with Adams, related how far the decline had gone by the time of Adams's arrival in the East (in April 1860):

> During our conversation, Grizzly Adams took off his cap, and showed me the top of his head. His skull was literally broken in. It had on various occasions been struck by the fearful paws of his grizzly students; and the last blow, from the bear called "General Fremont," had laid open his brain, so that its workings were plainly visible. I

remarked that I thought that was a dangerous wound, and might possibly prove fatal.

"Yes," replied Adams, "that will fix me out. It had nearly healed; but old Fremont opened it for me, for the third or fourth time, before I left California, and he did his business so thoroughly, I'm a used-up man. However, I reckon I may live six months or a year yet.[11]

Other accounts, more reliable and respectable than Barnum's, substantiate the extent of the head injury; it was almost an open wound, a thin layer of skin between the open air and the brain. Of course, there is no knowing what frightful assortment of internal complications accompanied it and Adams's other wounds, but the result was inevitable. In late October 1860, back in the care of his wife in Neponset, Massachusetts, Adams finally succumbed to the wear and wounds of his wilderness days. He may not have meant it this way, but his life was a testament to the whimsical truth of something published the next year by some unnamed Californian:

Hence the peculiar charm of a fight with a grizzly! If you kill your bear, it is a triumph worth enjoying; if you get killed yourself, some of the newspapers will give you a friendly notice; if you get crippled for life, you carry about you a patent of courage which may be useful in case you go into politics. . . . Besides, it has its effect upon the ladies. A "chawed-up" man is very much admired all over the world.[12]

Chapter Three

Wilburn Waters

*T*HE eastern black bear usually took human settlement hard. Bear populations were quickly thinned, along with all the other "varmints," once cabins had begun to spring up within sight of each other and cornfields and pigpens became an important part of human life in an area. Once the Boones and Crocketts had passed through, and communities began to take some pride in their civilization, bears were not to be tolerated.

We now know that the black bear is among the most adjustable of large game animals and can do just fine in the company of humans. Research in the past two decades has proven just how flexible the black bear is. For example, Gary Alt's lengthy study of Pennsylvania black bears has shown that the bears are amazingly able to get along in good numbers in a locality with a huge human population. The black bear needs only a little understanding on the part of its human neighbors to do quite well in the modern eastern forest.[1]

But it wasn't seen that way a century ago, when bears, like wolves, "panthers" (one common name of the eastern cougar), and rattlesnakes were pursued and persecuted out of existence in many areas. It wasn't a simple process, by any means; well after the first wave of settlers had passed, and some signs of polite society had appeared, most regions still had pockets of wilderness where the old conditions prevailed. In many cases, these last strongholds of "beasts of

raven" gradually shrank away under the encroachment of more settlers. But in other cases, they, too, were cleaned out by men whose
hearts were more in hunting than in farming. Such was more or less
the situation in southwestern Virginia in the years before the Civil
War, and such a man was Wilburn Waters.

We owe most of what we know of Waters to Charles B. Coale
(1807–1879), a newspaperman in Abingdon, Virginia, from the
1830s until at least the 1870s. Coale, having heard stories of a hermit
hunter who lived alone on White Top Mountain, sought the man out
(apparently in the 1850s), eventually doing for Waters what Hittell

The poorly preserved Clark portrait of Waters. (Photo courtesy of L.C. Angle.)

did for Grizzly Adams. Coale became the chronicler of the aging mountaineer's adventures, doing us all a favor by preserving at least a few episodes from a lifetime of rugged living in the southern Appalachians. In 1874, Coale wrote down what he had heard from Waters and included it in a book that was mostly about the early history of southwestern Virginia. All of the book except the Waters narrative had first appeared in the *Abingdon Virginian* over the years.[2]

I would have preferred a better chronicler than Coale, grateful though I must be to him for having done the job at all. I don't mind reading the high-flown style of writing so popular in those days; I've read so much of it over the years of my study of sporting history that I now find it almost pleasant at times. I am certainly willing to deal with the occasional bigotry, it being nearly universal in southern sporting writing in those days. Coale somehow manages to irk by sheer self-righteousness and preachiness, though I gather that he has also irked local historians by his inaccuracies as well. One local historian I spoke with expressed dismay at some of his information, and one of the copies of Coale's book that I examined had old, faded, marginal notations by some disappointed reader with comments such as "mistake in date," or "error." That doesn't do much for my faith in his accurate reporting of Waters's life, but we have little else to go on, and I suppose there's no reason to think he would have missed the major details of a bear story by much. It's a chance we have to take, now and then, in tracking down these hunters. Even the most reliable of sporting chroniclers make mistakes; in his great work *The Wilderness Hunter* (1893), Theodore Roosevelt, one of the most careful sporting writers of any generation, mistakenly referred to Waters as *Wilbur* Waters and said Waters did his hunting after the Civil War when in fact he did most of it before the war.[3]

Wilburn Waters was born on November 20, 1812, in Wilkes County, in northwestern North Carolina. His parentage was sufficiently romantic for a much more glorious story than he became. His father was French, a Huguenot whose hot temper led his friends to suspect that his presence in North Carolina was not entirely a matter of personal preference—that he might have been fleeing the law in some other state or the Old World. His mother was half white, half Catawba Indian, which made Wilburn, in the parlance of the day, a "quarteroon," or quarter-breed Indian.

Wilburn Waters was the youngest of five children, and his mother died when he was no more than three. He had little recollection of her except for her nearly floor-length black hair. His father unceremoniously dumped the children on relatives, remarried, and vanished, leaving Wilburn to be reared by a variety of relatives and strangers. In his fifth year, young Waters served a brief apprenticeship to a saddler, then went to work for the sheriff of Wilkes County, staying there for eleven years.

At that age, Waters was already well on his way to becoming a hardened outdoorsman, and had already had his first encounter with a bear. When only twelve, he got too close to a pet bear owned by a neighbor and was almost mauled. The animal was staked on a short chain, and seemed friendly enough when Waters tried to feed it, but soon the bear had a paw on each of Waters's shoulders and then suddenly attempted to entangle the boy's legs with its hind feet. Waters, realizing his predicament and suspecting that the bear intended to hold him or harm him, found it possible to gradually back away to the full length of its chain and then suddenly pull free. "He did so," Coale related, "leaving part of his clothing in possession of the bear, which became terribly enraged at his escape."

The rest of Waters's childhood and young manhood were spent in adventures and conflicts with deer, wolves, snakes, and society, the last of which seemed least to please him. Coale, in a characteristic burst of bigoted indignation, observed that at age seventeen, Waters began "to show the spirit of retaliation and vindictiveness of the Indian." At that age, having been punished for some misbehavior, Waters ran off with only a knife and a tomahawk, living the better part of three months on a mountain near the home of one of his older brothers. Though he finally returned to civilization, he was frequently in trouble; he had a gift for fistfighting that seemed to attract others with similar gifts.

At the age of nineteen, for reasons that remain unclear, Waters went to live with a country parson in Ashe County, the extreme northwest corner of North Carolina, where he established himself as the county's foremost turkey hunter and began to make a reputation for himself as a wolf hunter as well. Word of his skills got around, and he found himself in demand with farmers whose stock were being killed by wolves; he also found some income in bringing in wolf scalps, which he sold for as much as $20. He was once paid $175 by grateful farmers for taking a pack of five very destructive wolves in one day. It was in this new home that Waters also began to get himself involved in the sort of hairbreadth escapes and derring-do that makes his name so famous even today on the North Carolina–Virginia line.

One of Waters's first real adversaries was a huge old female wolf that had outwitted trappers and farmers for years, killing sheep almost at will. Waters, invited to try to take her, applied his unusual skills at trailing (Coale credits the skills to Waters's Indian heritage) and in time found a wolf trail, followed it to a marsh, and set his trap in a spot where any animal passing would have to put its foot. Returning later, he found that the wolf had fallen for his trick but had escaped from the trap with the loss of two toes.

Now that the wolf was hurt and unable to travel far, Waters rushed to the nearest settlement and sought the help of some local men. The hunters and their dogs soon "started" the wolf (that is, flushed it from cover) and chased it to a small cave. The dogs were sent in, but came out in tatters, so Waters decided to get the wolf himself. Removing his coat, leading with his gun (presumably a flintlock of some sort), he slid on his belly into the cave. There was little or no light—he himself must have been blocking most of it—but he was able to make out some reflected light, two spots of it, ahead of him in the darkness. Assuming them to be the eyes of the wolf, he quickly fired in their direction. The spots disappeared, so he reversed direction and snaked back out of the hole and sent the dogs in. Soon they emerged, dragging the wolf's carcass with them. It didn't take many incidents like this, especially with witnesses, to start the legend.

Waters experienced a religious conversion at about age twenty, going as far as to associate himself formally and permanently with the Methodist Church. We get a better idea of the actual degree of his hermitage when we learn that he rarely missed church, summer or winter. Late in life he was even named superintendent of a "Sabbath school," much like what we would call a Sunday school, eight miles from his home, and he attended faithfully every week. I wouldn't want to lean too hard on this idea, but I suspect that his newfound Christianity strengthened rather than weakened his enthusiasm for hunting. Now, with the full armament of Old Testament doctrine to back him up, he could add religious virtue to his reasons for subduing the wilderness. I don't say that to throw a shadow over his obviously substantial religious convictions, but I imagine that it worked that way. I suspect that Ben Lilly, the subject of Chapter Nine, thought along similar lines. Waters, however he may have been otherwise affected by his new faith, certainly showed no lessening of interest in wilderness adventure.

At the recommendation of friends, Waters moved in his twentieth year to the immediate vicinity of White Top Mountain, just across the line into Virginia. According to Raus Hanson's *Virginia Place Names*, White Top is the second-highest mountain in the state, at 5,520 feet: "Formerly called Iron Mountain. 500 acres across the crest has a fine white grass which glistens like a glacier; this explains the mountain's name." I'm not sure if this is an example of what are called "balds," those being large permanently open areas on the tops of various southern peaks. It appears that some settlers grazed stock on White Top, and that may have affected the summit. In any case, it was here that Waters found the homesite he wanted, in a little "cove," or sheltered valley, where he lived most of the rest of his life, the first four years in a tent. He filed a claim on 640 acres, and lost no time in hitting the trail for whatever big game he could find.

For all his previous hunting, Waters had apparently never seen a bear in the wild. The first of the six he killed that year he came upon near his camp while deer hunting. The bear was standing on a log, facing him, and Waters shot it through, the ball entering its head, going through the heart, and continuing to the animal's rear. (Stories of this sort cause some confusion to modern readers who have heard that early-nineteenth-century firearms were often not up to hunting the largest, most dangerous game. But the variables—

including powder load, make of firearm, size of the bear, and so on—are so numerous that any one situation cannot be used to prove anything. Waters was a good shot, and he must have had a pretty powerful weapon, unless this was a young, small bear.)

None of Waters's first few bears was any greater challenge than that, but late that first fall his hunting career was almost shortened dramatically. Snow had come, and he was hard on the trail of a large bear late in the day, so he decided to camp where he was rather than return to his tent, in order to have as fresh a trail as possible in the morning. The snow did not let up during the night, though, so the bear trail was completely lost. Waters soon crossed the trail of a raccoon, and being both fond of coon meat and ravenously hungry after a day without dinner and a morning without breakfast, he followed. Quite by accident, he thereby came upon the recumbent form of a large bear asleep in the snow.

At first Waters took it for a bearskin left by some other hunter, but what little he could see of the skin was slowly moving up and down as the bear breathed. Getting up close to it, he was still unable to tell, from the small patch of black fur that was visible, just how big this bear was, but he finally decided it was just a cub and that any shot would probably kill it. He shot.

Up from the snow rose an enormous bear, twice his size, "surging and whirling as if it had been stirred by a hurricane into a column of fog," towering over the hunter and infuriated by pain, locating the source of the pain and charging all in one swift explosion of snow. Waters, with no time to reload and lacking the instructive aid of many modern movies that surely would have taught him to wrestle the bear and stab it to death with his pocketknife, resorted to that oldest of bear hunter's tricks—running away. And, though he was new at this, he also knew that he could not hope to outrun a bear, so at the first opportunity he circled a large tree. At the instant he was out of the bear's sight behind the trunk, he leaped for a branch, held it with one hand (his other still held the useless rifle), and bunched his legs up under him as high as he could.

Make sure you've pictured this right. Waters is hanging only a few feet up. He told Coale his feet couldn't have been much more than four feet off the ground. A bear as big as this one, standing on its hind legs, would easily reach him. But a bear running on all fours, as bears do everywhere except in the movies, would be less than three feet at the shoulders. I've read enough odd accounts of bear encounters to give what happened next the ring of truth; in fact, it doesn't seem like the sort of thing Waters would have made up, even if he wasn't a churchgoing man.

What happened, of course, was that the bear, nose to the ground and in a great angry hurry, raced by right under Waters as he hung there swinging slightly back and forth. Bears aren't known for their eyesight, and this one had no reason to think its enemy would suddenly become airborne; it just kept going, assuming Waters must be somewhere in the snow up ahead. But it didn't go far, probably because it picked up his scent right there. And so Waters had to hang on for a few minutes while the bear ripped up the undergrowth all around below him in its rage. What Waters saw it doing to the rocks, brush, and small trees was sufficient incentive for him to hang on tight.

Finally, the bear took off back down Waters's track, giving the hunter a chance to drop down and reload. Waters heard the bear thrashing around in the heavy vegetation nearby, apparently engaged in some more landscaping, so he cautiously followed it. Peeking through the brush at the edge of a small opening in the forest, he saw the bear "making a furious attack upon a rock that protruded out of the snow." It was, at that point, relatively easy to shoot him in the head, which Waters did. The bear, we are told, weighed nearly four hundred pounds.

Coale did more than record Waters's own reminiscences. He saved the story of at least one other man who hunted with Waters, though he does not give us his name. It's a funny story, the kind of self-deprecating humor that is too rare in modern outdoor writing. (It reminds me, in fact, of Charles Dudley Warner's little gem of a bear story, "I Kill a Bear," in his book *In the Wilderness* (1878), itself a small and neglected classic.)

In this story the writer, a native of the area who had never hunted bear, decided that he should "knock up the trotters of one bear during a residence of a normal lifetime within sight of their foraging grounds," so he asked Waters if he would serve as guide. Waters happily agreed (he seems to have been a pretty sociable hermit), and invited the novice (as he called himself) to spend the night. By the conclusion of dinner, the novice was already having second thoughts:

> The hunt being determined upon and arranged, we had bear-meat, corn-dodgers and wild honey for supper, and the long ride through the rarefied air of the mountains that day having whetted my appetite to a pretty keen edge, and having stowed too large a portion under my vest, I was fighting, shooting at, and running from bears the livelong night, in my troubled dreams, and rose from my bed of skins in the morning with very serious misgivings as to the wisdom of bear-hunts in general, and of the present one in particular.

He was committed, though, and would see it through. At dawn, Waters, his dogs, and the novice were on their way to a certain slope of laurel. All along the way, Waters had been coaching the novice on just how to shoot the bear, and it all seemed clear enough until the actual hunt was at hand. As Waters stationed his new friend at an appropriate stand and went off to drive a bear or so to him, panic gripped the bowels of the novice. He found he had opened his eyes wider than ever before, and that he was unsure he would ever be able to close them again. He began to wonder if bear hunting was a sport at all,

> whether or not it was right and proper to stand behind a tree and murder an innocent bear in cold blood while going about his legitimate business! The more I thought about it the worse I felt, until my knees grew singularly weak, and if I didn't have an old-fashioned shake of ague, it was something so near akin to it that I couldn't well tell the difference; but when, a few minutes after, the perspiration broke out all over me in great big beads, I was ready to be qualified that I had the real *bona fide* Arkansas fever

and ague, and thought it not only in very bad taste, but criminally imprudent, for a man in such a wretched state of health as I was at that moment, to be standing away out there on the mountain-side without a physician, or quinine, or a bottle of French brandy.

As the novice was standing there absorbed in his mortal prospects, he heard the baying of the dogs and, soon after, "the tread of something coming that seemed to be as heavy as the march of an elephant," which turned out to be a squirrel hurrying by. Then he heard Waters's rifle fire, and in a moment it fired a second time. The first shot relieved him, as it suggested a dead bear. The second shot revived his panic, as it suggested a *wounded* bear.

Every sound, every minute, gave the novice new opportunities for dread and self-loathing, so that soon he stood there, frozen to the spot, his grip tight enough to leave fingerprints on the lock of his gun, waiting for the bear to come roaring at him from the thicket. In this state he was shocked, then relieved beyond words, to feel a hand on his shoulder, and to hear Waters's calm voice say, "Stop, friend, hadn't you better spring your triggers and cock your gun before you shoot?"

Not that shooting was necessary; Waters had killed both of the available bears already. Which news was greeted with rejoicing by the novice, who found that "the cold sweat had vanished like the dew of the morning; I could open and shut my eyes with the facility of a frog, and have not felt a symptom of fever and ague from that day to this."

Life was not always that easy for Waters, nor hunting that simple. The Civil War, surely the greatest domestic intrusion on American life ever, had its effects even in the remote highlands. There was little powder for hunting, and few hunters about, so those areas not devastated by battle or foraging troops experienced a recovery of game populations that was not always welcome. Waters hunted less, if at all, and stayed close to home to protect his modest property. The bears, of course, flourished.

One day around the time the war ended, Waters was hiking along a trail when he came upon the familiar bear signs. It was too much to pass up. He hurried to his place, got his gun and dog, and was happily lost in another chase. This one led to the top of a mountain, possibly White Top itself, where the dog had treed a mother bear and three cubs. Waters decided that he wanted to capture a cub alive, so he shot the sow and the other two cubs, set a fire at the foot of the tree, and left his dog to stand watch so the cub wouldn't try to escape if the fire went out. He then hurried a few miles to a cabin he knew of, but could find no men to help him, only two women who, as it turned out, were more than willing to help. He arranged to meet them at the tree in the morning, returned, and spent the night tending the fire and watching the cub climb nervously about in the branches.

The women arrived as promised, and he stationed them nearby with appropriate gear for tying and securing the cub. The cub, seeing the fire out and growing restless, finally descended the main trunk. Just as it was about to step onto the ground and escape, Waters was there to grab the hind feet.

It's at this point in the story that it becomes clear that this is not a springtime cub, not a little five-pound bundle of cuteness. This seems instead to be a late-season cub, perhaps even a yearling still hanging around from the previous year. It sounds to me that it must have weighed forty pounds, at least. It was big enough, in any case, to run with its front legs, as "away they went down the mountain side wheelbarrow fashion, at a rapid rate, regardless of whatever imposed." Knowing something of the ruggedness of that country, I am confident that many things *did* impose. But somehow Waters managed to move up from the hind legs and even get a grip on the bear's neck, more or less riding it partway down the mountain, all the time being snared, gouged, ripped, and grabbed by passing bushes and rocks. By the time they got to the bottom, Waters was pretty well undressed, still having one good sock, his suspenders, and a shred or two of his pants, but otherwise being stripped to the skin.

The women, chasing down the hill at a slower pace ("as they had no bear to ride," quipped Coale), did not miss the assortment of shredded garments along the way, and were quick to take Waters's suggestion—called to them from the cover of a mountain laurel— that they let him take care of the cub and just go get him some help for hauling out the carcasses of the other bears. The women left, and Waters made a suitable rope from his suspenders, tying the cub well enough to get it to his cabin, where he also got some whole clothes.

That was not the only bear Waters rode, nor the most dangerous. It was New Year's Day, 1873, and the hunter of White Top, now sixty years old, was no longer living on his little homestead. He lived with Clark Porterfield, an avid hunter who maintained a good pack of dogs.

The footing was wretched, snow over ice, so that travel in the mountains was adventure enough without trying to find a bear to shoot. But despite Waters's reluctance, Porterfield persuaded him to go. Soon enough, the dogs were off on the trail of a bear, and the old hunter felt the thrill of it to the point that he soon outdistanced Porterfield and scrambled recklessly up the slopes—falling, rising, slipping, crawling, but always climbing—until he broke into a little clearing and saw that the dogs had treed not one but three bears. Picking the largest one, Waters took a shot with his shotgun, trying first the barrel loaded with a ball, which had no effect, then the barrel loaded with buckshot, which brought the bear down the trunk of the tree and into the midst of the dogs.

In seconds, one dog was crippled and the bear had another one by its head. As the bear and dog slipped away from the tree and rolled down a steep gorge, Waters was after them, armed only with a tomahawk. This seems less cautious than his behavior as a young man, but, as Coale said, it all happened "before he had time to reflect on the situation." When Waters arrived in a cloud of snow at the bottom of the ravine, the bear let go of the terribly wounded dog and turned on him. There followed a frantic dance of swipes and parries as the bear tried to get him and as he gave it what punishment he could with his tomahawk, which, judging from the effect it was having, must have been a steel-bladed ax. The bear turned from this fight and rushed for a cliff, apparently, to Waters, in the hope of jumping from the cliff to nearby trees and then to safety. But Waters grabbed a handful of back fur and found himself mounted, loosely, on the back of the retreating bear. He took this opportunity to give the bear a really authoritative smack on the skull with his tomahawk, which brought it down just as its front end slid to a halt hanging over

An artist's rendering of Wilburn Waters, based on the David Clark portrait of him.

the cliff. The ride would have gotten a lot worse from there on out, and Porterfield was overjoyed to find his older companion safe. No-body even minded that the other two bears got away.

At least one other writer left us an account of Waters in a hunt. A southern artist named David L. Clark hunted with Waters and Coale during the Civil War (the exact date is not known). Clark, who later painted a portrait of Waters, wrote an autobiography in about 1895, *The Roving Artist, A Biographical Sketch*, a book now difficult to find, and devoted most of a chapter to the hunt. I will quote most of it, because it's such a rare first-hand account of a man who we know only slightly, through the eyes of an amateur biographer.

Yet I must ask the privilege of submitting a brief sketch of a bear hunt in which Mr. C.B. Coale and myself figured; neither of us getting the bear or permitting the bear to get us; and yet we were emphatically going for bruin— This being in the days of the confederate war, when it was much more congenial to the feeling of us both, to attack a bear, than to enter into deadly conflict with the enemy of our own flesh and blood.

Capt. John M. Preston, an acquaintance and friend of ours residing at the Seven Mile Ford (17 miles distant) dispatched to Mr. Coale and myself to come at once, stating that a very large bear had been seen in one of his cornfields, and that he had already dispatched for Wilburn Waters, who would join us in the hunt. Whereupon we immediately set out for the home of Captain P., armed and equipped for the emergency. At about 2 o'clock at night we were rapping at the door of our friend, who kindly conducted us to a room for a few hours sleep, and whilst thus refreshing ourselves preparatory to the hunt, the voice of the old hermit hunter came sounding in our ears. This was the first time I had ever seen Wilburn Waters, and here he stood with his unerring gun and faithful dog, Jack, who seemed as anxious and eager for the hunt as did his master. Never had my eyes fallen upon a more remarkable man, one who had killed hundreds of bear, deer, wolves [and] all manner of wild beasts and fowls, with which that wild mountain country is inhabited. But the most remarkable characteristic of the old hunter was his power of imitation, he could imitate, almost to perfection, the very cry or note of the victim of his gun, when describing it to you and what seemed still more remarkable, he could throw himself into a very close resemblance of the animal itself—Wilburn bid us hasten to the chase. The sun had scarce dispelled the darkness of the night when all parties were in the field. Here were most striking indications that bruin had been about, and yet the trail was too cold for Jack, though I had never seen a dog hunt with more energy. But I was more particularly impressed with the actions of Wilburn, than his dogs, though each seemed to understand the other, and both kept close together in the hunt. One moment scenting thro' the broad and open field, and the next moment, as it were, climbing over cragy [sic] rocks and precipices which would seem almost impossible for mortal man to reach. There was in his veins just enough of Indian blood to make him a perfect hunter. We found several bushels of corn deposited in a piece of woods, near by the field, which had evidently been borne there in the arms of bruin. We called to Wilburn to bring his dog. Soon the old hunter was at the spot, but Jack could not catch the trail. Yes, Wilburn remarked, the bar has been here sarten, but it is not about here now or Jack would a bin axin him some questions. But where do you think he is Wilburn, I enquired? Well, replied the old hunter, he may be ten, twenty or thirty miles from here now. And yet you say that perhaps he may return to this corn tonight. Why yes, that is just the nator of the brute, a bar don't mind traveling 50 miles more'n you mind traveling one mile.

Controlled entirely by the judgment of the celebrated old bear hunter, we deemed it unnecessary to pursue bruin any further on that day an all parties repaired to Capt. P's for refreshment and rest. But passing down the river, we discovered that Wilburn had wandered off to himself and was sitting on a log seemingly in a pensive mood. Neither of us could imagine what change could have come over the spirit of the old hunter's dreams. Mr. Coale suggested that perhaps one of our party may have used profane language in his presence, and if so that we were done with Wilburn. This proved, however, to be only some plans that were revolving in the mind of the old hunter by which he might overtake bruin. We were soon all together again, listening to Wilburn's marvelous hunting stories.

The party then went fishing, but Clark said that Waters was not interested:

> But this was too small a business for Wilburn Waters, there was not enough of the wild adventure in it for the old hermit hunter, he had not come here to fish but to hunt bear. And soon Wilburn and his faithful dog, Jack, were seen wending their way back toward their wild and secluded home in the Whitetop mountain.

Unlike many hermits and other social oddballs, Wilburn Waters has been remembered with affection in his neighborhood. His association with camp meetings and various other religious activities made people think more of him, and he lived in a day when cleaning out wolves and bears from the forest was heroic work. Anybody going off to live on a mountain by themselves now would either be labeled a misfit or ridiculed as a budding young Thoreau trying to do something worth writing about. Waters fared well in public opinion, and even at the time of his death, in 1879, he was recognized as being, in his own peculiar way, a useful and important citizen.

Over time his reputation grew, so that he now has a secure niche in the history of southern Virginia and northern North Carolina. Coale's book, or portions of it, has been republished twice—in 1929 and 1960—and at least one novel has been based on his life.[4] In 1957, Reverend M. D. Hart, of West Jefferson, North Carolina, a grandson of one of Waters's close friends, led a successful effort to have a monument erected to Waters, and even so long after Waters's death, contributions were received from more than a hundred people. Wilburn Waters may not be known at all more than a few hundred miles from White Top, but close to home he's still a lively topic of conversation.

Chapter Four

Wade Hampton III

*T*ODAY, when the term "outdoor sport" is as apt to mean bass fishing in Texas, elk hunting in Montana, or grouse shooting in Vermont, it is hard to imagine that there was ever a time when a region of the country could have held a preeminent position as the land of great sportsmen. But something like that was in fact the case before the Civil War. Though there were, of course, sportsmen—and wonderful sporting opportunities—in all parts of the country, there was a leading sporting region: the South. As a writer in *Harper's New Monthly* magazine, in October 1855, said, "The planters of the South, more than the citizens of any other section of the Union, indulge in the manly excitements of the chase; they are, without exception, excellent horsemen, and have a thorough knowledge of woodcraft." When Henry William Herbert, writing under the pen name of Frank Forester, published his *Field Sports of the United States and British Provinces of North America* in 1849, it opened with this dedication:

To COLONEL WADE HAMPTON, &c., &c., &c., of "The Woodlands," South Carolina, This book on the Field Sports of the United States and British Provinces of North America, is very respectfully dedicated, as a tribute of homage to The First Sportsman in the land; By his Obd't Serv't Frank Forester.

Colonel Hampton was the father of the subject of this chapter. He was a great hunter and horseman, owner of a famous stable and many famous racehorses, and he, the entire Hampton family indeed, represent the pinnacle of the Old South's social system as it was manifested in sport. In fact, Wade Hampton III was so described at the time of his death in 1902, by a writer in the *Sewanee Review*:

> There is probably no name in recent Southern history that stands out more conspicuously as the representative of the old order of things now rapidly passing away than that of Wade Hampton, the soldier-patriot, whose long and eventful career terminated at Columbia, South Carolina, on the 11th date of April last.

Nowhere near enough has been written about the sporting life of the Old South. Nowhere near enough historical—or sociological—research has been done into the sporting way of life the Hamptons represented. Southern historian Clarence Gohdes, writing in his handsome and engaging collection of antebellum stories, *Hunting in the Old South* (1967), offered a similar lament, but hardly anyone seems yet to have noticed. Like other aspects of our sporting tradition, this is one that we risk losing simply through neglect and ignorance.

It didn't just happen that the South became so famous for sport. There were political, social, and geographical reasons for it. Much of the country was sparsely settled, compared to the more industrialized North, so there were still good gamelands and abundant habitat for wildfowl. There was a patrician class, wealthy planters supported in good part by the slavery system, with ample leisure to breed fast horses and make extended hunting trips to wilderness camps peopled with dozens of helpers and slaves. There was, under the circumstances, the opportunity for a wealthy sportsman to own huge amounts of land, sometimes holding it simply for the hunting.

While some writers stressed that *everybody* in the South, regardless of race or money, enjoyed good sport, it was to the likes of Hampton that prominent sporting writers and editors such as Forester, William Porter, and John Skinner (founder of the *American Turf Register and Sporting* magazine in 1829) looked with greatest admiration, apparently not any more troubled by the slavery system than were the southern planters.

They hunted everything (they were much more associated with hunting than with fishing), from woodcock to wild cattle, from wildcat to elk. They hunted with the British formality of the fox hunt and the aboriginal wildness of a bayou alligator hunt. Like many another generation of expansionist settlers, they saw it as their patriotic duty to clear the land of predators and vermin, and as their gentlemanly prerogative to enjoy the hell out of the effort. I can think of no other place or time in American sporting history where the hunting of the bear became more a fully established tradition—a rite of passage and even a manhood rite—than it did in the Old South. Especially from the Smoky Mountains of eastern Tennessee and western North Carolina to the Big Thicket of eastern Texas, bear hunting was for those ardent sportsmen almost a religious activity.

Bear hunting inspired, among countless other tales, the story that many literate outdoorsmen consider the finest piece of sporting fiction in American literature. I don't see how any one story in such a huge body of writing could be so judged, but I would at the very least insist that William Faulkner's "The Bear" (partly published first in magazines, then in its entirety in his 1942 book *Go Down, Moses*) is extraordinary. Set, like most of his work, in the fictitious Yoknapatawpha County of Mississippi, it is a powerful tale on many levels. Even a reader with no interest in or knowledge of its social themes will be swept along by the story of Major Cassius Despain, General Compson, McCaslin Edmonds, the boy Ike McCaslin, the Indian guide Sam Fathers, the crossbreed Boon Hogganbeck, the great untamed mongrel dog Lion, and the wise, ancient, mighty wraith of a bear, Old Ben.

A correspondent to the *Spirit of the Times* wrote in the 1840s:

As regards our hunting ground, "it is the great Mississippi swamp—which we are about to say is no swamp—that is to say it is not a morass; and when we invite the huntsman to the boundless wilds of the great 'father of waters,' we invite him in November, to the finest and most delightful hunting ground on the continent . . . The Mississippi swamp is nearly level—a perfect forest—in some places free from any undergrowth; in other places, the undergrowth is palmetto, from two to seven feet high. There is no difficulty in riding over it, at least in our region, with the exception of the cane brakes and the palmetto swamps; for although it is quite wet during the latter part of the winter, yet in the fall season it is as dry and firm as a turnpike; it is intersected in its whole extent by the numerous rises that pass through it, by little rivulets and bayous, by magnificent lakes and ponds. The banks and margins of these various water courses generally compose the most elevated lands in the swamp, and are generally covered by cane brakes, twenty and thirty feet high, and the cane as close together as it can stand on the ground—and these cane ridges are commonly from one hundred yards to one mile in breadth, and usually bear some relationship to the size of the stream they border upon. These cane ridges are skirted by ridges of green mar thickets of the smilax genus. Bears are almost invariably found in the largest cane, and are very partial to those places in the cane brakes where the cane has been blown down and tangled by the wind. These places are called *drifted cane*.[1]

The author of those words was Thomas Bangs Thorpe. Thorpe, you may recall, we met earlier, in Chapter One. He was the author of a number of early bear articles, including the famous "Big Bear of Arkansas" sketch, a prototype American bear tale. His description of the canebrakes is not much different from what Crockett encountered farther north in Tennessee, and it was the hunting ground of several of the hunters featured in this book.

A camp scene from a bear hunt in the Old South, published in *Harper's New Monthly* magazine, October 1855.

For the wealthy planter, unlike Crockett and his uncultured colleagues, the bear hunt was a social event of many parts. For one thing, it involved a much more professional attention to the matter of the dogs. As with the fox hunt and various types of bird hunting, the involvement of the dogs became a key element of the chase, and the chase was usually far more exciting and adventurous than the kill. Riding after the bear dogs through this biological mayhem of cane and palmetto was a wild and woolly version of the more manicured rigors of riding after the fox hounds.

Crockett never told us what his dogs were. He mentioned at one point in his autobiography that he had "eight large dogs . . . as fierce as painters," but we know little or nothing about the breeds involved. There remained a lot of informality in the breeding of these animals, for many years; some hunters seem to have cared little for such details as long as they got certain general characteristics.

But, of course, more thoughtful hunters and breeders went to work early, even in the 1700s, to perfect good bear dogs, and eventually breeds such as the still-famous Plott hounds were developed and maintained. Unfortunately, most of the early bear-hunting accounts do not tell us too much about the breeds involved. Thorpe, certainly a leading writer on bear hunting before the Civil War, was typically vague:

> The description of dogs that are preferred for bear-hunting, is a cross of the hound, bull, and cur dog. This cross is very generally admitted by the old bear-hunters of Arkansas and Louisiana, to be preferred, for several reasons. This mongrel has, in a great degree, the fine nose and bottom of the hound, with the speed and fierceness of the genuine cur. Now, the term "cur," is very vague and indefinite, and is applied to many varieties of dogs. The dog we allude to, is an active dog, of a yellow colour, a pointed nose, an ear that is partly erect and partly dependent—a watchful, sprightly guard-dog. This half-breed, crossed again on the bull-dog, produces a heavy and more powerful dog. The full-bred bull-dog makes but a very indifferent bear dog; he cannot smell well, and of course is no hunter. He is a slow runner, and when he comes up with a bear, he seizes hold of it, and the bear kills him as quick as thought; and, even if so disposed, he has not sufficient activity to get out of a bear's way;—when the bear makes a charge upon the dogs, the same objection that applies to the bull applies to the hound.

Variations on these comments appear in many early accounts. There seem to have been a good many variations on the bear-dog theme, even among the planters who had access to the best breeders. As we will see in Chapter Seven, informality of breed never really vanished from bear hunting; each hunter had his own idea of what was needed.

"The Bear at Bay," from *Harper's*, 1855.

Around the dogs and the hunters, then, was built a bear camp, gathering place and private resort for the great fall hunts portrayed so vividly by Faulkner. In the wild country of the Mississippi, just getting to camp was a major accomplishment. Here is the *Harper's New Monthly* magazine author again:

> To accomplish their wishes more perfectly, some en-thusiastic sportsmen provide themselves with jolly little steamers, made for no other purpose than for the trans-portation of horses, dogs, guns, provisions, and men, into out-of-the-way places, where a camp is formed, and days, and sometimes weeks, are dedicated to following the amusements incidental to such life.

One eyewitness to the hunts participated in by Wade Hampton

III left an account of the scale of the event in a memoir, not published until 1954:

> The day after our arrival we were joined by Wade
> Hampton and his party, who came by steamboat from
> Lake Washington [the site of one of Hampton's plan-
> tations] to the mouth of Lake Dawson Bayou, thence
> by barges, skiffs and dugouts. These annual hunts
> would last for a month or more each year after the
> frosts had scorched the trees and the flies, gnats and
> mosquitoes had been thinned out, and the nights were
> crisp and cool. . . .[2]

The editors of this memoir further observed that "Wade
Hampton also brought a good many negroes with him and at night
there was music and dancing and all kinds of plantation songs from
the fiddlers, and banjo players around the camp fires."[3]

There was something approaching pageantry in all of this, a
grandness of scale to suit the grandness of the country. No doubt
many of these men could have afforded such a hunt even if they
hadn't run it on slavepower, but it seems to have been seen as a great
lark by all the participants, from the whitest hunter to the lowliest
camp lackey.

But it still came down, at last, to the hunt itself. The horn rang
through the forest to call the dogs together, and rang during the hunt
to signal the parts of the chase, that wild galloping pack of horses behind the even wilder pack of dogs. After hours of such reckless
riding, whether it ended in a successful bay, a treed bear, or a pack
drifting here and there in search of a lost scent, it must have been
good to get back to camp and wait for the venison roast to cook. Few
early sporting subjects evoke such a mixture of excitement, danger,
and frustration as do these southern bear hunts. Here is one account
from *Harper's Weekly*, February 28, 1863, that suggests how little
one knew of the way the day would go.

> On some days he [the bear] is surprised in his hold,
> where he sits on his hams with quite a Fitz-James "come-
> one, come-all" expression on his countenance, and re-

"Fight of Dogs and Bear," from *Harper's*, 1855, shows why it was often necessary for the hunter to close with the bear and use the knife in order to save the dogs.

gards the dogs with what they consider a by no means inviting manner. Then comes the excited rush of the hunters, who, hearing the baying of the pack, dismount; and each hurries through the cane or brush as best he may, to get the first shot. At other times the quarry has a shrewd guess as to what is in the wind when he first hears the cry of the hounds, and puts his best leg first to get as far into the impenetrable recesses of the cane-brake as possible; the stout bamboos bend like rye-grass before his weight, and close in his rear, making it very difficult for the dogs to follow, and impossible for the hunters, who have to ride the best way they can, guided by the yelling of the hounds. I have known a bear to get clear away very often owing to the impassable nature of the jungle. Clumsy as the beast looks, he is by no means inactive, and can travel very fast.

But sometimes not fast enough. One more quotation from Thorpe is in order before we move on to Wade Hampton himself. Here is how the hunt would commence at a canebrake's edge.

> Having arrived at a place where there is a reasonable probability of getting a start, one or two of the party dismount, and having called the dogs together by a few blasts of the horn, got into the cane-brake and pass through the most dense places they can find—sometimes creeping on their hands and knees under drifted cane. The rest of the party having galloped down the margin of the cane-brake, dismount, one at a time, at considerable intervals, and at such points as the bear usually cross it occasionally. One or two continue on horseback and gallop several hundred yards in advance of the dogs, dismount and hurry into the

"Shooting at the Bear from the Tree," from *Harper's,* 1855, is probably mistitled. It should have been "Shooting at the Bear *in* the Tree," or "Shooting the Bear from the Tree." Notice that one man has lit a fire at the tree's base to smoke the bear from its lair into the open.

cane, and endeavor to meet the bear as he passes. In the mean time the dogs have come to a bay, and then there is a general scramble to get into the heart of the cane-brake and get the first shot—for the honours of the day are borne by him that kills the bear. Some one has now got within sixty or ninety feet of the bear, with his ears laid back, and his hair erect, with the dogs formed in a semicircle around him; the most courageous have approached within a few feet—when, with a bound or two, he makes them all give back; and, having made the dogs stand back a little, he makes a stand, when he receives a shot; but the shot has not been fatal, and the bear starts off at the top of his speed, with the whole pack in hot pursuit; he has got nearly out of hearing distance, when the barking of the dogs at one place notifies the hunters that the bear is again at bay. The hunters, in the mean time, have made their way out to the edge of the cane, where they have left their horses, and having once more mounted, make speed in the direction of their dogs. The bear now makes another *break*, and again the dogs are in hot pursuit, indicated by their yelpings and short barkings. The hunters continue at half speed, and are now pretty much scattered, each taking the course he expects the bear to take; the bear is again at bay, and one of the party hurries through the cane— now losing his cap, which has been caught by a brier, and again, getting tangled drifted cane, falls prostrate on the ground. At length he comes in sight of the bear, that has been slightly wounded by the first fire, and who now, with fatigue and rage, fights the dogs most furiously, now and then making a pass at them, and occasionally giving them a rake with his claws. At length, having made a momentary pause, he receives a ball about the lower part of the breast, near the belly, when with a few groans, he struggles with the whole pack, and falls dead.

It was that kind of chase, and that kind of rugged, exhausting hunting, that Wade Hampton III inherited from his sportsmen-ancestors.

Wade Hampton III, honored general of the Confederacy, South
Carolina governor (1876–1878) and senator (1878–1890), and one
of the nineteenth century's most distinguished southern political
figures, was born in Charleston, South Carolina, in 1818. His grand-
father, also a general, served with distinction in both the Revolu-
tionary War and the War of 1812, and also was twice a congressman.
The first Wade Hampton was (according to *Who Was Who in America*) "reputed to have been [the] wealthiest planter" in the country
at the time of his death in 1835, and both his son and grandson were
well set up from childhood on.

Hampton's public career does not especially concern us here, but
it was a fascinating one. As the epitome of the southern aristocrat, as
an officer beloved by his troops, as a stalwart and controversial Reconstruction politician, and as a figure in various federal adminis-
trations, he was a prominent citizen of his age.[4] In fact, considering
the extent to which he was known and reported on, it is surprising
how little we actually know about his sporting adventures. Bear
hunting history has come close to losing the story of one of its most
famous characters.

Everyone seemed to know that Wade Hampton was an avid and
skilled bear hunter. That's not the problem. The problem is—at
least for those of us who want to see the proof—that so little information has survived. There are some impressive testimonials in his
behalf. There are occasional vagrant references to bear hunting in
his correspondence. There is a thriving, almost legendary in fact,
notion that he was one of the greatest of all bear hunters. But when it
comes to hard information on his actual adventures as a hunter, the
surviving record is disappointing. With the generous assistance of a
modern Hampton scholar, we will hear a great story of the hunter
momentarily. But first let me share the puzzle with you.

By now you may have noticed that I'm an avid reader of old sporting books and periodicals. There are still hundreds of volumes of
periodicals I've never reviewed, still many obscure memoirs and
local histories I've not seen. But I've been looking hard for bear history material for about ten years now, and in that time I've gotten a
pretty thorough education in the big names in bear hunting.
Through that process, as incomplete as it has been, I long ago began

Wade Hampton III in 1878, about the time he lost his left foot as the result of a hunting injury.

to wonder why I didn't see more of Hampton in print. It had seemed to me, in my various readings, that if a man gets well established as a sportsman, especially if he is a man of some public notability, his companions and acquaintances cannot resist putting into print their experiences with him. With Hampton, the extent of his fame has not been matched by the extent of the written record.

I even have encountered doubt that he was all that great a hunter. In 1979, Harry R.E. Hampton, a great-nephew, published a book of reminiscences called *Woods and Waters and Some Asides* in which he suggested that Wade Hampton had perhaps only once killed a bear with a knife. He further pointed out that "Teddy" Roosevelt, when writing about Hampton, had said that he killed "no less than 80 bear with his hunting knife," and that Teddy was known to exaggerate these things.

As near as I can figure it, the distance from Hampton's time— seventy-seven years from the date of his death until his great-nephew's book was published—must have made the killing of bears with a knife seem more of a feat than it seemed at the time. Lots of hunters did it. Once the dogs were swarming around the bear, a shot was often impossible, and the knife was commonly used by hunters. Furthermore, the Roosevelt quote is simply in error, as we will see in a moment; and Roosevelt has long been recognized as among the most reliable of writers in such matters. He did not exaggerate.

When I contacted Clarence Gohdes, whose beautiful book *Hunting in the Old South* I mentioned earlier, he, too, was skeptical of Hampton's reputation. His research, like mine, was not terribly successful, and he concluded that, "My guess is that Hampton and his sort didn't do much bear hunting if any."

After the searching I've done, I can't really blame Gohdes for deciding that, but the evidence now at hand is sufficient to prove that Hampton was quite a bear hunter, and I don't doubt that there's more yet to be found. Professional historians, as Gohdes and I have both complained, have not gone out of their way to interest themselves in something as, well, *insignificant* as sport. I think that's a mistake, because sporting attitudes reflect all sorts of cultural influences, but that's the way it's been.

I didn't expect the published biographies of Hampton to say much more than they do; most devote only a page or two to parroting the accepted historical image of Wade Hampton as a great hunter, and they repeat the same fascinating little pieces of information: that he could hoist a dead adult bear onto the back of a horse; that he killed many bears with a knife; that he was the finest rider in the country, perhaps even in the entire English-speaking world.

If all these wonderful things were true—and I remain convinced they were—I cannot yet understand why stories of his hunts are so hard to come by. I therefore assume that I've just missed the necessary issues of the necessary periodicals, where surely his friends' remembrances were published. I'll keep looking. If I'm lucky, some reader of this book will have some information for me.

In the meantime, I will show you why I'm so sure of Hampton as a bear hunter.

My search began when I first read an account of him as a hunter. I knew the name, and was vaguely aware from some reading I'd done in sporting history that he was a famous hunter, but that was as far as I could go. Then I read Theodore Roosevelt's account of him in *The Wilderness Hunter* (1893). Roosevelt and Hampton were at least slightly acquainted, and Roosevelt probably got his information straight from Hampton. In any case, Roosevelt devoted a page or two to explaining that Hampton had "probably killed more black bears than any other man living in the United States . . . " He went on to say that Hampton had killed "thirty or forty" (not eighty) with the knife, and was only hurt once, when he was "rather severely torn in the forearm."[5]

Roosevelt was probably wrong that Hampton had killed the most bears. He believed Hampton had "been in at the death of" five hundred bears, "at least two thirds of them falling by his own hand," and that he had killed sixty-eight in one five-month period in Mississippi. There were other hunters, even in Mississippi, who had by 1890 killed more bears than that. Roosevelt simply hadn't heard of everybody, and was certainly unaware at that time of both Bob Bobo and Holt Collier (who appear later in this book).

According to Roosevelt, Hampton's two largest bears, weighed on scales, were 408 and 410 pounds. Hampton did most of his hunting near Greenville, Mississippi, near his favorite plantation there. Roosevelt *never* made this kind of stuff up, and though I and others have tried to locate a published source of this information, we have not been able to. The only surviving correspondence between the two men, at least the only items I have been able to locate, have nothing to do with hunting. Roosevelt was an incurable gatherer of such data, and could well have cornered the old man in some congressional hallway in the 1890s and subjected him to a vigorous fifteen-minute interview, scribbling notes furiously as he asked question after question. Hampton did not do much writing for the popular press, and as far as I have been able to determine, he left no diaries of the sort that would contain hunting experiences.

But he left a marvelously intriguing trail nonetheless.

We find, first, that he was a Hampton in the grandest tradition in his abilities as a horseman. Hampton was a thickset, powerful man, a shade under six feet tall; it was said his legs were so strong he could, while astride a horse, squeeze his legs together until the horse groaned. But, much more important, he was both a lover of horses and a brilliant rider. Edward Wells, in his biography, *Hampton and Reconstruction* (1907), told of an incident that occurred at Hampton's "Wild Woods" plantation in Washington County, Mississippi, before the Civil War.

> It was here that he was so famed as a bear hunter, and was the only one known who could, unassisted, put a dead bear on a horse to be carried home. On one occasion a young Englishman was his guest, a man of the class who are bred from boyhood to hunt across country, and he himself was a noted daredevil rider, following the hounds through thick and thin. After the first day's hunt was over, he remarked to a fellow guest:
>
> "There are few men in England who can ride with him," indicating Hampton.
>
> After the second day's hunt, he said:
>
> "There are not three men in England who can ride with him."
>
> On the third evening, he made no remark for a while, and then said quietly:
>
> "There is only one man in England who can ride with him."
>
> On the fourth night, he sat after dinner silently and

thoughtfully smoking his cigar in front of the generous chimney, where were blazing the huge yule logs cut from the adjacent forest. At length he jumped up, turned his coattails to the fire, and as he stood before it toasting that portion of the human form divine which most touches the saddle, exclaimed excitedly:

"By Jove! There is not a man in all England who can ride with him!"

Hampton's stature in American field sports was such that in 1846, when he was not yet thirty years old, he was already recognized as a great figure in the outdoors. In that year, William Porter edited and annotated the first American edition of Hawker's classic British hunting book, *Instructions to Young Sportsmen in all that Relates to Guns and Shooting*, adding dozens of new chapters on American game and producing one of the most important early-American hunting books. It was dedicated, in an effusive two-page dedicatory essay, to "Col. Wade Hampton, Jr., of Lake Washington, Miss., Formerly of Columbia, S.C." It said, in part, "If you did not excel in all Field Sports, from deer and fox-hunting to quail-shooting and fly-fishing—indeed, if you were not 'up to every thing in the ring,' and 'a trump' whenever coolness, sagacity, strength, or activity is required, I should hesitate in expressing the hope that this work may meet your acceptance." That kind of deference, coming from a man generally recognized to be the foremost arbiter of good taste in American sport at the time, was the highest praise imaginable.

There is also ample evidence of Hampton's steady involvement in bear hunts. The relatively few letters of the Hamptons that have been published indicate a long and successful career as a hunter. Here are a few examples.[6]

First, two letters from Wade Hampton II, our subject's father, to Mary Fisher Hampton, our subject's sister. These were written from Walnut Ridge, the Mississippi plantation of Wade Hampton II that would become one of his son's numerous Mississippi holdings in 1858 after the father's death. The first letter, dated April 22, 1855, reported that, "Your brother Wade has had some sport the last week. Some gentlemen from the upper part of his county have been hunting with him. The first day, they killed two bear, and the last three more and one deer." Then, on November 17, 1855, he wrote that, "Your brother Wade will leave by F. Lyon, on his return home, and will I hope reach it simultaneously with this letter. Dr Blanton has been spending a week with him, and Sunday excepted, they have been bear hunting every day. They have killed ten bear, and have had seven dogs killed."

On May 22, 1857, Wade Hampton III wrote to his sister that his friends "Portman and Mr. Townley seem to enjoy themselves very much, altho' they have not had a great deal of sport as yet. But I hope they will soon be able to kill some bear. Yesterday I killed two and caught a cub."

On November 7, 1857, Wade Hampton II wrote again to his daughter, that, "Your brother Wade has a large English party now with him, Lord Althorpe and his friend, whose name I have forgot, Cap Tower of the guards, and Mr and Mrs Portman. They are all hunters but they have killed but few Bear, and no deer at all."

Wade the son followed up that letter the next day, and came near to telling a story about the English guests:

> Two days ago, on our return from hunting, I found here *another* Englishman, Capt. Tower of the Guards, who was in every action of the Crimea. He called to see the Duncans and not finding them, he came here as he had a letter to me. He is a very nice fellow, and seems to regret much not being able to stay here longer. But he says he will come back. Today I took them bear-hunting and we killed *four.* Unfortunately I could not get them in to the death, as they are not accustomed to the sport. Lord Althorp (or as Sam calls him "Lord") was with me and he literally had his clothes torn off. I had to furnish him with my *drawers*, so as to enable him to come home decently.

Racing through the cane on a horse must have built up a lot of friction, or the lord's own drawers may have been insufficiently

Wade Hampton III late in life at home. Courtesy of the South Caroliniana Library, University of South Carolina, Columbia, South Carolina.

stitched. There are a few other mentions of hunting, and of dogs, in the letters, well into Hampton's later years, even though he lost part of a leg in a hunting accident in 1878. The South Carolina Department of Archives and History holds a letter written in 1883 from Johnson Hagood to James Conner, two close friends of Hampton's. Hagood wrote of Hampton, then sixty-five years old:

> "The Old Chief" writes to me occasionally. His last letter was from Mississippi & after some little matter of business was filled with his bear hunting & pack of bear dogs. He says they had got five out of six bears striked and the chief of course was happy.

As late as 1894, Hampton was considering a Montana bear hunt. As archivist Paul Begley put it, in sending me the reference to this hunt (which was not made), "Pretty ambitious for a one-legged, Septuagenarian, wouldn't you say?" Yes, I would say, but considering Hampton's enthusiasm for bear hunting, I guess I'm not surprised, at that.

What we end up with, after a review of these pieces of evidence, is plenty of reason to believe that Wade Hampton III did, as Roosevelt wrote, enjoy a half-century of bear hunting, and did kill a lot of bears. He often owned more than forty dogs. Among his numerous Mississippi properties was one called "Bear Garden," a 2,085-acre tract in Washington County that he and some friends purchased as a hunting preserve in 1853. He seems always, whether his personal fortunes were rising or falling, to have found time for hunting and fishing.

And, on at least one occasion, a companion of his took the time to record the excitement of a bear hunt with this singular man. On October 1, 1872, the *Phoenix*, a daily paper in Columbia, South Carolina, reprinted a story from the periodical *Turf, Field and Farm* entitled "My Bear Hunt with Gen. Wade Hampton." I summarize a lot of what I tell you here, but I'm going to give you all of this one because it's such a great period piece. It's written in the gushy, overdramatic style of the day, by a correspondent whose pen name was "Greybeard." He said the hunt took place "more than fifteen years ago," so it occurred at least in 1856 or 1857. He mentioned having gone west in 1856 to hunt, and having met Hampton on his way back east, while making a side trip down the Mississippi, so I imagine it was late 1856 or sometime in 1857. Hampton would have been at his best.

Hampton, at that time known as "the Colonel" by more than a few people, invited this man to join him on a bear hunt as part of a hospitable visit to Wild Woods. After a restful visit to the plantation and a good night's sleep, the party set out, riding ten or so miles from the house to the site of the hunt.

"Now," said the Colonel, "if you are not familiar with the bear, be careful. Don't take him into close quarters. Put a ball through his heart before he can reach you with his paw; but if you fail to do this, stand not on the order of your going—leave! And, by the way," he added, "whatever you do, save the dogs."

I knew as much about bear hunting as I did about elephants; had seen the beast tame in menageries, and once or twice encountered a live one, but no rifle-shot of mine had ever yet penetrated the shaggy coat of a Bruin, and my ambition was on edge to be gratified. Besides, I had just come from "the Plains," and felt big with the reputation which all fledglings innately enjoy who have knocked down a dozen or twenty buffalo. Well, we separated and got to work, I taking the stand which the Colonel had assigned me, to await his movements and those of the dogs, who were to drive up the game while he made a circuit. Whither he went or what he did, I have no knowledge. I only remember that for nearly two hours I waited patiently, listening to every sound, trembling with expectation, and brave down to the pulp of my index finger, that rested on the trigger of my trusty rifle. In fact, I had begun to grow dreamy, and thoughts were wandering among the scenes of home-life far Eastward. Suddenly, there was a long halloo—a shot, and then another. The dogs were baying, and evidently in full pursuit of game. What it was, whether of deer or bear, of course, I had no means of knowing; but instinctively I felt that it was coming toward the little branch whereon I had been stationed.

It was a question of less than five minutes, but in that interval I enjoyed the keen zest of a sportsman's expectation. I had it settled in my mind where I was to send my rifle-ball, where I would bleed my trophy when down, and what I would do in various triumphant contingencies that were pictured in my mind. But, alas! the schemes of men "aft gang agley." Bruin—for it was a full-sized beast of that nomenclature—made his appearance with a rush, tearing through the cane-brake, a hound hanging to one ear, and the pack close on his heels. I raised my rifle and fired, and have long been satisfied that the bullet sped at least fifteen feet above its mark. At any rate, it didn't hit him, while the sound of the discharge served to draw his attention to a new and unexpected adversary, and that was your humble servant. Despite the fact that he carried the weight of a dog and a bullet from the gun of Gen. Hampton [Greybeard makes a field promotion here], he turned his blood-red eyes [Greybeard warms up his rhetoric here] on me, and with an ugly expression around his mouth, which I regarded at the time as physiognomically dangerous, made directly for the position I occupied. At the same instant, a brace of hounds, God bless 'em! dashing through the cane with a glad yelp and a bound, seized the bear, one by the haunches and another by the flank. The digression saved me. I had no other resource than to take to a tree or the bush. I never was good at climbing, and chose the latter, plunging pell-mell into the cane, with an impetus like unto that of a demoralized locomotive. Fortunately, I struck a path—one of those narrow openings which are sometimes worn on the Mississippi bottoms by animals making their way to water. But, horror of horrors! I had not proceeded fifty yards before I heard close behind the sound of the pursuing bear. Frantic with the pain of the chawing bites every instant penetrating his flesh, and unable to shake off the faithful dogs, Bruin had doubtless taken one of his old routes, and instinctively hoped to brush or shake his tormentors off in the thick un-

dergrowth. On he came—closer and closer—the brittle
reeds crackling under his feet; the hounds giving their
short, sharp, ugly yelps, and I dashing forward as best I
could through the almost impenetrable mass. It seemed as
if I could feel the hot breath of the brute upon my back,
and I realized, as only a man in such an emergency can do,
that if once he laid his claws upon me, I was a dead man.
My knife was already drawn. Life seemed to hang but by a
thread, and I was prepared to do battle over that thin tie
while there was a muscle left to put forth its strength.

Yet stay! Suddenly—in less time than I can describe
it—there was a crashing of reeds in front of me. In an instant more, Gen. Hampton, hot and flushed with pursuit,
his clothes torn, and his fine face lighted up with that
keen, bold expression which I can fancy illuminated it on
many another occasion in the hour of danger afterwards,
stood face to face with me. It was but a second. He took in
the situation at a glance. Like myself, he could almost feel
the presence of the bear now twenty steps behind. Seizing
me by the breast, he pushed me back into the wilderness
of canes perhaps three or four feet—at any rate, out of the
narrow path—and exclaimed, as I fell backward, "Stay
there, as you value your life. Don't move an inch!" At the
same moment, darting forward, he dropped on his knee,
and, cocking his rifle, waited. I can't describe the interval,
it was so short; but it seemed as if before I could gasp, the
bear was on him. He fired, coolly and steadily as if he were
shooting at ducks. The bear gave a groan, but the pace was
unslacked. He dashed on, up to the very muzzle of the remaining gun barrel. The General was in the act of pulling
the trigger, when a cane, slipping from under his feet, flew
upward, like a spring, and striking the weapon, the gun
was discharged high in the air. In the twinkling of an eye,
the General was on the ground, struck down by the forepaw of the enraged brute, but knife in hand, and as cool as
if promenading his own piazza. I sprang forward to his
assistance, but he shouted to me to stand back. He was

lying almost at full length with the bear, while the latter
was being torn and distracted by the dogs, now in full
force, and doubly frantic, seeing their master in his power.
It was but the work of a moment, but I shouldn't forget the
scene in a month of centuries. The General's right arm
and knife were under the animal, but with a motion as
quick as a flash, he threw the other arm over the body, and
clutching the knife, drove it deep into the heart of the
brute. There was a spasmodic stroke of the paw in the direction of the stroke of the blade, for a bear always strikes
out in the direction from which it experiences pain—a
fact, by-the-way, which saved the face and body of the
General—and after a short convulsive spasm, the monster lay dead. And that is all. The dogs, with their jaws all
bloody, were called off, save one, who lay in the brake
panting its death agony from wounds it had received. The
General recovered his feet without a scratch; gathered his
gun, wiped the bloody knife in the dark fur; sheathed it in
an every-day sort of fashion; the negroes came up, and
after extravagantly pouring forth their congratulations
with true Ethiopian enthusiasm, secured the carcass, and
the whole party re-united around the camp fire at night
fall, well satisfied with the adventures of the day.

I would like to think that someday there will be enough interest
in sporting history that someone could do a thorough job of tracking down *all* of Hampton's sporting adventures, including bear
hunting, bird shooting, fox hunting, horse racing, and fishing. I
am as intrigued by his fishing as by his bear hunting. In a letter
written in 1896, when he was almost eighty, Hampton discussed
his sporting plans for the summer. He was at the time U.S. Com-
missioner of Railroads, and was writing to W.G. Curtis of the
Southern Pacific Railroad.

My Dear Mr. Curtis:
I hope very much that you will be able to meet us this
Summer at Ogden, and that Mrs. Curtis will also join us at

some time on our travels. Dr. Taylor and Capt. Lowndes
will both be with me this year. My departure has been delayed by a Confederate Re-Union at Richmond on June
30–July 2, and I will make short stops at Chicago and
Denver, so that it will be rather late before I reach California, and I am afraid the fishing season will be pretty well
over. My intention is to come back this year over the
southern route through Texas, as I want to go over that
road, and then the tarpon fishing in the Gulf is said to be
fine. If the salmon are running, I would also like to have
another try at them in the Willamette River, but unless it
is good I do not care to make the trip to Oregon this year. I
hope to be able to make a longer stay in California this
year than heretofore. Please let me hear from you. I am,

> Very truly yours,
> WADE HAMPTON

He was nearly eighty, and he was anxious to have a go at tarpon and salmon. Someone who was that indefatigable a
sportsman deserves a better celebration than we've given him
so far.

Chapter Five

William Pickett

I N 1900, the great naturalist Ernest Thompson Seton published what has become perhaps the best-selling of all bear books, *The Biography of a Grizzly*. It could well be that some of the mass-marketed children's books, such as the Pooh series, have sold more copies than the *Biography*, but of books about "real" bears, Seton's is probably the most successful. My personal copy, published in 1928, was the nineteenth printing, and I believe it has stayed continually in print since then. It was made into a movie by Walt Disney.

Today, I suspect, practically all of its audience is children; to the modern eye it reads like a children's book. When it was published, I think it had a much wider appeal. Our understanding of wildlife, especially of "bad" animals like grizzly bears, was relatively primitive at the time, and this tale of an orphaned cub growing up in the wild country to the east of Yellowstone Park must have had great appeal with readers of all ages.

Seton proved himself a fine student of nature in his long career, but today we have to admit that his anthropomorphism—that is, his ascribing of human qualities to other animals—was pretty heavy-handed. Mind you, I don't entirely disapprove of anthropomorphism; humans have too often attempted to unreasonably distance themselves from other life forms, either for the sake of feeling superior or to justify some cruelty or mistreatment. Seton, however, tended to go pretty far, certainly a lot further than most modern naturalists would accept. He succumbed, I think, to what some modern sportsmen have called the "Bambi Syndrome." His little bear cubs were little people.

"Grizzly Killing a Steer," from Theodore Roosevelt's *The Wilderness Hunter* (1893).

Now, this is deep stuff, field for involved philosophical and psychological ruminations that are outside the scope of this book. I bring it up because it's necessary stage-setting for introducing my present subject, William Pickett, who appeared prominently in Seton's book.

In the first chapter of the *Biography*, we are introduced to "Mammy" ("just an ordinary Silvertip, living the quiet life that all Bears prefer, minding her own business and doing her duty by her family, asking no favors of any one excepting to let her alone") and her four cubs, Frizzle, Mooney, Fuzz, and Wahb. As we watch, Mammy helps the cubs kill a mess of trout (fish apparently not being animals that were allowed to let her alone): ". . . the little ones rushed noisily on these funny, short snakes that could not get away, and gobbled and gorged till their little bellies looked like balloons." After this merriment, Frizzle and Mooney rolled down a hill while wrestling, provoking a charge by a "huge Range-bull" that happened to be wandering by. Luckily, Mammy came to the rescue: ". . . she dealt him a stunning blow, and before he could recover she was on his shoulders, raking the flesh from his ribs with sweep after sweep of her terrific claws."

Then, in the second chapter, this peaceable, fun-loving family meets its doom. Here is Seton at his emotional best, so I will quote the whole episode.

> Old Colonel Pickett, the cattle king, was out riding the range. The night before, he had seen the new moon descending over the white cone of Pickett's Peak.
>
> "I saw the last moon over Frank's Peak," said he, "and the luck was against me for a month; now I reckon it's my turn."
>
> Next morning his luck began. A letter came from Washington granting his request that a post-office be established at his ranch, and contained the polite inquiry, "What name do you suggest for the new post-office?"
>
> The Colonel drew down his new rifle, a 45-90 repeater. "May as well," he said; "this is my month"; and he rode up the Graybull to see how the cattle were doing.
>
> As he passed under the Rimrock Mountain he heard a faraway roaring as of Bulls fighting, but thought nothing

of it till he rounded the point and saw on the flat below a lot of his cattle pawing the dust and bellowing as they always do when they smell the blood of one of their number. He soon saw that the great Bull, "the boss of the bunch," was covered with blood. His back and sides were torn as by a Mountain-lion, and his head was battered as by another Bull.

"Grizzly," growled the Colonel, for he knew the mountains. He quickly noted the general direction of the Bull's back trail, then rode toward a high bank that offered a view. This was across the gravelly ford of the Graybull, near the mouth of the Piney. His horse splashed through the cold water and began jerkily to climb the other bank.

As soon as the rider's head rose above the bank his hand grabbed for the rifle, for there in full sight were five Grizzly Bears, an old one and four cubs.

"Run for the woods," growled the Mother Grizzly, for she knew that men carried guns. Not that she feared for herself; but the idea of such things among her darlings was too horrible to think of. She set off to guide them to the timber-tangle on the lower Piney. But an awful, murderous fusillade began.

Bang! and Mother Grizzly felt a deadly pang.

Bang! and poor little Fuzz rolled over with a scream of pain and lay still.

With a roar of hate and fury Mother Grizzly turned to attack the enemy.

Bang! and she fell paralyzed and dying with a high shoulder shot. And the three little cubs, not knowing what to do, ran back to their Mother.

Bang! bang! and Mooney and Frizzle sank in dying agonies beside her, and Wahb, terrified and stupefied, ran in a circle about them. Then, hardly knowing why, he turned and dashed into the timber-tangle, and disappeared as a last *bang* left him with a stinging pain and a useless, broken hind paw.

That is why the post-office was called Four-Bears. The

Colonel seemed pleased with what he had done; indeed, he told of it himself.

But away up in the woods of Anderson's Peak that night a little lame Grizzly might have been seen wandering, limping along, leaving a bloody spot each time he tried to set down his hind paw; whining and whimpering, "Mother! Mother! Oh, Mother, where are you?" for he was cold and hungry, and had such a pain in his foot. But there was no Mother to come to him, and he dared not go back where he had left her, so he wandered aimlessly about among the pines.

Whether or not Seton's tale succeeds in twanging your heart-strings, I should tell you that there is much truth to this story, though the details and chronological sequence are hopelessly fouled up. Pickett did, indeed, shoot four bears one day (though not three cubs and a sow), and a post office was, indeed, named for the incident. But Pickett himself was a much more interesting and varied character than Seton's portrayal of him as the evil cattle baron would allow.

He was, above all else for our purposes in this book, an honored outdoorsman, given a magnificent tribute by George Bird Grinnell:

> For many years Colonel Pickett was one of the vice-presidents of the [Boone and Crockett] Club, representing Wyoming, and has had an experience in hunting the grizzly bear greater probably than that of any man who ever lived. A keen sportsman, a lover of outdoor life, and a Southern gentleman, Colonel Pickett represents the ideals of the Boone and Crockett Club.[1]

Speaking as a historian of American sport, I can think of no one— *no one*—from whom such a tribute would be more gratifying than from George Bird Grinnell. Grinnell, with Theodore Roosevelt, founded the Boone and Crockett Club. He was a widely traveled naturalist and anthropologist; he was the founding force behind the Audubon movement; he was for many years editor and voice of one of the greatest of all sporting periodicals, *Forest and Stream*; he was, in short, a leading literary, intellectual, and political force in American sport. It was even more a tribute to Pickett that, when his *Memories of a Bear Hunter* were published in one of the Boone and Crockett Club books in 1913, Grinnell personally undertook to edit them and provide extensive commentary in footnotes.

William Pickett's portrait from the frontis of *Hunting at High Altitudes*, a Boone and Crockett Club book edited by George Bird Grinnell in 1913.

William D. Pickett was a native of Alabama.[2] Born near Huntsville in 1827, he moved to Kentucky as a child and received an education that prepared him for a career in engineering. He served in the Mexican War, though his duties were in fighting Comanches in Texas rather than in Mexico itself. He was a civil engineer following that war, making a name for himself in railroad construction in the Midwest until the time of the Civil War. He enlisted with the Confederacy, and by the close of the war he had worked his way up to the rank of Colonel, serving in numerous engagements with distinction.

A local legend in northwestern Wyoming said that Pickett, bitter over the outcome of the war, immediately came west to the Territory to hunt, while living a hermit's life[3]; Pickett had a way of getting people's attention and arousing their curiosity, so such legends were probably inevitable. (It was also believed, and even reported in later historical journals, that he was both secretary to Jefferson Davis and secretary of war of the Confederacy.[4]) Actually, Pickett went back to engineering after the war, and it wasn't until 1876 that he came west, first to hunt and then to settle. During a hunt in 1882, he came upon a lovely spot near the upper Greybull (then spelled Grey Bull) River not many miles west of the present town of Meeteetse, which is about thirty miles south of Cody. He liked this isolated area so much he decided to settle there and build a ranch, which he did. He stayed there until 1904, when he sold his ranch and returned to Kentucky.

Pickett seems to have done much less hunting after 1883, the year he first came to his new ranch; from then on, he was busy with his Herefords, as well as with state politics. He was twice a state representative from Fremont County, once before and once after statehood, and later served as a state senator from Big Horn County. In fact, "to the intelligent and untiring work of Colonel William D. Pickett," according to one historian, "goes the credit of the creation of Big Horn County."[5] He is now remembered as the "father" of that county. Among other things, he is credited with pioneering game laws in that part of the state.

But even today, Pickett is most often remembered as a bear hunter. Some believed he was the most skilled grizzly-bear hunter of his day, even granting that he had the advantage of getting into his country early in its settlement when bears were pretty thick and not especially shy.

Pickett got his first bear in 1877. The hunt occurred on a visit to

Yellowstone National Park, which, in 1877, was still without most of the "improvements," as they called them then, that would make it into a tourist mecca.

It was a wild year in that part of the West, mostly because Chiefs Joseph and Looking Glass and a large band of Nez Perce Indians were engaged in a running battle with U.S. forces across Idaho and into the park that fall. Pickett happened to be at Bozeman, Montana, not far north of the park, at the time of the tribe's flight through the park, and he later met some of the tourists that fled from or were captured by the Indians. (Pickett had the good taste to realize the injustice of what was being done to these Indians, who through no fault of their own were deprived of their rightful lands.) The attacks delayed his visit to the park, but on September 11, he finally started from Bozeman for the eighty-mile ride to the park. He had hired a guide, Jack Bean, and carried a .45-90-450 Sharps. (This may have been the weapon Seton was referring to in his book, but Seton called it a repeater when actually it was a single-shot breechloader.)

Passing evidence of the recent hostilities here and there, Pickett and Bean made their way to the Washburn Range in north central Yellowstone, country I know something about. The slopes of Mount Washburn are some of the best grizzly-bear habitat in the park area. In 1986, my wife saw her first wild grizzly bears on Mount Washburn, a sow with cubs, only a few hundred feet from the road.

But 110 years ago, it wasn't a pleasant auto tour. Pickett and Bean hit heavy weather the morning of the sixteenth; from their description, it sounds as though the blizzard was raging by the time they reached the 8,000-foot elevation, well below Washburn's 10,000-plus summit and more than a thousand feet below the pass they sought. It was hard going; they had to wade through nearly twenty inches of fresh snow, leading their horses.

The slopes were—are—a patchwork of meadows and forest, often giving travelers a long look at wildlife a mile away. While crossing one of these clearings near the pass, Pickett and Bean were surprised to see a large bear coming across the slope toward them, apparently unaware of their presence in the heavy storm.

I'm pretty sure what the bear was doing up there; in the fall,

Yellowstone grizzly bears move to high country to feed on the "nuts" in whitebark pinecones, and this bear was probably hard at work when the blizzard hit. Pickett, more concerned with getting his first trophy than with bear ecology, excitedly slogged through the drifts to some trees within a hundred yards of the bear, waited until it passed an opening in the trees, and fired into its side. Bean had come up beside Pickett, and as the bear took the shot and raced down the slope more or less toward the hunters, the guide told Pickett to hold his fire. Pickett had loaded another shell, however, and he fired again as the bear passed within about twenty yards of them. Bean, seeing the bear show no signs of injury, opened up with his .44-40 repeating rifle as Pickett reloaded and fired again. The flurry of shots took effect, though it seems unclear how many actually hit the bear; it fell, and the hunters, fearful of being caught in the storm on the high range, had to abandon it without even taking the skin.

Lots of shooting, a wasted trophy . . . not an auspicious beginning for a man who would later be called "the most noted bear hunter in the West."

In case you're wondering, this hunt was perfectly legal. Yellowstone Park's wildlife was open game until 1883, when concerned sportsmen (Grinnell, of course, in the lead), seeing the slaughter of animals by both tourists and market hunters, applied political pressure that resulted in park regulations against hunting. These early conservationists saw the park as a reservoir of wildlife that could provide surrounding gamelands with huntable animals forever. With hunters of Pickett's ability coming into the region, that reservoir was going to get very important very soon.

Pickett returned to the Midwest that fall, and it wasn't until the following August that he was again in the West, this time for a hunt in the Judith Mountains of central Montana. I am always impressed with the patience these early sports had about their arrangements. Pickett left Chicago on July 17, and, traveling mostly by steamer, reached Cow Island (now a Montana state recreation area) on the Missouri in central Montana on August 24. He wasn't sure how to set up his hunt, so a local Army officer let him know that a British sport named Messiter was also scheduled to arrive in the area, and offered

to arrange a hunt they could share. Pickett, in full confidence that
something would work out, agreed; Messiter was supposed to be on
the next steamer coming up the Missouri (whenever that had been
decided; however reliable Messiter was; however certain the date of
the next steamer's arrival was . . .). So Pickett engaged a guide named
Fishel, along with a "teamster" (to handle the wagon and stock) and a
cook, and set out for the Judith Mountains, a four-day wagon trip (the
first three without water except as carried), in hopes that Messiter,
with his own team, would rendezvous with them in a few days. Thousands of miles of travel, vague directions, a-day-here-and-a-day-
there imprecision of scheduling, and, sure enough, Messiter and his
team showed up at Pickett's camp, all his baggage intact, a couple
days after Pickett got there. Better than the airlines.

Messiter got there just in time, for Pickett and Fishel had been
busy scouting the area and killing a few bison, leaving the carcasses
for bait to attract grizzly bears. The morning after Messiter's arrival, they awoke to three inches of fresh snow. Fishel, examining
their baits through binoculars, discovered that one of the carcasses
had been moved. Hastily climbing the foothills for a better view,
they saw a large grizzly fleeing from the bait.

As the heat of the morning turned the snow to slush and mud,
Pickett, Messiter, and Fishel mounted up and took up the trail, but
soon lost it as the melting snow began to drain and obscured the
bear's tracks. Pickett went one way, Messiter and Fishel another,
and it was Messiter and Fishel who got lucky, more or less, and
found the trail.

Not waiting for Pickett, they followed the bear's tracks to a
stretch of a small stream engulfed in a long thicket of willow. For
about a hundred yards of its length, the meandering little creek was
cloaked in dense brush, the sort that could hide half a dozen bull
moose, much less a crouching grizzly bear. Cautiously circling one
end of the thicket, the two riders had just reached its far side when a
six-hundred-pound grizzly bear hurtled from the brush toward
them. The horses, surprised and probably shocked into inaction,
took a second to react. But once underway, the horses were able to
outrun the bear, which quickly retreated to its cover.

I am reminded of the first of my still-too-few rides in grizzly country. I was riding with two rangers on a backcountry patrol in northern Yellowstone Park, following them down a trail along the Yellowstone River. The lead rider was having a little trouble with his horse, which kept spooking at things we couldn't see but that the horse could apparently smell. This, naturally, led me to wonder aloud what I should do if we encountered a grizzly bear. I further wondered, supposing we did encounter a bear, if I should get off the horse at that point. My companions both laughed, explaining that if we surprised a bear, my horse would know *exactly* what to do, and I should just try to pay attention and stick with him.

Anyway, after the hunters' horses realized exactly what they should do, and did it well enough to leave the bear in a spray of snowmelt, Fishel headed back to camp to get Messiter's greyhound. On his way he met Pickett, who immediately hurried on to the thicket. Messiter, who had taken up a position on an overlooking ridge, was waiting for him.

As they were trying to figure out what to do, Fishel rode up with the greyhound, which had the good sense to refuse to have anything to do with the thicket. A bear in a thicket is a bear with every advantage. The hunters certainly weren't willing to go in there themselves, so they could hardly blame the dog. Visibility in a willow thicket is a few feet, at best.

So, not being willing to go in, they tried to drive the bear out. Having a pretty good idea of where the bear had gone in, they opened up with their rifles, crisscrossing the thicket with a searching fire that finally forced the bear into another charge, this time directly at Messiter's little hill. As the bear came on, both Messiter (who was dismounted) and Pickett (who was not) managed to hit it, driving it back to the thicket badly wounded but still terribly dangerous. They now could locate the bear by the sound of his rough breathing, so again they laced the heavy brush with shots.

Again the bear rushed out, this time at Pickett, who missed a shot at the charging grizzly and barely turned his horse in time to escape the claws.

For another half an hour, the three men tried to flush the bear, while the bear waited for its chance, which came just as a snowstorm hit the valley. Pickett, not thinking the bear was close to his position, was almost taken by surprise. The bear broke from cover, eating up the ground with great, thumping strides as it closed on the mounted rider. Pickett's first shot seemed to do it in, hitting it in the chest. The bear dropped flat, but no sooner had Pickett shouted, "I have got him!" than the bear was up and rushing toward him again. Pickett hit it again with a hastily loaded second shot, then spurred his horse and escaped the reaching claws by inches. Yet again the enraged and injured animal retreated to its thicket.

Now it came to a decision. It was snowing furiously. Going twice blinded—by snow *and* vegetation—into the thicket after the badly wounded grizzly would have been stupid. The bear had taken no telling how many bullets, and suffered no telling what damage, but the job was badly botched, for there was no choice except to go back to camp and wait for the weather to clear. With luck, Pickett reasoned, the bear would die of its wounds in the meantime, or would at least be further weakened enough to be less dangerous when the hunters returned.

The storm had not eased when the hunters reached camp, a little after five in the afternoon, "disappointed that we had been obliged to leave the bear hide on the carcass." They had a hot dinner, huddled around their fire in the falling snow, and planned for morning.

The storm had passed by dawn, and the thicket was quiet when the hunters reached it. Their hope that the bear was dead (and their commitment to finally finish the job if it was not) was sufficient to get them off their horses and into the most ticklish of hunting situations, searching for dangerous, wounded game at close quarters in heavy cover. Moving slowly, leading always with their rifles, fanning the brush aside with the barrels as they checked every step, Pickett and Messiter invaded the thicket just where they expected the bear to be waiting. They thus moved to the densest middle portion of the willows, where they gingerly spread the curtain of brush apart and, to their vast relief, found the bear dead and cold.

Pickett and his colleagues were armed with weapons a generation advanced from those used by the likes of Crockett and Adams, and yet at times they still seemed unable to make a clean (to say nothing of safe) kill. It was the occasional grizzly like this one in the willows that gave the bear such a reputation for toughness. Adams would have envied Pickett his firepower, though, to say nothing of the convenience of reloading even the single-shot rifle, which used nice simple cartridges and didn't involve messing around with loose powder and shot. And, as it turned out, Pickett's generation of hunters was decidedly more efficient at making clean kills. Here is Pickett discussing his 1881 season, after he had learned something of grizzly bears and how to shoot them, and after he had learned more about his cartridges:

> For great beasts like the buffalo a heavy solid bullet is the thing, but during the season of 1881, after I had become familiar with the habits of the grizzly bear, I killed, using an express bullet with 110 grains of black powder, twenty-three of those bears, of which seventeen required only a single shot.

Having quoted that, it's probably only fair that I let Pickett tell you what an express bullet is:

> The express system is the combination of a solid bullet with a hole of varying diameter running back from the point of the bullet about three-fourths of the ball's length. The diameter and length of the hole depends in some degree on the caliber and weight of the bullet. Such a bullet, with a heavy charge of powder behind it, giving a muzzle velocity of from 1,750 to 2,000 feet [per second], constitutes an express bullet. A suitably designed ball with this velocity, after penetrating the skin of the animal, bursts into many small fragments with sufficient momentum for these fragments to reach the opposite ribs of the animal and make a dozen perforations of the vitals, instead of a single large perforation, as in the case of a solid ball. The express bullet expends its momentum on the vitals in a space about equal to a circle with a six-inch diameter, whereas the solid ball makes a clean cut hole of the caliber of the bullet,

which, passing wholly through the animal, expends much
of its energy after it has passed out.

Pickett encountered an equally durable grizzly bear in 1880, but
ultimately it wasn't his powerful weapon that saved him.

Before the opening of the season that year, Pickett had been given
a dog he named Nip (he later acquired another dog that he
named—of course—Tuck). Nip's previous owner, Jack Smith of
Bozeman, Montana, was an avid bear hunter himself, and had produced Nip by crossing a Scottish terrier with a collie. The resulting
dog, according to Pickett, "was not afraid of any grizzly that wore
hair, but knew enough of their habits, and had sufficient activity, to
keep out of reach of their teeth and claws." Nip was a great help to
Pickett in his hunts that year, often serving to harass a bear or distract it during a close session with the hunters, and always showing
just enough respect for the bears to stay alive.

"Bear at Elk Carcass," from Theodore Roosevelt's *Hunting Trips of a Ranchman*
(1885).

Pickett was hunting that year in the drainages south of the Stinking

River (now called the Shoshone) east of Yellowstone Park. His guide and companion was a veteran army scout named George Herendeen. It was early November, and they had been in the field for several weeks, killing much game, when this incident occurred.

Their camp was ideally located up a small stream that fed into the Shoshone. Deer and elk were migrating down the slopes as the snow deepened in the high country, so food was plentiful for the hunters, and the leftovers from the carcasses of their game were helpful in attracting bears. One day Herendeen took a flying shot at an elk that escaped. He reported the animal's direction to Pickett, who decided he'd go see if the animal had died nearby. He found the carcass up a narrow dry gulch, and he was pleased to see that a grizzly bear had already been feeding on it.

Returning to camp, Pickett got Herendeen and Nip, and the three of them set up a lookout post. (Herendeen's job was to keep Nip from chasing the bear before Pickett got to shoot; Nip loved to chase bears.) Pickett led them to a high slope well away from the bait but apparently along the bear's approach route, where they made themselves comfortable and waited.

They were not disappointed. The bear soon appeared in the distance, moving confidently down the slope to the carcass. When the bear had disappeared into the little gulch with the dead elk, Pickett began a slow stalk, coming down the hill to a point in the gulch below the carcass, slipping into the little ravine and reconnoitering.

Something was wrong. From his chosen approach route, Pickett could see neither bear nor bait. It was getting late, and would soon be dark. He eased himself out of the gulch, circled wide of it in an uphill direction, and again slipped into the gulch, this time sure he was only a short distance *up*hill of the bait.

Again, no carcass, no bear. After a moment's puzzlement, Pickett realized that the bear must have dragged the carcass some distance down the gulch, where it could not be so easily seen. This told him two things: that he was dealing with a big bear, and that he was dealing with a careful bear.

Without a sound, Pickett removed his heavy hunting boots and inched forward, peering into the premature darkness of the gulch. Things happened then, a lot faster than they could be described.

Pickett somehow crept within about thirty feet of the carcass; the bear must have been pretty busy eating not to sense him, but somehow he did get that close. Rifle to shoulder, the hunter rose slowly, taking aim at the dark shape of the bear hovering over the carcass. The bear was facing away from him (a lucky break), and he feared missing a head shot in the miserable shadows, so he fired into the shoulders. At the impact of the bullet, the bear leapt from the carcass, scrambled up the side of the gulch—taking a second shot on his way—and made for a nearby grove of pines. As Pickett was reloading for a third shot at the rapidly disappearing bear, Nip, uncalled, came racing through the gulch and past Pickett in hot pursuit of the bear. Pickett, worried about hitting the dog instead of the bear, fired too high with his third shot, just grazing the bear as it made the safety of the trees.

Disappointed and angry over having possibly lost the bear, Pickett climbed out of the gulch on the side opposite the bear's and hurried uphill to get a better look at the bear's sanctuary. As he did so, Nip and the grizzly, fields reversed, came, as the saying goes, boiling out of the grove toward him.

Here is where Pickett learned the quality of his dog. He knew that a poorly trained dog would have run straight for his master's legs, not caring that a bear was right behind him. But he quickly saw that Nip was not that kind of dog:

> With an intelligence quite human, it seemed to me, he kept just far enough ahead of the bear to lead it on, the dog's head turned first on one side, then on the other, always with one eye on the pursuer. He led the bear straight across the open ground, causing him to expose his side to me, and saying as plainly as could be, "Now, boss, give him a good shot." I took advantage of the opportunity, hitting him in the side. The ball should have knocked him down, but did not. On the contrary, he turned from the dog and rushed straight toward me. In reloading, the shell stuck in the chamber and the breech-block could not be closed. The bear was near the brink of the gulch, evidently about to jump over.

Again, Nip to the rescue. The eager dog rushed in, snapping at the bear's rear legs and grabbing a mouthful of fur just long enough to distract the bear from Pickett. The grizzly spun on the dog and resumed his chase back toward the trees, allowing Pickett to fuss with his rifle, get it working, and shoot. This brought the bear on another charge, one the brave little dog could not distract it from. When the bear was bounding toward him, almost to the opposite edge of the gulch from Pickett, another bullet slammed into it, and rather than jump into the gulch and come up after Pickett, the bear slumped over the edge and rolled to a stop. Pickett, with a formality that he could not have felt at the moment, observed that, "If the bear had succeeded in jumping the gulch, I do not know what would have happened."

Here was another of those legend-building bears that "took a lot of killing." This one received, according to the Colonel, "six bullets from a high-powered rifle loaded with 106 grains of C. & H. No. 6 powder, with 340 grains express bullet."

These close calls didn't happen all that often, even for a hunter as active as Pickett, and especially once hunters were armed with something more than a single-shot muzzle-loader. Thomas McNamee, in his excellent recent book, *The Grizzly Bear* (1984), complained that "the story of America's conquest of the grizzly suffers, ultimately, from a deadening sameness. Bang bang bang. How I kilt the bear that almost kilt me. Bang."

True enough. There was a terrible slaughter of bears, and rarely did the bear do more than "almost" kill the hunter. By the time people in a region got around to recognizing the various worths of the grizzly bear—cultural, aesthetic, scientific, sporting, spiritual—their bears were in trouble or gone. I'm not happy today that Pickett and his fellow ranchers killed so many grizzly bears, but he was a man of his time, and was doing what his time, generally, saw as right. Grizzly bears were still only *marginally* thought of as game animals by *some* people. When Pickett was out killing bears, he had every right to believe he was doing the neighbors a favor. Not knowing any better isn't an excuse; it's simply the way it was.

More, the sport of bear hunting was undergoing evolution. Pickett was part of the first wave of grizzly-bear sport hunters in the

Yellowstone area, just as Crockett was in the vanguard of black-bear hunters in western Tennessee. It seems an unfortunate truth in American sporting history that we have to almost lose something before we realize its value and start to protect it.

A simplistic illustration, from *Harper's*, 1855, of a spring-set gun used to kill grizzly bears as they traveled their favorite trails.

But we're interested in hunting stories here. People who don't enjoy them, or find outdoor tales to have a "deadening sameness," aren't likely to have their minds changed by any defense I could give these early sportsmen anyway. I am sure, at least, that Colonel Pickett, standing there in his socks on the edge of that gulch in a sudden rushing silence—that is, standing there looking down at the warm dark form of a grizzly bear that came so near killing him—did not find a deadening sameness in the moment.

Pickett recounted many other bear adventures in his memoirs, two of which stand out in my mind as the sort of odd things that happen to someone who really puts a lot of time in a specific sport.

He spent several weeks in the summer of 1882 camped near Heart Mountain, an 8,100-foot peak not far north of present Cody, Wyoming. His party had left portions of an elk carcass in a meadow near camp, and before long there were signs of grizzly bear near it. Pickett spent a few evenings waiting for the bear, but it always showed up after dark, each night hauling the carcass farther from the meadow toward the trees.

Finally, one day Pickett tied the remainder of the carcass to a tree, taking care to pull the elk up high enough so that the rope was out of reach of the bear. The added cover of the trees had the desired effect: well before dark, given added confidence by the gloomy forest, a grizzly bear came in to feed. Pickett, perched on a nearby limb, killed it neatly with one shot.

The next morning, this bear was skinned, and *its* carcass was also hung up, with a rope through the hamstring to hold it good and high. Pickett resumed his post, and just at dusk in came another bear; it came within sixty yards before spooking and making off into the woods. But after Pickett left for the night the bear returned, cut the carcass's hamstring, and hauled it off for a leisurely meal nearby. After feeding, the bear buried the remaining meat and left.

The next morning, upon discovering the relocated carcass, Pickett again constructed himself a little seat in a nearby tree, and was on duty by evening. Right on schedule, the bear appeared, but it seemed confused. It kept watching the spot Pickett had been hidden in the previous night (thus revealing what had spooked it before), and with a loud shaking of its head (flapping the mane and ears the way a dog does), it came on to the bait in an agitated state of mind. As it approached in that smooth, rolling gait, Pickett took aim and fired an express bullet at the shoulders. The bear was spun and felled by the shot, but was up instantly, running full tilt back up its trail.

Pickett jumped from his tree and raced after it, into deeper and deeper shadows in the heavy timber. At last it became clear that the bear was not mortally wounded, and that Pickett's pursuit was quite dangerous. Visibility was limited by the trees and the gathering night, taking away from Pickett the one sense advantage—sight—that he might have had over the bear. Time to go back to camp.

First thing in the morning, Pickett was back with his guide, Corey. With Corey leading, hunched over looking for any sign of track or blood, they cautiously advanced into the dense stand of pine. Pickett was immediately behind Corey, so immediately that his rifle barrel extended over the tracker's back. Both had their jobs, and no mistakes were permitted. For a mile they moved like that, through one thicket after another, sometimes finding blood, sometimes not, in what must have been an incredibly draining exercise in concentration, listening for that warning snap of a twig, that inhalation of breath before a growl, that trouser-wetting crash of undergrowth a few feet away that would signify they had found what they were looking for.

They were to find no such relief. Corey eventually realized he'd crossed another bear trail, and could no longer be sure which one he was following. The bear got away.

Why this is unusual is that the bear seemed to *really* get away. Four years later, on a hunt near his ranch some seventy miles to the south, Pickett killed a large grizzly with three shots. Upon skinning it out, he found not only two of his own bullets, but what was left of a .45 bullet, exactly like those he had been using four years earlier, and in exactly the spot he'd hit on the bear that got away.

He was fairly sure this was the same bear. As he said, seventy miles was "a distance not outside the range of the grizzly bear." Though most may not travel that far routinely, some will take it in their heads to do so, either because of some disturbance in their own range (like being shot, I suppose) or for some reason only bears are aware of.

The other incident occurred in 1880, in October, in the same area where Nip had saved Pickett from a grizzly. Pickett had seen evidence of a grizzly at one of their elk carcasses, so he set himself up in a perfect blind, looking down over the carcass from about thirty yards' range, with the wind in his face. At dusk a bear came in, and Pickett, on the watch, crept in to take his shot. (He was wearing moccasins; after a few years in the woods, he had learned to move with complete silence.) He came to within twenty-five yards, and was just taking aim at the bear when it suddenly swung to one side, took two quick leaps, and stared right at him, as if to say, "I *thought* someone was watching me."

Pickett was so unnerved by his sudden exposure that he shot recklessly and missed. The bear bolted away, taking a bullet amidships as it went, and with Nip hot on its trail. After a hard and harrowing chase in the dark, Pickett got close enough to the bear to hear it making what must have been terribly rude suggestions to the dog, but it was too dark to follow any more, so he called Nip back and they returned to camp.

Pickett, obviously a practical man, never got over an eerie feeling about that bear. He was positive it did not hear him, and it could not possibly have scented him. He remained sure, years later, that the bear reacted to Pickett's surveillance just as people do when they sense they are being watched. This bear suddenly somehow knew it was not alone, and it knew where Pickett was. The former is not unusual, as bears are often described by hunters as appearing restless, or knowing something is amiss. But this one, for no apparent reason, also knew right where to look to see Pickett.

Maybe it sensed him. Maybe it didn't. Maybe, with its superior hearing, it heard something Pickett couldn't hear, a moccasin brushing against a root, or a dog's tail hitting a branch. But I'm inclined to think Pickett could have been right; humans are nowhere near as tuned in to their surroundings as are wild animals, and a bear could have all sorts of senses we can hardly imagine. As much as we've learned about them through modern science, we still know very little about how their minds work.

William Pickett's activities are hard on modern sensibilities. He killed more than seventy grizzly bears, most in what is now called the greater Yellowstone ecosystem, an area whose bears are the subject of intense scientific scrutiny and endless public controversy over their management. We are likely to exercise retroactive indignation when we hear that a century ago some rich guy was out here blazing away at these endangered animals, killing elk and bison to bait them in, shooting even the cubs.

But as I've said, Pickett doesn't need my defense. He knew what he was doing and what it meant. Cubs, he believed, grew up to be stock killers. He loved to hunt grizzly bears, but he didn't want them around forever, the way he must have wanted elk and deer around. Grizzly bears were still there to be thinned out, and Pickett and his colleagues were pretty good at that. They weren't able to kill off the bears in the Yellowstone area, but by 1911 they had wiped them out of the Bighorn range east of Cody, and even earlier they had seen to it that grizzly bears no longer appeared around Thermopolis, a hundred or so miles southeast of Meeteetse.[6] Almost a century later, though, when the famous Craighead research team was in Yellowstone (also killing bison to bait in bears, but this time to livetrap them), there were still bears making a comfortable living on the Stinking River, wandering the same hills Pickett had left behind so long ago.

And I think I've figured out what was bothering Seton. I've wondered for a long time what could have gotten that very famous author so riled up against a private citizen like Pickett that he would openly make him the villain of a work of fiction.

Pickett was, by all accounts, a pretty forceful character, certainly one with political and personal adversaries. I came across mention of some of these in my readings, especially a man named Abraham Archibald Anderson, who seems to have come to the upper Greybull area in about 1886.[7] He was, like Pickett, a man with a substantial financial reserve, and at first the two men seemed to hit it off. Then Anderson said he intended to hunt in the area that Pickett liked most, and there the friendship seems to have ended. Exactly what was said is unclear, but a grudge was quick to develop and slow to heal. Anderson spitefully filed a claim on a 160-acre homestead only ten miles from Pickett's ranch. Being an artist, he named his new home the Palette Ranch.

This information was squirreled away in my mind's chaotic filing system, with no likelihood of ever needing to be used, when just the other day I got to browsing through Seton's *Biography of a Grizzly* for perhaps the hundredth time. I tripped over the dedication:

> This book is dedicated to the memory of the days spent at the Palette Ranch on the Greybull, where from hunter, miner, personal experience, and the host himself, I gathered many chapters of the History of Wahb.

So there it was. Seton didn't pick Pickett, so to speak, merely because he was a famous bear hunter, or because he was a hunter at all. Seton's "host" was a hunter, too. Seton most likely got a heavy dose of Pickett poisoning just by sitting on the verandah at the Palette, hearing various partisan authorities hold forth on the many sins of the big rancher down the hill.[8] To Seton, the feisty old rebel must have seemed the perfect adversary for the fictional, near-mythical grizzly bear of the *Biography.*

The irony is that Pickett, if asked, would almost certainly have agreed.

Chapter Six

Robert Eager Bobo

ONE of the ethical problems that many nineteenth-century sportsmen struggled with was the killing of huge numbers of animals. By the 1830s, when the sporting press was well enough established to publish such things, avid anglers vied in print over who had killed the most trout in one day on such and such a creek. Totals of three hundred and more were not uncommon. Incredible numbers of game birds and mammals were also reported, though quite often this kind of killing was done by market hunters rather than amateur sportsmen.

Historian John Reiger has already devoted much of a book, his *American Sportsmen and the Origins of Conservation* (1975), to the gradual move away from such resource-exhausting kills, so I won't cover that ground again. What interests me about them here is the effect they had on our estimation of a sportsman. In those days, when game management was a rare thought, when so many parts of the country seemed to have inexhaustible numbers of animals, and when a lot of sportsmen really didn't care that excessive killing now would mean no hunting later, a hunter proved himself in different ways than now.

Certainly the best tracker, and the best shot, and the best companion were all admired and considered good sportsmen just as they are now. Certainly the well-mannered hunter who gave his friend the first shot, or the well-tempered angler who showed a companion the best fish of the day, were as appreciated as they are now. But for a large segment of the sporting public, at least up until the late 1800s, a hunter could also achieve notoriety on the basis of sheer numbers of game taken. A "great" hunter was often just a very successful hunter in terms of meat brought home. In some regions, there were so few sport hunters that large kills were possible for a long time. But eventually, more and more people had the leisure to hunt, and there were more and more people, period. The more people hunting an animal, the greater its value as an individual trophy. No doubt a lot of modern hunters would be content to take one black bear in their lives, to say nothing of a grizzly bear or a polar bear.

But numbers alone weren't enough. It seems that the few bear hunters who gained more than local reputations, and more than temporary fame, had to have more than numbers going for them. That's how it was with Wade Hampton, for example, who was admired throughout polite sporting society not only as a killer of many bears but as a fine gentleman. And that's how it was, as well, for Bob Bobo.

The Bobos were French, originally settling in Virginia in the 1720s, moving into South Carolina in the 1770s, and on west to Mississippi in the 1830s. Spencer Bobo came to what is now Coahoma County, Mississippi, in 1834, and his brother Fincher arrived not long after. Fincher married Sara Eager, and in 1842 a son arrived whom they named Robert Eager Bobo.

Little is known about the boy's childhood, except that it was spent in a relative wilderness, where hunting the likes of that experienced earlier by Crockett in Tennessee was still possible. Young Bobo enlisted in the Confederate Army in about 1861, and it is at the close of the Civil War that his record begins to clarify. An unpublished 1971 memoir by his grandson, Robert Bobo, Sr., gives what little is known about the start of Bob Bobo's Mississippi adulthood.

> After serving four years in the Confederate Army he returned home to find much of the County under water. You see, there were no levees and most of the land was subject to overflow from time to time. So, in an effort to

find a spot out of water, he got in a canoe and started South and saw no dry land until he reached the spot where Bobo now is. So, he staked his claim there. Years later, when the railroad came through, they depended on the land owners to give them right of ways, which they usually did, providing the trains would stop at their headquarters. These stops had to be given names and they were usually named for the donors of the right of ways. Hence, throughout this area, we find such stops as Sherard, Stovall, Clarksdale, Powell and Bobo.[1]

That list of stops means a lot to bear hunters. Curt Clark and John Holmes Sherard were frequent hunting companions of Bobo's, and were admired hunters in their own rights. The town of Bobo, unincorporated yet, still exists, a few miles southwest of Clarksdale, home of Robert Bobo, Jr. There was nothing there in 1865 but a canoe and a man with a dream; Bobo had returned from the war, according to one account, with "little more than the clothes he wore."

His home was pitched in the midst of a far-reaching and almost impenetrable forest and canebrake, where wild beasts flourished in such abundance that the work of all the hunters that have scoured the country since that time has not sufficed to exterminate them.[2]

That was written in 1902 in Bobo's obituary. He died a prominent and celebrated southerner, having parlayed his first claim, through savvy investment and hard work, into "an estate of some 2,000 acres, 900 in cultivation, and including some of the best hunting ground yet left in Mississippi, worth probably something like $100,000." That was a level of solvency that even Wade Hampton, who died the same year, would have found charming.

Bobo was like Hampton in another way, apparently. He did not take much to publicity. He loved his bear hunting, and he cordially entertained hunters from other parts of the country, but he avoided interviews, photographers, and talking about himself. For that reason, most of his adventures are lost. Fortunately, his fame in the region has never died, and both local historians and his descendants have preserved a fairly good record of his activities.

There are, of course, the occasional indirect references that tantalize historians. Here's one from W.A. Williams's *History of Bolivar County, Mississippi* (1976), Bolivar County being the county directly south of Coahoma along the Mississippi River.

> At the Sears home, Messrs. Bob Bobo, Felix Payne, Sam Dunn, and others with about seventy-five dogs would gather for a week of bear hunting. Sometimes the kill would be eight in a day. Choice cuts were roasted and eaten, the rest boiled in huge pots outdoors for the dogs.

Three views of hunting in the southern cane "jungles" that were often nearly impenetrable and yet were an integral part of the southern bear hunting experience. These illustrations are from Alfred Mayer's *Sport with Gun and Rod* (1883), but were first published in *Scribner's Monthly* in 1881.

Hunting brought its hazards. Once during a hunt one of
the boys with a bear at bay shot a gun which failed to fire.
While the dogs held off the bear, he cut a big cane and
sharpened it. At first he aimed it poorly and struck the
bear's side, breaking at once both the bear's rib and the
cane. While the dogs and wounded bear fought, he
resharpened the cane and thrust again—this time at the
bear's heart—fatally.

But we don't have to settle for such accidental history in our
search for information about Bob Bobo's bear hunts. He didn't leave
as good a record as, say, Grizzly Adams or Theodore Roosevelt, but
he left enough for us to know he earned his reputation.

He hunted in the style described in Chapter Four, with a large
number of hounds—Walkers and redbones were his favorites.[3] According to an interview with his grandson in 1974, Bobo had
adopted an unusual training program for his hounds:

"Colonel Bobo trained the dogs with the aid of a pet
bear. He would put a collar around the bear's neck, tie him
to a wagon, and lead him through the woods. Later on, he
would turn loose the young puppies that he wanted to
train to chase bear," Mr. Bobo said.[4]

He often used the knife, closing with a bear that could not be
safely shot without risk to the dogs. During a period when he preferred to carry a Colt pistol rather than a rifle, he had one of his
closest calls with a bear.

He had discovered that there was a serious disadvantage to the
pistol. In order to be used reliably, the pistol had to be fired from
very near the bear, so near that the noise of the shot spooked the dogs
as they attempted to fight and hold the bear. The result was that the
dogs would sometimes back off when they saw him coming, which
made his job just that much harder. A bear not distracted by dogs, he
found, is a hard bear to kill with a knife.

According to his own account, published as part of a rare interview in *Forest and Stream* on March 24, 1887, his hounds had

brought a wounded bear to bay, and as he stepped up with the knife, the hounds must have eased off their attack. The bear turned on him, and in an instant had his knife hand in its mouth. The guard on the handle was big enough to keep the bear's mouth from closing, but its teeth had bitten into his hand deeply enough that he could not pull away. Thus held, with hardly any time left to him before the bear realized his predicament and clawed him to death, Bobo reached his left hand across in front of him and managed to pull his revolver from his belt, and found it easy enough to fire point blank into the bear's head, killing it and releasing himself.

In his younger days, he admitted, he was even foolhardy enough to hunt bear with only a knife and dogs.

On one occasion Curt [Curt Clark, his stepbrother] and I went into the woods, taking two negroes with us, to cut a hack (a blaze line) as a guide in hunting. We agreed not to take our guns as they would be in the way, and probably divert us from the business we were upon. After a while one of my dogs came to us. Then another, and another, until there were half a dozen. As we proceeded with our hack, we crossed a fresh bear track, and the dogs gave chase. They treed the bear quite near us. We went to the three and saw that it was a large bear. The sun was only two hours high and we were five or six miles from home. Curt Clark, who was a regular dare-devil, said, "Bob, let's kill him with our knives." I was a much younger man then, and equal to anything, so I agreed. The negroes promised to stand by with their axes. We pulled a grapevine, which caused him to come down the tree. I expected to kill him at the first blow, standing behind his back as his hindfeet touched the ground. But my knife struck a rib and did not penetrate. Instantly we were all in a promiscuous pile. Curt and I, the dogs and bear, in a rough-and-tumble fight. The negroes ran away. Curt and I used our knives for all that was in them. Curt tripped and fell on his back. The bear was on top of him. He gave me a look which said, "it all depends on you, now." I would rather the bear had

killed me than Curt. I made a desperate lunge and struck
his heart with my knife. He was already badly wounded,
and sank down dead upon Curt.[5]

Undated photographic portrait of Robert Eager Bobo. (Photo courtesy of Robert
Bobo, Jr.)

Even in his later years, when he usually had firearms with him, he
never lost his sense of excitement about a hunt. Another of his companions, railroad man and fellow sportsman Thomas Divine
(spelled Devine by some writers), told of a hunt when the two were
host to a British sportsman named Noel Money (also to become famous as a fly fisherman). Colonel Bobo (the origin of his title is
unclear; some early writers refer to him as Captain Bobo as well)
promised his companions that he would let Money actually shoot
the bear when they caught one.

But, as Divine said, Bobo's "impulse to kill bear was irresistible.
He would frequently invite people down there to hunt, and would
take a solemn promise not to kill a bear himself, but leave it for the
visitor to dispatch. But when the time came and the animal got

within range of his gun, he could not resist the impulse to administer the quietus. Then he would be sorry that he had done it."[6]

That's how it went for Noel Money. After a hot chase, as the hunters drew near the dogs and bear, Bobo found himself just ahead of Money. As the Colonel came within range, he didn't know that Money was only yards away wrestling through the dense cane toward the noise of the hounds, and as usual he couldn't wait; he fired, and Money raced up just in time to watch the bear die.

Despite this bad habit, which he openly acknowledged was his great weakness ("Anything other than a bear is too tame," he said[7]), Bobo was widely respected as a great sportsman. He was a perfect host and ran a "model plantation." His dogs found so many bears that his companions surely had ample opportunities to shoot a few (and I suspect from the context of the story that Divine was having a little joke, and overstating Bobo's bear-killing obsession for effect), and, besides, the bear hunt of the Old South was rather like the fox hunt: being "in on the kill" was usually enough of the excitement for most participants. The chase was the thing.

Exactly how many kills Bobo was in on is impossible to know now. He was, as I said, reluctant to talk about such things, and the various newspaper reports and articles from his day disagree. Figures of 150 to 300 bears in a season are usually used. The 1887 interview in *Forest and Stream*, probably the most reliable of the published sources, quotes Bobo himself:

> One year, I think in 1869, we had rented out a farm and spent nearly the entire time out in the swamp. We didn't come out for three months at a time, but had a couple of negroes with us, and sent them out for what we needed. We kept a memorandum of the game we killed and the score stood thus: Bears, 304; deer, 54; wildcats, 47; panthers, 9. One season I killed 150 bears before my dogs and lost only two runs.

Bobo himself had something to do with the wild reports of his kills that occasionally surfaced in the press. He admitted once to telling a naive newspaper editor that he'd killed twenty-seven bears in one day, just because he was uninterested in the interview and because one of his companions put him up to leading the editor on with a big number. He did tell the *Forest and Stream* interviewer, though, that his real personal high was nine adult bears in one day, though he said he let others kill most of them after his dogs had cornered or treed them.

His largest, Bobo said, was a huge one, weighing 711 pounds:

> I killed him at night in the cornfield about half a mile from the house. We took down the express wagon to bring him home, but four of us couldn't put him in, so we tied him to the hind axle and dragged him to the house.

That is a very big black bear, but not an impossible one by any means. On a steady diet of fat pork and corn, a black bear could get bigger than that. In fact, Bobo's remarks on bear weight are one reason I'm inclined to accept his stories on other subjects. The *Forest and Stream* interview contained the following exchange between Bobo and his interviewer, a *Forest and Stream* correspondent who wrote occasionally to the magazine in the 1880s and 1890s, using the pen name "Coahoma."

[Bobo asked] "How much do you suppose she bears will average in weight?"

"About 300 lbs.," I ventured.

"They won't average over 150," he said.

In the literature of bear hunting, such a remark is a powerful antidote to the countless tales of thousand-pounders. Bobo was one of the responsible ones, and it's too bad that he didn't write about his hunting just for the sake of balancing out the reports of bears almost as big as elephants. Black bears of five hundred pounds, and grizzly bears two or three times that, seem to have been everywhere a century ago, and still appear with disproportionate regularity in the press. Even allowing for the greater likelihood that big, rather than small, bears will get written about, hunting writers seemed to kill way too few small bears.

I suppose, from my reading, that this problem was at its worst with grizzly bears. I've seen reports in sporting magazines of the late

1800s of grizzly bears in the Lower Forty-Eight weighing more than a ton. Absurd stories like that were constantly fought against by the better naturalists and sportsmen. George Bird Grinnell turned the pages of *Forest and Stream* over to reliable authorities for just such purposes, but there was no stopping the stories completely; who could be sure, even at *Forest and Stream*, that a report sent in from the wilderness of some exceptionally large bear was not a rare case of a truly gigantic old animal that grew hog-fat on an unusually good food source for many years?

But in general, saner perspectives prevailed, at least in print. On December 16, 1893, Grinnell published an excellent paper by Arthur Erwin Brown of the Philadelphia Zoological Garden, in which Brown reviewed what really was known about North American bears. His comments on bear size shed some interesting light on the subject of Chapter Two, John Adams.

Size is, furthermore, quite as variable with these animals as any character can be, and thereon I am about to state conclusions, which will certainly be scorned by those fortunate followers of Nimrod who slay 1,500 or 1,000 lbs. grizzlies. It is a curious fact in the geographical distribution of animals—for which an explanation might be sought among ethical rather than physical causes—that 1,000 lbs. bears are not found inhabiting the same range of country as Fairbank's scales. I have seen but one grizzly actually weighed, and that was a male which died in the Philadelphia Zoological Garden in 1881; a larger and finer specimen than the average, and which weighed a trifle under 500 pounds.

By far the largest of these bears that I have seen were one from the Sierra Nevadas, known as "Sampson," who with his owner, old "Grizzly Adams," was the delight of my schoolboy holidays, thirty years ago, in Barnum's Museum at Broadway and Ann Street, New York, and the male of a pair now in the Cincinnati Zoological Garden, which, I am informed by Mr. Stephan, the superintendent, were captured in San Joaquin county, California, in

1871. Quite recently this bear was under discussion between Mr. F. J. Thompson, the former superintendent of
the Cincinnati Garden, and myself, and we independently
estimated his weight at 800 lbs. I am disposed to believe
that is quite as large as "Sampson." Not infrequently
bears are offered to me for sale, by parties in the West,
weighing 1,200 or more pounds. In such cases I always
offer a sliding scale of prices, so much a pound up to 600
lbs. and an increased rate for each 100 additional. It always happens that the weight finally comes down to the
lower limit, and the owner acknowledges that the one first
given was estimated. I confess myself profoundly skeptical as to the present existence of a bear weighing 1,000
lbs., anywhere between the Gulf of California and—say
the Mackenzie River.

Brown may have gone a bit too far in his justifiable skepticism; a
thousand-pound grizzly bear was and is possible in that geographic
region, and has been scientifically documented. But such a bear is
somewhere off the high end of any curve of averages.

Black bears grow surprisingly big in some areas, as the 711-
pounder weighed by Bobo proves. Pennsylvania, with its rich
natural food sources, grows unusually big bears, and of course
anywhere the bears have access to human foods in garbage dumps
you may see a jumbo. In most circumstances, a four-hundred-
pound male is a very big black bear. But, as with grizzlies, there is
something about a black bear that makes us think it's bigger than
it is.

In his very fine book *The Wild Bears* (1986), George Laycock
tells a wonderful story about a sportsman's club in Pennsylvania
that arranged a project involving a caged black bear. The bear, which
weighed 320½ pounds, was put on exhibit and the public was invited
to guess its weight. The highest guess was 1,650 pounds, and many
estimated more than 700.

I was taught a helpful trick for estimating bear weight by a fellow
ranger in Yellowstone. He was trying to get some visitors to give him
an estimate of the size of a bear they'd seen. They didn't know how

to make a guess, so he suddenly got down on all fours in front of them and said, "How would it compare with me?" When you see a bear, imagine how it would compare in height and girth with you if you were crouched by its side. Just don't go crouch by its side.

In 1959, *The Clarksdale Press Register* published an article on the early days of the town of Bobo, based in part on an interview with Mrs. Fincher Bobo, the daughter-in-law of Bob Bobo. She married Bobo's son Fincher in 1900, and recalled the last days of the old hunter, when sportsmen still traveled from far away to hunt with him. There was a festival mood in their setting out for the wild country, with the string of four-mule wagons, the dozens of dogs racing here and there, and the hunters themselves, mounted on their fine, high-spirited horses. She recalled the long hunts, when the men were gone for weeks and lived on bear steaks and stew. The bear meat, she said, was "quite coarse and tough but good."[8]

Bobo and friends with the captive bear he used to train his hounds. (Photo courtesy of Robert Bobo, Jr.)

It seemed to be those later hunts that had much to do with Bobo's fame. When he attracted well-known men to hunt with him, he and his skills—as well as his hospitality—reflected well on the community and the region, and he became even more well known as a citizen.

And he did attract a variety of people. Kit Dalton, a captain under the infamous guerrilla Quantrill and later a member of the James gang, recalled a visit he made to Coahoma County with members of the gang.

> ... we were in Clarksdale, Mississippi, visiting relatives of the James boys, who received us most cordially and caused us to meet a Mr. Bobo, a famous bear hunter, who gave us the glad hand of welcome and arranged a bear hunt in our honor.
>
> It was our first experience in that kind of sport and though we enjoyed listening to the yelping pack, there was little fun in trying to keep up with it through the terrible forests of canes and bamboo. We were scouts of many years' experience, but we had never encountered a Mississippi jungle before, and I will never tackle one of them again unless that were the sentence passed on me by the authorities for some of my misdeeds of the long ago.
>
> In the chase we rounded up one bear—that is, Mr. Bobo and the dogs did, for not a bear in all Mississippi jungleland could get through one of those almost impenetrable canebrakes easier and with less damage to himself than our honorable host.
>
> When the bear was brought to bay behind an upturned tree root, the dogs were crowding in on him, and I have no doubt but for Mr. Bobo's interference would have made quick work of him. But he had taken us out for the chase and wanted one of us to have the pleasure of bagging the little black rascal. The lot fell to Wood, who dispatched him with one shot from his big pistol.
>
> That was enough for us. The honor of killing one bear was enough for all three of us.[9]

Bobo also attracted the journalist and novelist Emerson Hough, a onetime *Forest and Stream* writer who in 1904 published a novel, *The Law of the Land*, based on a fictional version of Coahoma County with a leading character modeled after Bobo. Hough, a leading sporting writer of the time, was apparently a frequent visitor to the county, and an avid hunting partner of Bobo's.

Unfortunately, for a time in the early 1900s Bobo's name was unfavorably associated with a hunt he did not even participate in. It seems a shame that after such a long and successful hunting career he should have a shadow cast on himself at the very end of his life, and it also seems that it now has been straightened out and his honor restored, but for a while in 1902 it looked pretty grim for him.

That was the year of Theodore Roosevelt's famous bear hunt in Mississippi, a hunt that will be described in a later chapter. It was also the year of Bobo's death. Indeed, Bobo was in declining health when the President arrived for his hunt.

What seems to have happened was that Bobo was already busy with a scheduled hunt with some visitors from Illinois when word reached him that the presidential party would like him to join them and bring his dogs for a week of bear hunting. The visitors from Illinois were special friends; earlier in the year, while in Chicago, Bobo's cancer had made him ill enough to need a great deal of personal attention, and these people were the ones who offered him hospitality and cared for him. He was taking them hunting and entertaining them at his plantation out of gratitude.

When the message came from Stuyvesant Fish of Roosevelt's party, Bobo and his friends had just emerged from the woods after several days of hard hunting. The dogs were exhausted, and, considering that cancer would claim Bobo's life in only a few weeks, he must have been pretty well beat himself. His guests were scheduled to stay several more days. He politely declined the invitation.

A reporter on a Memphis paper cooked up a story that Bobo had refused to hunt with the President because not long before, Roosevelt had entertained Booker T. Washington at the White House. Bobo, upon hearing of the story, wrote letters enough to state his own position, but it was a sad thing to happen to the old sportsman in his last days, and it must have heartened him to see the press come to his rescue. Even *Forest and Stream*, still watching over the scruples and activities of sportsmen, published his letter, and concluded that "the next time the President wants a bear hunt, it is to be hoped he will go to Bobo direct. The Bobo bear pack is by comparison the only one in the State of Mississippi. It is a pleasure to see it when it moveth itself aright on its accustomed grounds; and when Bobo goes after bear, he gets bear."

The last remark, besides being a testimonial on behalf of Bobo, was a gentle jab at the planners of the presidential hunt, which turned into a fiasco in which Roosevelt not only did not get a bear, but got a mascot he never really wanted, and a whole lot of ribbing from the press.

But there is something else to the incident of Bobo and the Roosevelt hunt, something that intrigues me. It connects, in my mind, with another piece of western Mississippi folklore that I came across in my research.

There is a persistent tale, one with no documented proof that I can find, of another hunter's being approached about joining the President on his hunt. According to this story, which is a part of local oral tradition, an old black man of some local reputation as a hunter was asked if the President could use his bear dogs. The old man refused. His questioner explained to him that the bear hunt was for the President, but the old man was adamant, and said something to the effect that he didn't care if it was for Booker T. Washington, they couldn't use the dogs.

I wonder if that story, which obviously has been making the rounds for years in Mississippi, somehow grew out of the other story, of Bobo's supposedly not wanting to hunt with Roosevelt because the latter had been friendly to Booker T. Washington. Local legends are born in just that way, as a tale is passed around and ornamented by each generation until its originator hardly recognizes it.

I find it satisfying to know that, even in his last weeks, when cancer was wrecking him, Bob Bobo still had the spirit and stamina to get out and hunt, and still maintained his high standard for hospitality even in the face of a presidential invitation. The scandal over the hunt seemed not to diminish his fame in the region, and when he finally died, in a Chicago hospital in the middle of December 1902,

his obituary reported that "strong men in Memphis who are not related to the family by ties of consanguinity wept like children this
morning, and every one who knew the deceased had a kindly word to
drop to his memory."

Chapter Seven

Theodore Roosevelt

A boy growing up in the years just before and during the Civil War heard about the deeds of Crockett and Adams with an immediacy we can't imagine. Those famous early bear hunters were real; some were still alive, and even after they died their stories lived on. The books and magazine articles about them were not obscure old rarities, as they often are now; they were news, on the front shelves in the bookstores.

That is the way it was for a boy growing up in the 1860s. The boy I have in mind, Theodore Roosevelt, was born in New York in 1858. He had what must be called an advantaged childhood, and though it presented many opportunities to a child interested in nature—an uncle, next door, of great renown as a hunting and fishing writer; a father among the founders of the American Museum of Natural History; and a flood of writers, scientists, and adventurers as guests—I don't suppose any of his adult acquaintances could have imagined how fully he would embrace the outdoor life.

But Roosevelt grew up reading the enervating tales of Mayne Reid (books of boyish wilderness adventure with no pauses for civilized relaxation), and the epic novels of James Fenimore Cooper. He fell in love with taxidermy, with birdwatching, with guns of all sorts, with physical hardship for a good cause. He fell in love with many things having nothing to do with the outdoors, too—poetry,

"Close Quarters with Old Ephraim," from Roosevelt's *Hunting Trips of a Ranchman* (1885), shows Roosevelt shooting his first and largest grizzly bear as it rises from a daybed. Roosevelt's books were published in the heyday of the great sporting illustrators of the late 1800s, and featured the best work of A. B. Frost, Frederic Remington, Henry Sandham, and others. Frost produced this reasonably accurate image of the hunt described at the beginning of this chapter.

ships, literature of all kinds, all manner of polite pursuits—but for a long time there, as he was growing up, it must have seemed that the outdoor world had the firmest grip on his interests. It still must have seemed that way to many when, in his mid-twenties, Roosevelt found himself camped at last in the midst of scenes from all those marvelous boys' books about great adventures in the wilderness.

It was almost the middle of September, a time of frosty nights and brisk, eager dawns in the Bighorn Mountains of northern Wyoming. Roosevelt's hunting companion, William Merrifield, was one of the cowboys on his new ranch back near Medora, now in western North Dakota. The two discovered that a grizzly bear had been feeding on a black bear carcass (killed earlier in the hunt by Merrifield) near their camp. They then saw that the bear had moved on to feed on the carcass of an elk killed by Roosevelt. They sat up by the carcass that night, but the elk was unvisited until after full dark, when they could hear the snap of a branch near the carcass. Not even the rambunctious Merrifield would go for a closer look in the blinding dark.

In the morning, they found the tracks of a truly giant grizzly bear; even these two newcomers, neither of whom had ever seen a grizzly in the wild, knew they were on the trail of a huge one. With Merrifield leading the way across the floor of the pine forest, the two moccasin-footed hunters made their way after the bear.

Luck was with them. After a few hundred yards of hard trailing in the pine needles and moss, they saw the tracks turn onto a well-worn, dusty little game trail through the trees. Now they could well see the size of the grizzly's feet, and could follow much more quickly. The bear seemed to have fed much of the night, so they knew it was near.

The track left the well-established trail and entered a thick brush of the sort so many bear hunters seem eventually to encounter. But Merrifield knew his business, and, by a faint sign here, a disturbed clump of moss there, he led them on, each moving with painful care, not uttering a sound. Merrifield, in the lead by a step or two, had just passed a pile of downfall—wind-felled pines that make travel so slow in such forests—when he rounded a tall stump. Giving a silent start, he dropped to one knee, and, "his face fairly aflame with excitement," turned expectantly to Roosevelt, who advanced past him, heart racing, and looked in the direction of Merrifield's attention.

And there rose, from its comfortable daybed, the boy's dream, the man's challenge. Only yards away, the grizzly rose, and rose, until it stood hindlegged-upright, its massive head looming a yard above theirs in the questioning pose of a bear that has not yet decided what to do, a bear that has heard or scented something but is still wondering what it is.

From its position in the bed, it rose with the hunters to its side, but as it looked around, it picked them out of the forest gloom. The bear's hackles stood, it turned toward them, and it came down on all fours in their direction. As it did so, Roosevelt, drawing a bead, put one bullet perfectly centered between its eyes and the great bear slumped down, dead in seconds.

One of the many things that makes the study of Theodore Roosevelt such a pleasure is the wealth of information available. This isn't like sorting out the chaff in Crockett legends, or separating the promotional hype from the genuine Grizzly Adams. The historical scholars working in the "serious" fields, such as diplomatic history or presidential politics, have an enormous amount of stuff to work with, of course; every word and move of a President is recorded, chewed on, argued over. But even those of us with more specialized interests, like sporting history, find we have a lot to work with. Not only did Roosevelt publish many exciting and detailed accounts of his own,[1] and not only was he written about by many others,[2] but he left a substantial legacy of unpublished material that fills in whatever gaps may remain.

Consider the hunt just described. Roosevelt told of it in his first hunting book, *Hunting Trips of a Ranchman* (1885). There are all sorts of backup sources that enrich the image, however. Being a writer, he naturally kept a good many notes. Being an incurable keeper of personal records (he was a respected and widely published historian, too), he liked to keep track of what he had done.

In his game book, the handsomely bound journal he kept that is now a part of the great Theodore Roosevelt Collection at Harvard College Library, is the following entry for that animal:

> old male; biggest bear I ever shot; short + poor fur. shot once, between eyes, at eight yards, 45-75 Winchester. Standing. With Merrifield.

In his personal diary, part of the Theodore Roosevelt Papers at the Library of Congress, Roosevelt said the distance was twenty-five feet. In a letter he wrote to his sister, Anna, a week after the bear was shot, he said the bear was "less than twenty five feet off—not eight steps."[3] Much of this letter, incidentally, found its way into the published account with few changes (fascinating process, tracking down Roosevelt's prose this way).

In his published account, he said the bear "must have weighed about twelve hundred pounds." In writing to his sister, he said it "weighed over a thousand pounds." In his game book, he didn't say. But his game book may be the least primary of all these sources, at least in the case of this bear; the entry must have been written later, or how could he know it would be the biggest bear he ever shot?

So you see what we have to work with when we go to study Roosevelt. He left us a marvelous record of a great life of sport. He was one of the greatest of outdoor writers, producing a series of books in his spare time that would rival the books of our best modern full-time outdoor writers, both in volume and in quality.

I've spent a lot of time with Roosevelt's record, and, even considering that this was his first bear, and that even he obviously had some doubts about its size—not being consistent in his writing about it—I don't doubt that it weighed over a thousand pounds.

It's not that a thousand pounds is a common weight for grizzly bears in that part of the Rockies; it isn't. When the Craighead team spent more than a decade (1959–1970) studying Yellowstone Park's dump-fattened grizzly bears, the largest one they weighed was 1,120 pounds, and the average of the adult males was about 675. Now, with the dumps having been closed for fifteen years and the bears feeding naturally, more the way they would have fed in Roosevelt's time (the Bighorns are the first major mountain range east of the Absarokas, along the eastern side of the park, so the comparison of bears in the park with bears in the Bighorns is probably reasonable), none approaches a thousand pounds and the average adult male weighs about 490.[4] So it isn't that a thousand-pound bear was an everyday thing. It's just that this was Theodore Roosevelt, a superb naturalist and an outstanding observer. Of all the hunters

I've included in this book, the only other one whose claims I'd trust as much as Roosevelt's would be William Wright. Roosevelt was one of the best-informed, most skeptical writers in the history of hunting, and if he said the bear weighed over a thousand pounds, the bear weighed over a thousand pounds.

But the bear's weight did not matter that much. It was the first, and the excitement of it was obvious. More, this was a man who desperately needed this restorative adventure, a man who earlier in 1884 had suffered the crushing loss of his young wife and the sting of a political defeat that seemed to end a short political career; a man who, in hastening to the West for the happily exhausting life of a ranchman, had written that "Black care rarely sits behind a rider whose pace is fast enough." He might have added that black care rarely can find any room in the mind of a man who is facing off at spitting distance with half-ton grizzly bears.

Bears did become very important to Roosevelt there for a while, at least judging from his correspondence with his sister. He told her that, "the woods fairly rang with my shouting when I brought down my first lordly bull [elk], with great branching antlers; but after I had begun bear killing other sport seemed tame.

"So I have had good sport; and enough excitement and fatigue to prevent over much thought; and moreover I have at last been able to sleep well at night. But unless I was bear hunting all the time I am afraid that I should soon get as restless with this life [as I] was with the life at home."

Roosevelt soon regained his emotional and political balance, and never again would it be as shaken as it was right then. And there was much more to his recovery than bear hunting. In time, he decided that his favorite big game was probably the elk. But he never gave up on bear hunting, and the thrill found in that first hunt did not fade in the later ones.

There were several more bears on that same Bighorn trip in 1884. Between them, he and Merrifield killed five grizzlies, Roosevelt getting three of them. One of Merrifield's might have caused a lot more excitement than it did, if Merrifield had had his way. The cowboy was a pretty wild sort, given to crazy impulses that kept Roosevelt on his toes.

Merrifield allowed that, as fine a bear as the first one was, he had been a little put out that there was no fight. He'd heard so much about the grizzly bear's reputation for ferocity and strength that he was hoping for a little more excitement. That should have warned Roosevelt, but it wasn't until the two of them had stalked another bear—this one feeding on an elk carcass—that Merrifield let on what he had in mind. They were only twenty yards from this one, a smaller, quicker animal that Roosevelt thought was probably more dangerous to them than the big one had been. Roosevelt wrote about Merrifield's plan with the sense of humor that comes from seeing an event safe in memory:

> . . . as Merrifield had not yet killed a grizzly purely to his own gun, and I had killed three, I told him to take the shot. He at once whispered gleefully: "I'll break his leg, and we'll see what he'll do!" Having no ambition to be a participator in the antics of a three-legged bear, I hastily interposed a most emphatic veto; and with a rather injured air he fired, the bullet going through the neck just back of the head. The bear fell to the shot, and could not get up from the ground, dying in a few minutes; but first he seized his left wrist in his teeth and bit clean through it, completely separating the bones of the paw and arm. Although a smaller bear than the big one I first shot, he would probably have proved a much more ugly foe, for he was less unwieldy, and had much longer and sharper teeth and claws. I think that if my companion had merely broken the beast's leg, he would have had his curiosity as to its probable conduct more than satisfied.

I can picture the two of them, crouched there in the woods, watching the bear. As Merrifield leans over and whispers his suggestion in Roosevelt's ear, the hunter's eyes start behind their spectacles and he jerks his head to the side and hisses a negative order through his flashing teeth. I think it's a lot more funny than Roosevelt must have at the time.

This account of a kill is pure Roosevelt in one particular: he never

passed up an opportunity to offer some interesting tidbit of information about the game he shot. In this case, it was the peculiar
self-inflicted bite of the wounded bear. In another case, it might be a
digression on the stomach contents and food habits of mountain
lions he had killed, or on the growth rate of antlers, or any of a hundred other things. Roosevelt was recognized by some of the
foremost scientific minds of his day as a leading authority on big
game animals—not merely on their chase, but on their life habits
and everything to do with their environment.

When I began reading about bears, especially when I was doing
reading for my first bear book, *The Bears of Yellowstone* (1980), I
found my way to Roosevelt's books just out of curiosity. His name
was closely associated with the history of American big game hunting, and I figured his would be one of the interesting "old-time"
accounts. Over time I read many such accounts, in sporting periodicals and books, by hundreds of writers, and I gradually came to
realize that Roosevelt was far more than just another bear hunting
writer. He was long ago recognized for his outstanding portraits of
game animals—bighorn sheep, elk, mountain goat, and so on—but
in my exploration of his writings I saw that Roosevelt studied no
one animal more than he did the bear. I saw that Roosevelt's writings on bears were the most comprehensive and reliable account of
the black and grizzly bear published prior to the writings of
William Wright, whose two books, which came out in 1909 and
1910, were the product of many years' intimate acquaintance with
bear country rather than of Roosevelt's often hurried visits to the
wild country he loved.

That discovery, of the magnitude of Roosevelt's contribution to
bear knowledge, and of the quality of his writing, of which I never
tire, led to my second bear book, in which I collected all of his bear
writings (some of them never before disinterred from their original
periodicals), *American Bears: Selections from the Writings of
Theodore Roosevelt* (1983). And that work, I am grateful to say, led
eventually to this book, because it was in Roosevelt's writings that I
first heard of Holt Collier and Wilburn Waters. I decided I wanted
to follow Roosevelt in his search for these remarkable bear hunters
and unfortunately forgotten characters. For as much as he was a

naturalist he was a historian, and the lore of the bear intrigued him as much as the natural history.

I am sure that is why I include Roosevelt in this book. He made a massive contribution to bear lore and literature, never mind that there were single months in which Crockett killed more bears than Roosevelt did in his entire lifetime. He then went on to do more for bears directly, through his conservation achievements, than had any American before him. But for his sake, let's keep one thing straight: neither he nor his companions considered him an outstanding bear hunter. He was an outstanding man who loved to hunt bear. He saw himself as a mediocre shot; his vision probably made him so, and his extended habitation of cities certainly kept him from developing the kind of wilderness skills his companions did. But what he learned he learned well, and what he saw he understood. It was, in fact, that gift of penetration, of perceptual clarity, that earned him his place in the history of bear hunting.

Roosevelt was a student of life. He was fascinated by everything, and he loved information. Things were there to be learned about, exuberantly and with no real need for a practical reason. He seemed to approach wildlife that way, but he also recognized, and preached about, the responsibility of the observant sportsman to preserve the knowledge won so slowly in wilderness experiences. He once summed up that attitude in a letter to his fellow Boone and Crockett Club founder, George Bird Grinnell, in 1897, when the two of them were editing the Club's books on sport:

> The geology and the beetles will remain unchanged for ages, but the big game will vanish, and only the pioneer hunters can tell about it. Hunting books of the best type are often of more permanent value than scientific pamphlets; & I think the B. & C. should differentiate sharply between worthless hunting stories, & those that are of value.

It would certainly thrill Roosevelt to know he was almost completely wrong about the fate of the big game animals he thought were vanishing, for he did all he could to preserve knowledge about them. He worked very hard to publish books "of value," and to take full advantage of every moment he had in the wild, taking time to note the birds he saw on a hunt, or to take a close look at any animal skin or skull that came his way. And he made the most of his many acquaintances in the outdoors. Through his correspondence he kept in touch with reliable professional scientists, asking them anything that occurred to him, challenging theories, proposing new ones, wondering about this or that. Through his less formal acquaintances, he learned as well; when he and his men were snowed in at some line cabin or he found himself dining alone at some tiny village along the trail, he availed himself of the local conversation, thus hearing the tales of the old trappers and mountain men who had lived their lives in the wildest corners of the West.

What made Roosevelt so special was not his enthusiasm for gathering such information, though we owe him a debt for many of the stories of other bear hunters that he has preserved in his own writings. What really set him apart was his extraordinary ability to discriminate between the likely and the unlikely. He said, for example, that the old hunters, however good they may have been at killing bears, were often lousy at understanding natural history; they'd focused only on the killing, and let the rest go by unnoticed. He also knew that the scientific authorities sometimes built fairly elaborate natural histories on the basis of laboratory study of specimens, with insufficient regard for firsthand observations in the field. And he knew that the public was gullible, that what started out as light literature had a way of hardening into something more, so that hoary legend became gospel over time. I suppose it was because of his childhood training in natural history, and because of his insatiable reading, as much as because of his remarkable mind, that Roosevelt was able to sort out bear lore and present only the most reliable parts of it. I daresay his bear writings were even more reliable than those of Ernest Thompson Seton, who became one of our leading nature writers in the early 1900s, and who gathered his information with just as much enthusiasm as had Roosevelt, but with a little less discretion.

This being a book about hunting, I'll let Roosevelt's natural history go for another time, merely adding that though it wasn't always

Listening for the hounds in Louisiana, 1907. (Photo courtesy of the Theodore Roosevelt Collection, Harvard College Library.)

perfect, it was outstanding for its day. The same was true of his analysis of bear behavior around humans, a foremost consideration of the hunter.

Roosevelt devoted many pages to this topic. He had studied the historical records and the older literature, so he could make informed judgments. Try these:

> Black bear are not, under normal circumstances, formidable brutes. They are not nearly so apt to charge as is a wild hog; but if they do charge and get home they will maul a man severely, and there are a number of instances

on record in which they have killed men. Ordinarily, however, a black bear will not charge at all, though he may bluster a good deal.

In fact bears differ individually in courage and ferocity precisely as men do, or as the Spanish bulls, of which it is said that not more than one in twenty is fit to stand the combat of the arena. One grizzly can scarcely be bullied into resistance; the next may fight to the end, against any odds, without flinching, or even attack unprovoked. Hence men of limited experience in this sport, generalizing from the actions of the two or three bears each has happened to see or kill, often reach diametrically opposite conclusions as to the fighting temper and capacity of the quarry. Even old hunters—who indeed, as a class, are very narrow-minded and opinionated—often generalize just as rashly as beginners. One will portray all bears as very dangerous; another will speak and act as if he deemed them of no more consequence than so many rabbits. I knew one old hunter who had killed a score without ever seeing one show fight.

It is just this unpredictability, this quality of individuality, that still makes travel in grizzly-bear country a matter of risk. A cub's upbringing and young adulthood contain so many influences, so many variables, that there is no sure way of knowing just how it will act. A veteran bear scientist, or a ranger with many years' experience at livetrapping bears, will develop a fine sense of what can and can't be done, and of when a bear is in an especially bad mood and when it can be maneuvered and manipulated. Scientific research is revealing many things about bear behavior that will make future backcountry travel safer for people and bears. But there will always be the two imponderables, the personalities of the bears and those of the people involved in any encounter.

Roosevelt only once felt he was in great danger in such an encounter. It happened late in the fall of 1889, when he was hunting along the Montana-Idaho line. On this hunt, he ranged from the valley of the upper Big Hole River down to the Red Rock Lakes, all along the border. Some of this country is still very wild even today, and holds some of the last authentic "Old West" ranchland in the northern Rockies.

Roosevelt's hunt had been interrupted by the incompetence of his guide, who, though he knew the mountains and the game well, was almost impossible to get along with. Finally, Roosevelt returned to camp one day to find the old man drunk on emergency whiskey purloined from Roosevelt's supplies. The guide and his outfit were dismissed; Roosevelt took a good mare and a small supply of camp gear and headed home on his own, walking and leading the mare.

This was a life Roosevelt loved, part of his childhood dream of wandering vast wildernesses alone with only his horse and rifle, relying on his ability as a hunter to feed himself. As on the other occasions when he made such trips (and this one must have lasted weeks, altogether, for "home" was clear across Montana, hundreds of miles away), he did just fine, and even found some adventure along the way.

On his second day out from the camp, Roosevelt was having a little trouble working his way through a convoluted patch of narrow valleys, trying to find a way through for the horse to follow. As evening approached, he stopped by a little stream, set up camp, hobbled the mare, and went in search of dinner.

What Roosevelt was after was a grouse or two. What he found, just at dusk, was a grizzly bear. He topped a rise, and there, about sixty yards away, walked a big bear. It did not see him, just lumbered along broadside to the hunter on an evening stroll. Judging the light adequate, Roosevelt fired a round into the bear's side, a shot the bear acknowledged with a grunt and a sprint for cover.

With Roosevelt running hard to get another shot, the bear made it to the safety of the brush, leaving Roosevelt to circle the hideaway warily, not willing to follow the bear in. It was a thicket some thirty by a hundred yards, and it offered the hunter little hope. He sneaked along the edges, "standing on tiptoe and gazing earnestly" in to see any sign of the bear. The bear was seriously wounded—a lung shot, as he would later determine.

"The Death of the Grizzly," another fine A. B. Frost illustration, this one from *The Wilderness Hunter* (1893).

With nightfall imminent, the bear's patience broke first. Apparently locating Roosevelt, the grizzly hurried from the opposite side of the thicket and moved up an adjoining hill. It might have escaped then, but it chose to stop, turn, and look back at the surprised hunter, who now could see it presenting its wide flank to him as it glared in his direction. (Roosevelt, never one to underdramatize, said that "scarlet strings of froth hung from his lips; his eyes burned like embers in the gloom.")

With light diminishing every second, Roosevelt did not hesitate. He fired a bullet into the bear's chest, actually hitting the heart.

But not killing the bear. Roaring with pain, the big grizzly thundered back down the hill (far be it from *me* to overdramatize; I have not been in the kind of danger Roosevelt was at the moment, but I *have* seen big grizzlies "thunder" downhill. It's a good honest verb), plunged through the thicket, and came straight on at Roosevelt, who held his fire until the bear was climbing over a log. Then Roosevelt put yet another bullet into its chest cavity, by all rights killing this animal a third time.

For all the visible effect the shot had, however, Roosevelt might as well have been firing Grizzly Adams's Navy revolver. The bear gave no hint of being dead, simply ate up the few remaining yards between it and Roosevelt, who was now down to his last bullet.

They were more or less eyeball-to-spectacle when Roosevelt fired his fourth and final shot. He aimed for the bear's forehead, but, what with the excitement of having an apparently immortal grizzly bear about to make his next hunting book a short one, Roosevelt's shot went into the bear's mouth, broke its lower jaw, and ranged back into its heavily muscled neck.

It couldn't have been much of a surprise at that point that the bear kept coming. At the last possible instant, Roosevelt leapt to the side, just as the long claws ripped through the smoke from his final shot. As the bear poured past him, Roosevelt was already reaching for more cartridges; he quickly got two into the rifle. But the bear was moving only on momentum now; the powerful shells were finally taking effect. The hopelessly wounded grizzly fell, regained its feet, tried to run again, and fell in a rolling tumble. At least three, and possibly all four, of the shots would have eventually proven fatal by themselves, given time. But neither Roosevelt nor the bear was given much time.

For all the danger of that charge—danger that he did not underplay when he wrote about it—Roosevelt did not hesitate to place such charges in perspective. His extensive readings and research into bear history had convinced him that the grizzly bear was not the monster portrayed in the popular press, and in fact convinced him that it was becoming less dangerous all the time:

> This is the only instance in which I have been regularly charged by a grizzly. On the whole, the danger of hunting these great bears has been much exaggerated. At the beginning of the present century, when white hunters first encountered the grizzly, he was doubtless an exceedingly

savage beast, prone to attack without provocation, and a redoubtable foe to persons armed with the clumsy, small-bore, muzzle-loading rifles of the day. But at present bitter experience has taught him caution. He has been hunted for sport, and hunted for his pelt, and hunted for the bounty, and hunted as a dangerous enemy to stock, until, save in the very wildest districts, he has learned to be more wary than a deer, and to avoid man's presence almost as carefully as the most timid kind of game. Except in rare cases he will not attack of his own accord, and, as a rule, even when wounded his object is escape rather than battle.

This was a theme Roosevelt returned to repeatedly in his writings. Bears were not as dangerous as many self-promoting writers and periodical publishers would like to think. He might also have added that bears were most often of danger to bear hunters; the great mass of people who travel in bear country, with no intention of bothering bears, are rarely bothered by bears. The one that Roosevelt shot only charged after having been shot twice; the first shot precipitated flight. (Elsewhere in his writings, Roosevelt also pointed out that hunters, having shot a bear, often mistake its attempt to escape for a charge.)

So Roosevelt was on firm ground in saying that grizzly bears rarely "won" in any encounter with a hunter. But he was on less firm ground in his statements about the change in bear behavior brought about by a century of hunting. It wasn't quite as simple as he believed.

Roosevelt was expressing a common belief of his time: that grizzly bears had "learned" to fear white men, and thus were less likely to attack. I find two problems with that. I don't doubt that behavioral change occurred, but I think it was both overestimated and misunderstood.

First, there is his belief that grizzly bears, before they became familiar with white men's weapons, were likely to charge without provocation. The Lewis and Clark expedition journals are seen as good evidence of this aggressiveness; grizzly bears chased those explorers all over the mountains. The question of provocation is complicated, however.

A few years ago I undertook a review of very early grizzly bear-man encounters, in an attempt to get a better feel for just what was happening back then. I hope someday to polish it up, to whatever extent such informal reports can be systematized and quantified, and somehow see it published. In the meantime, I'm comfortable making a few generalizations.

"A Cowboy and Bear Fight," by Henry Sandham, from *The Wilderness Hunter.* The cowboy is firing a peculiarly shaped and very small pistol.

For one thing, most of the "unprovoked" charges melt away in the face of careful reexamination. In many cases, the bear made its first charge only after it had taken a bullet or three from ambush. In many other cases, men surprised a grizzly bear at close quarters, say in timber or brush, and the bear reacted as it often does today in such situations: it defended itself from what it surely perceived to be a sneak attack. In other cases, the grizzly was approached while it fed on or defended a carcass, or while it was in the company of cubs or yearlings. Today, nobody at all informed about bear country is ignorant of the bear's proclivity for defending food and young; a bear doing so is not seen as exceptionally aggressive. In a few cases, grizzly bears seem to have actually stalked and killed humans for food, something that—troubling as many people find it—some grizzly bears still do today.

The point is that those early hunters and explorers knew too little, and cared less, about grizzly-bear behavior. Words like "aggressive," "belligerent," and "ferocious" were used lightly, with no real concern about truer meaning. If I shot the bear, and the bear had the gall not to fall over right away, but charged me instead, I told everybody I'd been attacked by one of those by-God crazy killer bears. I don't find the evidence at all impressive that these early-American grizzly bears were anywhere near as manic as later writers made them out to be.

But Roosevelt probably had a point when he said that bear behavior had changed. It certainly would, in the face of all that killing. Native Americans just weren't as able to kill grizzly bears as were Europeans. Bears are like most other animals; there's got to be a certain amount of plasticity in their behavior for them to survive.

But that's about as far as I can agree with him. The change in bear behavior, to bears' being more cautious around people, didn't happen through simple learning. To hear Roosevelt and his colleagues tell it, the grizzly literally learned to fear men with guns. But how could that have happened? If a bear was shot by a hunter, what did other bears learn from that? Only if there were other bears witnessing it, or if some escaped wounded, would there be a chance for the experience of the shooting to be passed along to bears in general. No doubt there was some of that kind of learning going on; look at how many bears got away from those early hunters with nonmortal wounds.

But there must have been more going on, and I—and some scientists I know—think that the change in bears happened on more than one level. Sure, some learned by being wounded, or by seeing their siblings killed, as Wahb learned when Colonel Pickett shot his fellow cubs and mother. But there was a greater effect of the killings, one with important genetic consequences. From each generation of bears, the ones most inclined to chase after people, or attack people, were certainly the ones most likely to be killed. The shy bears, the ones who for one reason or another (whether it be past experience or just a mother who was on the cautious side), were the ones most likely to live long lives, during which they produced just that many more cubs who themselves were taught caution. Gradually, that kind of genetic shift reaches through a whole population of animals, and a direction is established. Shy bears live longer. Bears that don't kill stock live longer.

This sort of development gives wildlife managers a lot to think about. It may be terrific, for example, that the population of grizzly bears you manage doesn't eat cattle, but it may not be so good that their genetic shift has also made them less aggressive about eating elk and deer, whose populations were in part regulated by such predation. If you tinker with the dynamics of several interacting wildlife populations, you don't know what you will get. If you have bears that mightily wish to avoid people, you may also have bears so shy that they'll easily be pushed off vital habitat by only light human recreational use. If you have bears that shy, you also have a dramatically altered sport-hunting situation. None of this could have occurred to Roosevelt, of course, but life is not as simple now as it was then, either for hunters or for bears.

In time, it even became less simple for Roosevelt. Once his political star had risen, he had less time for hunting, and even the hunting he had was less his own. He had his most trouble as a bear hunter during his presidency, those crowded years in the first decade of the new century.

I think I'll pass over Roosevelt's southern hunts of 1902 and 1907. Most people think of him as the central figure in those hunts, but I don't agree; I think those hunts are actually the story of other men, especially one I will introduce in a later chapter. Roosevelt was the most visible, but he also was—and I think he would agree with me—sort of along for the ride.

That leaves us with the famous Colorado bear hunt of 1905, a perfect example of what a man must go through in order to be a hunter while also being the most important man in the country.

First, just planning it was a giant nuisance. Roosevelt's time was

Roosevelt during the infamous 1902 Mississippi hunt. (Photo courtesy of the Theodore Roosevelt Collection, Harvard College Library.)

no longer his own. He could no longer take off with horse and rifle for a few joyously quiet weeks of hunting and camping. There had to at least be some presidential bodyguards, a presidential physician, perhaps a few presidential cooks and domestics, some presidential guides . . .

And then there was the press. Roosevelt's 1902 bear hunt in Mississippi, alluded to a moment ago, had been a disaster, in good part because the large entourage made it that way and the press told the world. Roosevelt, obviously still stinging from the whole experience, wrote to Philip Stewart, organizer of the Colorado hunt, about the problems in Mississippi:

> I have just had a most unsatisfactory experience in a bear hunt in Mississippi. There were plenty of bears, and if I had gone alone or with one companion I would have gotten one or two. But my kind hosts, with best of intentions, insisted upon turning the affair into a cross between a hunt and a picnic, which always results in a failure for the hunt and usually in a failure for the picnic. On this occasion, as a picnic it was pleasant enough, but as a hunt simply exasperating, and I never got a shot. Naturally the comic press jumped at the failure and have done a good deal of laughing over it.

Roosevelt's hunting was often treated shabbily by the press. In a letter to Stewart in 1900, setting up a mountain lion hunt, Roosevelt (then Vice-President) had remarked that, "I suppose we shall have every type of swine trying to take photographs or get interviews, but I guess we can stand them off somehow." He was so often mistreated by journalists who either didn't understand or didn't approve of hunting that he became quite shy about them.

But there was more to it than dealing with snaky journalists. He was President now, and everything he did was a reflection on the country. He had to worry about failure; how would it look for the President of the United States to fail as a hunter? The public, ignorant of the realities of hunting, could find substantial embarrassment in their President's inability to kill a bear. So, when he made arrangements with Stewart for the Colorado hunt, he had to be cautious. Late in 1902, he wrote to Stewart:

Finally, and most important of all, what about the game? As I say, I can not afford to make a failure of this hunt if I go. I should not say anything about the bears. I should simply say that we were going for mountain lions, because with Johnny Goff's pack we are certain to get a mountain lion if we can start one . . . If I were in private life it would never enter my head to try to get such information, and especially to endeavor to make sure that I could kill mountain lions or have a chance at bear. But the bitter experience with newspapermen, and with the extreme difficulty of doing anything alone, now that I am President, and the knowledge of the way the amiable nonhunting public looks at a failure to get game no matter from what cause, all join to make me feel that I would like what our southern friends call "sure enough" information before I am able definitely to make up my mind.

Other trips came up, and presidential preoccupations intervened, so it wasn't until mid-April 1905 that Roosevelt met Stewart and the guides Goff and Jake Borah, at Newcastle, in western Colorado, for the hunt. Thanks to a lot of planning and the skill of the guides, it was a grand hunt.

It was a new kind of hunting for Roosevelt, done on horseback behind dogs. He found it enjoyable, and hard enough work, but not like "still-hunting" bears on foot. The dogs and horses did most of the work, and provided most of the excitement. The actual kill of the treed bear was an anticlimax after the wild cross-country chase of several miles. Goff was a regionally famous guide (he also guided Roosevelt on the earlier Colorado lion hunt), and his and Borah's dogs were perhaps the most entertaining part of the hunt; Roosevelt's account is full of warm descriptions of the antics and heroics of various dogs. One tiny "black and tan" named Skip spent much of the hunt riding with the President, to jump off and be in on the kill. Both Skip and another, larger dog named Shorty could climb trees, and would pursue small game, especially bobcats, into the top branches of a tree. Skip and Roosevelt hit it off so well that the President was given the little dog and took it home to become part of the White House family.

The first day they caught a bobcat, but the second day their luck with bears began. The small group of hunters rode out with thirty dogs ("a pack," Roosevelt wrote, "in which performance counted for everything and pedigree for nothing," it included some singular crossbreeds, including a foxhound/Great Dane, an indestructible half-breed bulldog "who looked as if his ancestry had included a toadfish," and even a white bull terrier). Bucking through two or three feet of wet spring snow, they rode to the site of a bear trail they'd seen the day before. Locating the fresh scent on a ridge, the pack of hounds lit out after the bear, the hunters slopping along through the mushy snow as best they could.

A couple miles of such riding led the hunters to a steep slope scarred with gullies, where the dogs became confused and seemed to lose the trail momentarily, spreading out in all directions while the hunters sat helplessly hoping for the best. Just as it seemed the bear was lost, some of the pack could be heard "barking bayed" off on the far slope, and soon they came into sight, well up the mountain, surrounding a very large and formidable black bear. The hunters knew the bear was formidable when Badge, the toughest dog in the pack, came back to the men as if to say, "If you don't mind, we could use a little help up there."

Dismounting, Roosevelt and the others led their horses up the rocky slope until they were close to the dogs. As Roosevelt came to the edge of a gully, he could see the bear burst free of the ring of dogs; he had already killed one dog and done damage to six others, but the pack pressed him so closely that Roosevelt could not risk a shot. As the bear passed him on the opposite side of the gully, it was suddenly exposed, and Roosevelt's rifle sounded once, aiming for the only clear part of the bear, its "great round stern." The shot crippled it, and it slid and rolled to the bottom of the gully, the dogs moving in for the final fight. To prevent the death of any more dogs, now that they were determined to move in, Roosevelt jumped into the gully, slid down his side of it on his back and seat, and finished the bear with a second shot as it attempted to stand.

Shorty, incidentally, had been badly used. His habit was to go for

The first black bear killed during the Colorado hunt of 1905. (Photo courtesy of the Theodore Roosevelt Collection, Harvard College Library.)

the bear's face and neck, counting on the other dogs to keep the rest of the bear occupied. The strategy had not worked well with this particular bear, and Shorty was so torn up with head and shoulder wounds that he had to be carried back to camp. The hunters stuffed him with meat, and he slept for forty-eight hours. A few days later, he was fine.

Roosevelt's other bears on this hunt required fewer presidential acrobatics. The first bear, an old boar, was the largest, at 330 pounds postdenning weight. It was probably the most important for Roosevelt, because once he'd gotten a bear the public pressure was off; he could relax and enjoy the rest of the hunt, knowing that the hunt was seen as a "success" by the people who concerned themselves with such things.

Theodore Roosevelt has long been the darling of history-minded outdoor writers. He was the perfect hardy citizen-sportsman— outspoken, bold, emphatic, upright, and often wise. He has come down to modern outdoor readers in an unfortunately simplified form—the sophistication of his intellect and education are little appreciated, I fear, among outdoor writers. Perhaps symbolic of that problem, and certainly among the most persistently annoying of the injustices done him, is the way every popular writer insists on referring to him as "Teddy," a nickname that he despised and that none of his friends would have dreamed of using. John Gable, executive director of the Theodore Roosevelt Association and a leading Roosevelt scholar, tells me that for many years after Roosevelt's death (if you need a short name, call him T.R.), his family could tell bogus friends from real ones by how they referred to him. If they came up and announced they were an old pal of "Teddy's," the family knew they were no such thing. It's sadly ironic that modern writers—not only in the outdoor field, I must say—in their attempts to sound familiar with this great man, abuse his memory by using a silly and inappropriate nickname. "Teddy" is the name of a toy.

For Theodore Roosevelt, bear hunting was part of a complex and vigorous approach to life that was built on a traditional devotion to manliness. There was virtue in learning about animals, and there was value in writing well about adventure, but there was a fundamental affirmation of more deeply felt things, too. For him, the outdoor life was a reflection of a life fulfilled. One hunted to stay fit, and one stayed fit so that one could be a good man and a good citizen. Hunting was in a sense a training for war, just as it was a making of one's peace with nature. It was not a simple code, however forthright Roosevelt's pronouncements about its worth may have seemed to his critics.

Roosevelt didn't kill bears because bears were evil, or because they "needed" killing in any practical sense, though as a ranchman he would have had some sympathy with Colonel Pickett's crusade against cattle-killing grizzlies. He killed bears because in a way very basic to his outlook, killing bears was the right thing to do. It was part of being a good man. That sort of talk has gone out of fashion in many circles today, but I don't think the modern world has come up with any criticisms of bear hunting that Roosevelt did not hear in his lifetime. For him it was a useful, important pastime, one he would never stop celebrating, and one he celebrated as well as any other writer in American history has. He approached outdoor sport with a sense of balance that allowed him to revel in its thrills, dangers, and solitudes without ever losing sight of the reality that it was, after all, only sport, and only a part of the complicated opportunity provided by life. And he wrote of bear hunting as a kind of pinnacle of that sport, at least for the hunter who did not leave North America:

> The most thrilling moments of an American hunter's life are those in which, with every sense on the alert, and with nerves strung to the highest point, he is following alone into the heart of its forest fastness the fresh and bloody footprints of an angered grizzly; and no other triumph of American hunting can compare with the victory thus to be gained.

Chapter Eight

William Wright

IN September 1887, *Scribner's* magazine published an article entitled "Camping and Hunting in the Shoshone," by Reverend W.S. Rainsford. In twenty pages—much longer than a typical modern outdoor article—Reverend Rainsford regaled readers with his adventures over the previous twenty years, hunting bison, elk, grizzly bear, and other big game, mostly in the wild country just east of Yellowstone Park. This was the same neighborhood hunted so often by William Pickett.

Rainsford's article was not unusual; many writers published similar accounts of their experiences at hunting. But Rainsford's article is revealing to us today because of the response to it. The reaction he got said a lot about where bear hunting, and public attitudes toward bears, were going.

I'm thinking especially of the response in *Forest and Stream*, that magnificent periodical established by Charles Hallock in 1873 and run for many years thereafter by George Bird Grinnell (it would easily receive my vote for the best outdoor periodical in American history). Grinnell himself opened the debate on September 6, with a brief page-one comment on the stir created by Rainsford's article. Grinnell pointed out that one of the New York newspapers had sarcastically editorialized that the Reverend Rainsford's hunting was "applied Christianity," and had questioned the appropriateness of a

minister's shooting grizzly bears. Grinnell defended Rainsford,
saying,

> At this stage of the world's development he can. By and
> by, when the lion gets ready to lie down with the lamb, it
> may be different, and when that time comes, the senti-
> mentalists, who are unable to harmonize applied Chris-
> tianity with the killing of large game, can safely hug to
> their bosoms the sweet-tempered, edentulous and
> anonycous grizzlies of that period.

Starting off with religion, the quarrel could only get worse.
Grinnell published a letter in that same issue, from a prominent
sportsman (later a member of the Boone and Crockett Club),
Archibald Rogers. Rogers accused Rainsford of hunting (illegally)
in Yellowstone Park (a partly reasonable, partly incorrect accusa-
tion); of trapping grizzly bears and then shooting the crippled,
secured animals and calling it sport; and of killing other game animals to use as bait (elk carcasses) to attract bears to be shot. This
was a hot letter, so here's a sample:

> Every true lover of bear shooting should protest against
> this detestable practice of killing bears. They are unfortu-
> nately scarce enough as it is, without their being killed off
> by means of those cruel steel-jawed traps. Apart from the
> cruelty, of what earthly value is a trophy when attained in
> this manner?

This was great stuff, bound to stir other readers. Rogers was one
of many sportsmen who thought the grizzly bear was too important
and valuable a game animal to be wasted by trapping, which at that
time was causing the death of awful numbers of the species all over
the West. He was overstating Rainsford's supposed misbehavior—
Rainsford said in his article that such shooting was not much
sport—but he was acting the part of the modern sportsman of his
day, being sensitive to any seeming indiscretion or lack of ethical re-
finement in his fellow sports. He was also participating in a debate
that is still going on, over whether or not baiting bears is okay. Some

states allow it even today, and in many situations it's very difficult to get a bear even with bait.

Rogers's condemnation of baiting was more complicated than it first appears, though. He was objecting mostly to the use of game animals as bait. He didn't say he'd mind if someone used chicken guts or a dead horse. He just hated to see good game go to waste that way.

Oddly, he concluded his letter by pointing out William Pickett as a model of a good sportsman, though, as we have already seen, Pickett thought nothing of shooting a few elk for bait.

But Rogers didn't hold the field for long. The following week, a letter appeared, signed only "E.S.Y.," from Baltimore, Maryland. Here was a man who did not share the views of Rogers, Rainsford, *or* Pickett:

> I always looked upon bears as enemies of civilization. We, I and others, destroyed them by whatever means we could employ to do so. We canvassed all our resources to circumvent their cunning, and that they are possessed of a large degree of cunning no one who has hunted them will deny. When a boy of sixteen years, in 1844 and '45, I spent a year at the mouth of the Arkansas River. The country thereabout, at that early period, was almost a *terra incognita*, and game, deer, turkeys, ducks, etc., were abundant. Our stock, hogs especially, suffered from the inroads made by the bears . . . We never considered them game and did not hunt them as such. They are a mean, sneaking, cowardly animal, and always will "squeal" when hurt. There is no game in them, and the sooner the race is exterminated the better for all who live in the vicinity. I think any person who manifests sympathy for a bear in a trap should be sent to some locality where he would get all the bears he wanted and he would soon be convinced that his notions of kindness to bears were mistaken.

This was bear hating at its anthropomorphic (bears "squeal," which proves they are deficient in character) and anthropocentric (everything that exists, must exist to give immediate benefit to people, or it should be exterminated) best, and it was probably still the most common view, except among sportsmen and naturalists. To most people, bears were still varmints.

But then Rainsford got in a word, responding to Rogers in the September 22 issue (no subsequent correspondents paid any attention to E.S.Y.). He defended himself (about half successfully) against the charge of hunting in the park. He pointed out that "at least three out of five" bears are shot over baits. He said that whether bears are trapped or not isn't any big deal in the long run, because, as the bounty system then in effect over much of the West showed, there was a "common opinion, a very decided one, that bruin must go." In short, he showed that E.S.Y. was more or less expressing majority will, and he implied that he, Rainsford, was merely having a little fun while doing a public service.

September 29 was Rogers's turn. (One of the advantages of having a sporting weekly was that these wonderful debates could rage and live for months at a time without overtaxing the audience's attention span; outdoor magazines were really quite lively, with great reader involvement then.) Rogers offered proof that one of Rainsford's party was, indeed, apprehended killing game in the park, and he pointed out that a mere bounty on grizzly bears did not justify the unsportsmanlike act of shooting a bear in a trap as if it were more or less the same kind of sport as shooting a loose bear.

Which was a good point, if only Rainsford had not said, in his article, that it wasn't much sport. But now the heat was up, and the big guns rolled out. This letter appeared in the October 6 issue:

SAGAMORE HILL, Sept. 28—*Editor, Forest and Stream*: I think that all men fond of large game shooting are under an obligation to Mr. Rogers for protesting against the unsportsmanlike practice of shooting bears in traps. Of course, where bears or cougars destroy stock it may be necessary to kill them by traps or spring guns as vermin, precisely as I poison wolves on my ranch; but as a form of legitimate hunting to shoot a bear in a trap ranks with the old time Adirondack practice of killing a deer in a

lake while the guide holds its tail so that it should not sink
... Two or three of our New York and Brooklyn sportsmen have gained most unenviable reputations in the West
by their so-called "bear hunts," on which they carry with
them a number of huge, exceedingly heavy steel gins—
very proper gear for a professional fur trapper, but
entirely out of place as adjuncts to the rifle of a true
hunter.

THEODORE ROOSEVELT

And on it went. The debate going on then is what goes on today,
though most modern sportsmen are blithely unaware of its process
and importance. Bear hunting, like any other sport, is in a perpet-
ual state of evolution, as practices, ethics, and beliefs are
reevaluated. The faster we learn about an animal and its world, the
faster we are likely to reconsider the way we treat it for sport. Bears
were disappearing from vast portions of their range. Their status
as game animals was still not so secure that they were never considered "vermin," but they were gaining status, as leading outdoorsmen spoke on their behalf. By 1900, the outdoor magazines,
which had for decades preached conservation for many animals
(game and nongame), were taking a serious interest in the status of
bears. James McGuire, longtime editor of *Outdoor Life*, launched a
personal crusade to save bears.[1]

Of course, sportsmen weren't the only ones fighting to protect
wildlife. Other groups and individuals were in on it, some with mo-
tivations nothing like those of hunters, who, among other things,
didn't want all the bears killed today because that would leave none
to kill tomorrow. And the bear was nowhere near its present status in
the public mind; at this early date, there was not much talk among
hunters, for example, of the grizzly bear as a symbol of the wilderness. Bears still had a long way to travel down our conceptual road
before they would be subject to the bewildering variety of admira-
tions and longings they inspire today.

And, sad to say, bears were not gaining in status anywhere nearly
as fast as they were losing populations and habitat. But there was no
longer the universal assumption among sportsmen that "bruin must

go."[2] The second half of the nineteenth century was a bleak time for hunting-oriented conservation, but it was also a time of great promise, as more and more sportsmen began to recognize their responsibilities to the natural resources, and to realize that hunting was more than the cleaning out of gameland after gameland. What they were realizing was that the kind of sport practiced by Crockett—which amounted to killing off most everything of interest, then settling down or moving on—was not the only choice they had. Concepts involving the sustained yield of wildlife populations, long practiced in some areas and well known in Europe, sounded better all the time to sportsmen who would rather be able to shoot a few animals each year forever rather than a whole bunch this year and none ever again. The Boone and Crockett Club, organized by Roosevelt and Grinnell in 1888, was only one of hundreds of clubs in which sportsmen banded together to protect their hunting.

As interesting as I hope you find all of that, I haven't forgotten my goal of keeping this a book about hunting adventures. It's just that this series of letters in *Forest and Stream* are so suggestive of what sportsmen were going through, and of what it meant to bears and bear hunting, that I thought I ought to give you a look at them. Also, I could think of no better way to prepare you for the story of William Wright, whose career as a hunter-naturalist is such a perfect reflection of the times.

The trouble with William Wright is that there weren't more men like him. Starting out as a hunter, he became a remarkably observant student of grizzly-bear natural history. With no formal training—indeed, with practically no education at all—he schooled himself enough to write two outstanding books on bears, both classics of the genre and both still valuable reading today. In doing this good work, he became a strong voice for bear conservation and appreciation in a day when bears were in grave trouble over much of their range. It would be hard to measure whatever effects he had as a writer in his attempts to protect bears, but, looking back, it's plain the bear had no better spokesman in the early 1900s.

Wright was born, by his own account in *The Grizzly Bear* (1909), in New Hampshire in 1856. He was raised on a small farm, "little more than piles of rock fenced in by other piles of rock." While still a child, he saw his first grizzly bear, in one of P.T. Barnum's traveling circuses in Nashua, New Hampshire. The posters claimed that it was one of Grizzly Adams's bears, which it well could have been, even considering Barnum's reputation for promotion.

The name of Adams was not new to Wright; his family had somehow come upon Hittell's biography of Adams in the local library, and Wright and his brother had practically memorized it. The book, he said, was the "greatest influence" on his life, and set him to dreaming of one day having such amazing adventures.

Wright grew up learning the blacksmith trade, and as a young man found easy employment for his skills in shops around New England. But he spent all his free time hunting and learning the woods, never forgetting that great lumbering grizzly in the circus cage. His chance came in 1883, when he was offered a free train ticket to Oregon if he would manage two carloads of emigrants. His real goal was Australia, but when he got to Spokane, in eastern Washington, on May 13, he stopped a while to see if he couldn't find a grizzly bear. His first day there he witnessed a murder, on a main street in broad daylight, but the roughness of the place did not disturb him much, and soon he found work in a local shop, picking up extra money as a mailman and a carpenter. Australia faded from his mind.

Through the rest of the century and into the early 1900s, Wright lived and worked in the northern Rockies, sometimes in Washington, sometimes in Montana. His businesses were sometimes successful, sometimes not. He married, though we never learn anything about his wife or family in his books. After about 1889, he devoted himself more or less full-time to hunting, and guiding hunters, but after about 1897 he no longer hunted at all. His own statement of his change of direction is an eloquent testament to one sportsman's coming of age as a naturalist. He did not become opposed to the sport of hunting; he just left it behind as his interests changed:

> In the beginning, I studied the grizzly in order to hunt him. I marked his haunts and his habits, I took notice of his likes and dislikes; I learned his indifferences and his

fears; I spied upon the perfections of his senses and the limitations of his instincts, simply that I might better slay him. For many a year, and in many a fastness of the hills, I pitted my shrewdness against his, and my wariness against his; and many a time I came out a winner in the game, and many a time I owned myself the loser. And then at last my interest in my opponent grew to overshadow my interest in the game. I had studied the grizzly to hunt him. I came to hunt him in order to study him. I laid aside my rifle. It is twelve years since I have killed a grizzly. Yet in all those years there is not one but that I have spent some months in his company.

It took Wright a long time to get his first grizzly bear. He made several trips with new friends, sometimes getting close to grizzlies but never killing one, all the while getting to know the mountains and discovering that he had a gift for finding his way in wild country.

The rugged country of the upper Clearwater, now part of Clearwater National Forest, Idaho, was a frequent hunting ground of Wright and his clients in the 1880s and early 1890s. (Photo courtesy of the U.S. Forest Service, Clearwater National Forest.)

Finally, more than a year after his arrival in the West, Wright and a friend took a three-month pack trip up along the Idaho/ Montana border in the Bitterroot Range. It was near the headwaters of the Clearwater River (the still very wild north fork) that he got his chance.

Wright had pretty much decided he would once again get no grizzly bear on this trip, and wanted only to get an elk before leaving the mountains. He had heard of a natural salt lick along a small tributary of the Clearwater, and he made his way there, leaving the pack train far behind so he could approach on foot. It was an open streambed, with no trees nearby, so he huddled in some bushes and waited for the elk to show.

They didn't show. Wright spent the better part of the day there, waiting, and it was starting to get dark—and cold—before he gave up hope. It sounds from his description as though he was up about 5,000 feet in altitude, and September nights get cold there. He had not expected to spend the day, so he hadn't brought a coat. The chill had just about driven him back to camp when he looked up the stream and saw what he would have sworn was the very bear he'd seen twenty years earlier in P.T. Barnum's cage. It was a broad old boar grizzly, coming steadily toward the lick, even then only a hundred yards away.

Now, I should tell you about Wright's rifle. It was an ancient Winchester .44 with a badly used extractor mechanism that required the shooter, upon firing, to assist the mechanism in removing the spent cartridge, usually through the diligent application of a pocketknife. This was not a rapid-fire weapon, and Wright had been meaning to replace it for years. It served well against deer and black bears, but he really did mean to replace it.

This was the rifle, then, that Wright pointed at the big grizzly bear. As the bear walked past him at about forty yards, Wright took his shot. It was a good one, into the shoulder, but it didn't have the effect he was so used to in firing the rifle at deer and black bear. Instead of falling over, the grizzly turned and charged the source of the noise.

The rifle, right on cue, jammed. Wright threw it down and raced to the creek, where he jumped over a three-foot-high cutbank into the water, which was even colder than the air but offered some shelter from the bear. Snuggling into a hole beneath an undercut portion of the bank, submerged to his neck, Wright waited for the bear to come roaring over the bank. He hoped his hiding place would be overlooked, and that the bear would rush on in search of him.

The bear didn't come, so after sharing more than enough body heat with the stream, Wright cautiously peeked over the bank. Not seeing the bear, he belly-crawled very slowly back to his shelter, where he retrieved his rifle, extracted the spent cartridge, and reloaded, once again ready to hunt bear. Emboldened by his rearmament, and too cold to have any more patience, he stood up and looked around. He saw the bear, dead, only twenty feet from where his bullet had hit it. The shot had taken out the arteries above the heart.

Wright, like Roosevelt, didn't pass up opportunities to learn about bear behavior. And, like Roosevelt, he was suspicious of popular claims that grizzly bears always charged when shot. He thought it might be more complicated than that. He suspected, based on this and his many later experiences, that for some reason bears that were shot raced toward the sound of the shot, but that they were fleeing rather than charging. Perhaps they confused the shot's echo with the shot itself, or perhaps the bullet, after passing through the bear, ricocheted or hit loudly on their other side, spooking the animal away from that side. He gave another example of a case in which he shot a grizzly bear that immediately "charged" him, coming directly toward him through intervening brush. As the bear closed in, Wright made himself visible and prepared to shoot again, at which point the bear suddenly seemed to see him for the first time and veered off. Wright did not suggest that all such charges were false, but he doubted that many of them were real. Many of his opinions were of this sort, and they inclined to make bear hunting seem less dangerous than was widely believed.

In fact, Wright said he had only once personally known of a grizzly bear making an "unprovoked" charge (in those days, as I suggested earlier, unprovoked meant "before having been shot") on a man. The charge occurred on what was apparently the first occasion he had ever tried to hunt with dogs.

This trip must have occurred in the early 1890s, when Wright was guiding full-time. He had become curious about bear dogs, and through communication with a breeder had been introduced to a new client, John O'Brien, who had one of the breeder's dogs, Nebo, and brought it along on a hunt. O'Brien brought along a second dog, a hound, to learn the trade as well. The two hunters were joined by a friend of Wright's, Martin Spencer, and Wright splurged on two huge dogs an Indian told him were good bear dogs. Neither was of recognizable breed, but one was "a cross between a brindle bull and a staghound."

The party's hunting ground was once again the Bitterroot. As soon as they arrived, O'Brien's hound picked up the trail of a deer and disappeared from their lives forever. Nebo showed great skill in treeing grouse and ignoring bear trails. The two Indian dogs spent most of their time tied up in camp.

Nebo became the camp joke for his ability to miss bears. Late one day, Wright located some grizzly sign in a little valley, along a willow-lined stream, so he chided O'Brien (known as Jack) about it:

> ... I told Jack that there were some grizzlies out in the willows, and suggested (this having become a standing joke) that his dog might be able to find them. I also told him that there were some beaver in the small creek, since he had been abusing the country for its lack of beaver, and had been anxious for some beaver-tail soup, having heard that it was a great luxury. Taking his gun and dog, Jack now went over to the willows, thrashed around for a short time, and returned without seeing anything. He said that the tracks were old, as Nebo would pay no attention to them, and tying up the dog, he went back to the creek to watch for beaver. After a while we heard a shot, and soon he returned to camp, telling Martin that he had wounded a beaver, but that it had escaped to its house in the stream, and he was unable to get it. Martin proposed that they go and tear the house to pieces and thus obtain the animal, and Jack again loosed the dog, shouldered his gun, and, Martin taking a long-handled shovel which we had brought along to prospect with, they set out.

Jack's gun was a single-shot, .40-70 Winchester. He claimed that a good hunter should never carry more than four cartridges for a day's hunt, and consequently he never carried but that number. One of these was always in the gun, the other three were tucked away in his pocket, one in each finger of an old kid glove.

Wright stayed in camp. As the evening wore on, he heard four shots, interspersed with barks from the dog, but he didn't think much of it until Martin appeared.

... I heard a shout and saw Martin coming through the flooded bottom ten feet at a jump, splashing water as he came. His hat was missing and he acted like a limited express going through without stops.

And as he came he yelled: "Get your gun! Turn the dogs loose! There are some grizzlies out there and I guess they've killed Jack," I managed to make out. So I loosed the dogs, caught up my gun, and, without waiting to put on my shoes, made the water fly nearly as high as Martin had coming in. I jumped the small stream, and, landing among the stumps of some shrub willows that had been eaten off by the beaver, punched several holes in the bottom of my feet. I could not, however, stop for that, and as I hurried on I could hear the water splash behind me as Martin, having secured his rifle, hastened after me. Then, as I came into the open, I saw Jack standing at the edge of some timber, leaning on his rifle, while in front of him, sixty feet or so away, a large grizzly lay rolling and bawling as she rolled. In the willows across the creek there was a big commotion—bears bawling and Nebo barking; my curs joined in the uproar; a bear showed his head and I sent a slug into it; Martin came up in time to get a shot at another; a third appeared and was instantly killed. We had four bears down and there seemed to be no more coming.

Once everybody's nerves and dogs had settled down, Wright asked for the story. There is something desperately comic in Wright's own telling of it, so I'll quote it at length:

Martin, in telling of the beginning of the adventure, said that when they came to the small creek and looked over the beaver house, they decided that they would have to cut away a dam below it and run off the water. Jack, therefore, placed his gun against a tree and went forty or fifty yards down-stream to the dam. As they were about to begin cutting this away, they were attracted by a noise in the willows across the creek, and Martin had advised Jack to get his gun, thinking it might be a moose. However, as they heard no further noise, they went to work on the dam, and when they looked up again they saw an enormous grizzly standing on its hind legs and looking over the willows at them. The dog had then begun to bark, and the bear, accepting the challenge, started for them. Jack sprinted for his gun, and Martin, sticking his spade into the mud, shinned up a tree, prepared to referee the show. As Jack got his gun the grizzly appeared at the water's edge directly opposite, and before he could shoot, jumped for him, landing in the middle of the stream. Jack now put in a shot, and as his small supply of ammunition was unhandily packed, was compelled to strike out for the timber, digging for cartridges as he ran.

The bear-dog had been very bold when the bear was on the opposite side of the creek, but when it forded the stream Nebo with great discretion retired some two hundred yards across the bottom; and had Jack's life depended on the dog's attacks, he would probably have been slaughtered then and there. And yet, to do Nebo justice, his barking saved Jack's life in the end. Martin, from his perch, could see Jack's effort to reach the timber, and to reload his gun before the bear overtook him, and, as the latter got nearer and nearer, he called "Look out, Jack, she's after you!" Jack, with this stimulus, made the timber, and the barking of the dog seems to have turned back the bear. Jack now got at his cartridges and, coming out from behind his tree, took another shot at the grizzly from a distance of about thirty feet, but missed her, and she, turning, went after him again. Martin, from his observatory, again called out the news, and again, after Jack had reached his shelter, the barking of the dog drew the bear off. Jack reloaded again, fired again, and missed again, and this time the bear went for him in earnest.

Martin still acted as a bureau of information, but as the bear was now so close to Jack that he had all he could do to dodge her claws, this was hardly necessary. This time he had kept his cartridge out, and he loaded as he ran, and reaching a large tree he swung himself around it, and as the bear passed, fired his last shot—and made a clean miss. He was now forced to continue his flight, and as soon as he was out of sight Martin made for camp.

But Jack never got scratched. After the bear passed the tree she went back to the creek, having now begun to feel the effects of the first shot, which, entering her side, back of the ribs, had ranged downward and passed out of the groin between the legs.

That was when reinforcements arrived and killed the three large yearlings in the brush. The sow was so concerned about the barking dog because, unbeknownst to Jack and Martin (and possibly even to the dog), it was barking so near her young. She was torn between defending the young and attacking her attacker.

But for Wright, the big point was that here was a bear that, before being shot, charged a man. Looking at it now, with comfortable hindsight, we can say that of course it charged. Not only was it being spoken to unpleasantly by the big dog, it was sheltering three young. According to the modern studies of bear attacks, a sow grizzly bear with young, disturbed at close range by people (to say nothing of people with a dog), is about the most dangerous of all bears.

Wright said he knew all the mountain ranges inhabited by the grizzly bear from Mexico to Alaska, and he may have; at least he showed no hesitation about traveling great distances on several-months-long hunts. But his recorded adventures, both in his articles and in his books, mostly involve the northern Rockies, especially the Bitterroots in Montana and Idaho, and the Selkirks and ranges to the east in British Columbia and Alberta. He never gave his total kill, and may have even become embarrassed by it, later in life, when he took up the grizzly bear's cause so enthusiastically. Late converts, they say, make the best zealots.

But in the meantime, Wright fulfilled every imaginable childhood dream of adventures with bears. He trailed one wise old boar for days, almost tricked into losing the track now and then, sleeping wherever nightfall found him, gradually picking up ground as the bear stopped here and there to forage or dig out a ground squirrel or a marmot (also known as rockchuck, sort of the western equivalent of the groundhog), finally seeing a thicket the bear's tracks entered but did not leave, and killing it with one shot.

Wright seems often to have killed more than one bear a day; he was a deadly guide. On one trip in 1891, his party took thirteen grizzly bears. Hunting on his own, he must have put a frightful drain on local bear populations. When he found them in berry patches, he sometimes could get two, three, or even four in a quick fusillade with the single-shot .45-100 Winchester that had replaced the lame old .44. On one occasion, later written up by Wright in *World's Work* (August 1905), he got five with five shots, in less than five minutes.

But sometimes the work was harder. On one occasion, Wright and two dogs found themselves in a bloody scuffle with a small grizzly bear that Wright and the dogs finally finished off with only the dog's teeth and Wright's small knife.

This story of the bear, the dogs, and the knife is the sort that, if I read it in one of the early outdoor magazines, written by some unknown writer, I probably would not trust. But I assume it's true, because Wright is so regularly reliable in his other writings. He was so good at hunting grizzly bears that he had no need to lie (though I know some people don't need a reason to lie), so I'm inclined to give him this one.

This hunt took place in 1891, just after the big hunt that accounted for thirteen grizzly bears. Wright took two men, Dr. C.S.

Packstring fording the upper Clearwater, much as Wright and his parties did in search of grizzly bears a century ago. (Photo courtesy of the U.S. Forest Service, Clearwater National Forest.)

Penfield and James Adams (no relation to the John of this book), to the Bitterroot for bear, elk, and moose. His two dogs, Pete (the "Indian mongrel") and Jim (the bull/staghound cross), went along, having become part of his hunting team by now.

The hunt for bears was not successful for quite a while, though the party got plenty of other camp meat. They made camp on the banks of what he called the middle fork of the Clearwater (by which I imagine he meant what we now would call the Lochsa), wild, beautiful country, and as rugged as it is beautiful. Wright knew of an Indian campsite near theirs, so he decided, after getting camp set up, to go have a look around. He took no rifle, bringing only Jim, the dog, trotting along beside him.

While looking over the Indian campsite, with its empty drying racks for elk meat, and its ample piles of garbage, Wright noticed what at first he thought was a black stump at the forest edge. Then, as his memory reminded him that there was no such black stump on any of his previous trips through here, he looked again and saw it was a black-colored bear, rummaging through the discarded elk bones.

Wright was anxious to get his clients into some bear shooting, and even this black bear was welcome. He sicced Jim on it, and though it took a moment to understand what it was supposed to sic, the dog finally figured it out when Wright let out a yell and the bear rose to look at them.

Wright's idea was to tree the bear, then get Penfield and Adams so they could shoot it. So, with Jim in hot pursuit of the lumbering bear, and Wright running along behind yelling furiously for the hunters to come, the little parade made its way down the shore of the river.

For some reason Wright couldn't understand, though, the bear refused to tree; this was not the sort of sign the hunter should have overlooked, but I suppose he was pretty busy at the time. The bear worked its way along the edge of a high bank over the river, and finally stopped to take a couple of swipes at the dog that was grabbing at its rear end; both of them lost their balance and tumbled down the steep gravel bank to the water, crashing into the trees at the bottom of the slope. The bear, again choosing not to tree in the handy cottonwoods, waded into the water and turned to face the approaching dog. Wright could see that the water gave the bear an advantage, but before he could reach the dog, both bear and dog were grabbed by the current and carried off.

The two animals fetched up against some rocks in the shallows, where they again squared off, making no progress but much racket, while Wright hurried after them. He had decided to try to drive the bear across the shallow portion of the stream into the timber, where, he believed, it would surely tree. As he approached, the bear did break for the other shore, sloshing through the slippery shallows with the dog after it. Wright, still yelling for his companions, was heartened to see Pete, his other dog, run to the water after the others, which seemed to suggest the hunters were not far behind.

Wright caught up with the animals as they struggled through the brush, and at every opportunity let the bear have a whack on its back with a stout pole he'd picked up, finally breaking off most of the pole. The chase rattled on through the heavy timber until it came to a small creek. In a narrow spot in the creek, where the water ran between low banks about two feet high, two large trees had fallen across the creek so as to form a little square corral, or "pen ten or twelve feet square," as Wright called it. Into this solid enclosure the bear bumbled, with Pete right on its tail. There, as the two animals got acquainted, Wright was shocked to see, for the first time, the feet of this bear he'd been beating on: it had the unmistakable long claws of a grizzly. No wonder it wouldn't tree. *Great* wonder it had put up with so much.

By now, Wright was hoarse with screaming for his hunters. Jim and Pete were keeping the bear occupied in its little ring, each darting in for a bite when the bear turned to attack the other. The movements of all three were hampered by the enclosure and the close quarters, and none could ease up long enough to climb out, so a noisy, hairy stalemate was underway, Wright getting in a lick with his stub of a pole whenever the bear came near enough his side.

Here's the part that is hard to swallow. Wright's only weapon, he said, was a pocketknife. He rarely carried a traditional hunting knife, finding that a small three-inch blade was all he needed for most skinning work. This he drew from his pocket and opened. But he decided he'd better find a club instead.

But the bear wouldn't wait. It turned to Wright, ignoring the dogs, and was in the process of climbing over the log when Wright, in attempting to retreat, stumbled over a root and fell flat in the creek. He was sure he'd be killed, but the dogs both took their chance, grabbing the bear's flanks and forcing it back into the pen. The bear, having been virtually on top of Wright for a second, was close enough for Wright to make an exploratory jab with the little knife. When it penetrated up to the hilt with little trouble, he decided to try again. As the dogs and the bear continued their fight, he leaned over the log and stabbed again, this time having no effect as he hit fat.

The strangeness of the scene is what distinguishes it. After the racket of the chase, with Wright yelling, the dogs baying, and the bear growling, the forest became silent. With no more noise than the shuffling of feet and paws and an occasional grunt, the bear and the dogs turned with one another, reaching, darting, sparring, feinting, while the man stood alert, leaning in for his chance, a quick thrust into some likely limb or flank. The bear immediately grew wary of this strange antagonist, whose bite seemed so small yet so bloody, and in a few moments there was a good bit of bear blood around, the bear was getting harder to jab, and everybody was getting pretty tired.

And careless. Wright moved too slowly after one of his jabs, and found himself with a badly clawed hand. The bear found it harder and harder to move as fast as it had in avoiding the bites of the dogs. And the dogs, especially old Jim, were getting very tired. There came a moment when the bear, frantic with its inability to deal a definitive blow, gave everything to one quick lunge and caught the exhausted Jim around the middle with its forelegs. As it went about dismantling the captured dog, Pete rushed in, but no amount of biting and harrying would disturb the triumphant bear from its chosen kill. So Wright jumped into the pen, came up behind the bear, and drove the knife and most of the handle into the bear's side. With its last gathering of power, the bear rose and spun, its claws just whizzing past the retreating hunter's body. But the accumulation of wounds was too much, and the bear's spin continued until the animal was down, and out, on the ground. Both Jim and Pete survived. Wright was a real sight when he showed up back at camp covered with blood.

I don't know. Wright doesn't say how big the bear was, but he does say that when they skinned it they found it had seventeen knife wounds, three broken ribs (from the pummeling he gave it with the pole? from the fall down the riverbank?), and one especially deep wound in the heart, the one that killed it. He had witnesses to the wounds, men who presumably would have backed him up when the story was first published in *World's Work* in August 1909. A three-inch knife, with a three-and-a-half-inch handle, would have reached pretty well into the chest of a smaller bear. But this larger bear? I don't know. I guess the only certain thing we can say is that it was possible.

In time, as we know, the excesses of Wright's hunting caught up with him. Even in his earlier days, he seems to have experienced considerable remorse over the killing of a bear for no good reason—sport or skin being two reasons he did approve of. On one occasion, he stalked a few bears that were feeding on salmon in a small feeder stream. After watching them for many minutes, and learning a good bit about their fishing technique, he said he "was the victim of what nowadays would be called a game-hog feeling." He opened fire, killing two of the three bears still in sight, and missing the third one only because it was too fast into the brush for him to get a shot.

> But now that the excitement was over and I had time to take stock of my achievement, my satisfaction was short-lived. The hides were not worth taking off. It had been a useless slaughter and I was sorry that I had killed. I took the large teeth and the long claws of the dead bears, but since then I have never, but once, shot at a grizzly when it was fishing.

Wright expressed similar regrets over other kills, and it would seem that what had once been for him an exciting sport had become a little bit sickening. He seemed to be learning the lesson of moderation preached by Roosevelt, Grinnell, and others, and never learned by Crockett, Waters, and those of earlier generations.

But moderation was not Wright's answer; abstinence was. He simply stopped killing bears, cold turkey, so to speak, and devoted himself to studying them.

A central part of his study was photography. Even during his days of hunting and guiding, he had lugged an unwieldy 8 × 10 camera with him, experimenting with the clumsy old flash guns then in use in his attempts to get photographs of game in the wild. After years of experimenting, and after grizzlies were becoming rarer and harder to track, he decided to make an all-out effort to photograph them.

Luckily for Wright, there was still Yellowstone Park, with its healthy bears that were relatively easy to locate because of their regularity of feeding at the dumps. Wright found that the bears were still extremely cautious when they got away from the dumps, where they seemed so bold and sociable, and found it necessary to do practically all his shooting with the flash gun. Major John Pitcher was at that time acting superintendent of the park (which was under military protection from 1886 to 1918), and, being an enthusiast of such wildlife work, gave Wright permission to conduct his photographic work in the park.

This was an exciting, pioneering era in wildlife photography. In some of the wildest corners of the world, adventuresome photographers were taking great chances to get surprisingly good photographs of wildlife. A few were working with flash photography, an even more cumbersome process, often involving stretching a wire across a game trail so that the animal itself set off the shutter and took its own picture. The photographer had to haul piles of gear—batteries, plates, lenses, cameras, wire, and so on—and had to watch it being destroyed by some animal that didn't appreciate a sudden flash in its face in the middle of the night. Wright's account of his photographic expeditions is as entertaining as his hunting tales, and even more amusing.

Wright occasionally asked for some volunteer at the park hotels to assist him during his nighttime forays. Most of the time, the young men who eagerly volunteered didn't stay with him too long, what with the dark shapes of grizzly bears looming in and out of the forest nearby. As Wright put it, "Any one who has never seen a grizzly in such a setting is more than likely to experience a softening of the bones when one appears . . . " Crouching in the bushes, waiting for the grizzlies to get close enough to the set cameras for photography, was a wearing way to spend the night. Wright recalled one assistant named Frank who learned firsthand of the inquisitive, cautious nature of the grizzly bear.

> For perhaps two hours nothing happened, and we all three remained at our posts. Then the young man at my side whispered to me that there was a large brown bear [a brown-colored grizzly, that is] some twenty-five yards in our rear, and as I turned to look, I saw the huge grizzly that I had taken a snap at a few nights before sneaking up behind Frank with extended nose and every appearance of puzzled curiosity. Frank was still gazing between the roots at his camera and lazily swaying his switch, and, knowing that the big grizzly was aware of his presence and only trying to satisfy his curiosity, I made no sign. When the bear reached the dead tree that lay at right angles to

Frank's seat, he placed his forepaws on it, stretched his head out, and began to sniff—well, out loud.

Frank turned around casually at the sound, and for a hundredth of a second there was a tableau that I would have given a good deal for a picture of. Then Frank's switch began a frantic tatoo on the nearest root. Frank himself leaped to his feet and the fat old grizzly shot away sideways—as luck would have it—in our direction. His first two or three jumps covered more than half the distance between us, and, as it began to look as though we would be trampled, we also jumped up, when, with a loud snort, the old fellow again changed his direction and made off puffing and blowing. Frank allowed after that that, although he was not afraid of bears, he would just as soon not have anything to do with any animal of that size that could get up near enough to smell the back of his neck without his hearing them come.

Wright came as close as he ever did to being killed by a bear when he was working the park. One night, returning from his shooting, he nearly stumbled on some grizzlies feeding in garbage barrels behind one of the park concessionaire's mess halls. He was walking quietly along near the building when three grizzlies suddenly bolted out and ran for cover, apparently startled by him. He was not especially concerned, seeing no reason why the bears should bother him, but as he walked he inadvertently walked between the last bear—the largest—and the garbage, something that annoyed the bear, apparently, for it turned and came at him. Still not especially worried, Wright stopped and faced the bear, assuming it would figure out what he was and go away.

It didn't. It came on, rose up to face the standing man, and took a swipe at him, which he dodged. Wright returned the favor by swinging, with his right hand, his twenty-pound tin of batteries, which didn't hurt the bear but did surprise it and knock it back a bit. The bear's second swing caught Wright's camera, held in his left hand, and tore it apart instantly. And only by fast ducking did Wright dodge the third swing, an angry one aimed at his head. Bears may look lumbering and slow when moving along peacefully, but they are breathtakingly quick in a fight. Wright's hat was torn off by the swing, but, knowing he had no choice now but to try to stay on the offensive, he gathered all his power into a great overhand swing of the big metal battery tin and brought it down on the bear's head with a force that probably would have killed a man. There was a dull crash, a squawk from the bear, and the fight was over; the grizzly gave up the garbage, turned tail, and galumphed off, bouncing off a tree before it figured out where it wanted to go. Wright, hardened veteran of many bear hunts and close calls, got back to his camp before he realized that his hands were shaking almost uncontrollably and, as he put it, "it was several days before I recovered my usual absence of nerves."

Wright found his hat the next day. It had two claw holes in the brim, which meant the bear had missed his head by only a couple inches.

Yellowstone seems to have been the capping experience of Wright's grizzly-bear work. His account of the photographic work, and many of his best pictures, appeared in his grizzly-bear book. And by the time the book came out, in 1909, he was already publishing his conservation articles, raging against the wastes of trapping (including the use of game carcasses to bait grizzly bears, by the way) and such travesties as the sale of elk teeth to members of the Fraternal Order of Elks, who used them for ornaments without a thought to all the elk that were killed to obtain them.

But it is Wright the hunter-naturalist who interests us today, much more than any good he might have done in his conservation journalism. Wright, like Roosevelt, was an incurable observer. From the first day he went out he was learning, and he learned far beyond the needs of the hunter or fur trapper. Even in his early years of bear killing, he often went out of his way to simply watch a bear and not shoot it. He was that finest type of hunter, the type that nonhunters and antihunters have the most trouble understanding; he loved the bears he hunted. This love was never better revealed than in the story of the bear that inspired his second book, a bear he captured and took home. Its name was Ben.

Wright's great book *The Grizzly Bear*, mentioned earlier, has already been done the important service of reprinting. It is now available in a nice paperback from the University of Nebraska Press, with a thoughtful foreword by Dr. Frank Craighead. Wright's other book, *Ben, the Black Bear* (1910), still awaits revival. It is a smaller book, with little hunting in it, but it is a charming tale, with an extensive discussion of black bears in the wild. Like *The Grizzly Bear*, its classification of bears is now out of date, and it has a few errors of natural history, but it is still very important, and more deserving of being in print than many modern bear books.

This is not a hunting story, but so much of Wright's contribution to bear lore has nothing to do with hunting that I don't feel unjustified in digressing now and then. He observed the habits of black bears as well as he did those of grizzlies, and what he wrote about their feeding, mating, denning, and all other aspects of their lives in the wild was truly the best information available in his day and for quite a few years afterward. The story of Ben reveals why.

Wright acquired Ben on a hunt in the Bitterroot with Jack O'Brien and Martin Spencer, both mentioned earlier. I can't tell from the accounts if this was the same hunt, or another with the same men, but it was O'Brien who one day shot a sow black bear and helped the others catch her three cubs. All three men "adopted"one, but with various mishaps only one survived the rest of the trip, and his name was Ben.

Wright took Ben home. The cub became quite tame and playful, and even learned to ride on the back of one of the horse's packs, which the horse seemed not to mind. Eventually, the five-pounder grew to almost 350 pounds, still surprisingly gentle and playful. Wright's narrative of raising Ben is one of the best early accounts of the growth of a black bear cub, detailing as it does a mixture of curious behavior, fascinating intelligence, and the inexpressible cuteness for which bear cubs are legend. The cub showed an uncanny ability to find natural food, food its mother could not have trained it to find, and was quick to learn new things.

It also learned tricks, including a form of juggling of which Wright was very proud. Ben would lie on his back, four feet in the air, and roll a block on his feet. As an adult, he graduated to a section

Wright with "Ben," the black bear cub he raised to adulthood. Photos from *Ben, the Black Bear* (1910).

of log about twelve inches thick and a foot and a half long, which, according to Wright, "he kept for a couple of years and juggled it so much that his claws wore hollows in the ends of it."

When Wright moved from Spokane to Missoula, Montana, in 1894, he took Ben along, where the bear was immediately the center of attention for the local boys, despite Wright's warnings. The crisis came one day in early winter when Wright had just settled Ben, on a long chain, into a corner of the woodshed and secured the door with a nail, knowing it was time for the bear to sleep. Later that day, as Wright was at work at his shop nearby, he saw crowds of people hurrying toward his house, where, moments later, he was confronted by "most of the women of the neighborhood wringing their hands and calling down all kinds of curses on my head."

His warnings to the boys had not been enough. Three leaders of a group that had been harassing the bear earlier had broken into the shed. Wright had on occasion let boys wrestle with the playful bear, something that he would only do when he was there to supervise, and now the boys wanted more. As the rest of the little gang watched from the doorway, the boys had a great time with Ben, wrestling and playing, and no doubt Ben was having a great time, too. Then they decided to ride the bear, climbing on one at a time until all three were riding him in circles around the shed. But Ben grew tired of this, and all at once he spun on his back to unload them. One of the three, unfortunately, got tangled in Ben's claws, and without hesitation the big bear began to juggle the boy. As the others watched in horror, the good-natured bear put the troublemaker into a spin, using those big claws on the boy's head and legs.

After a moment of shock, the boys found a long pole and managed to disengage bear and boy. Of course, Ben still had no idea he had done something wrong—but the boy was a bloody mess, requiring seventy-six stitches in the back of his head and heavy bandages over his legs (Ben was a good juggler; the kid had no damage at all on his face, arms, or torso). The boy's father demanded that Ben be killed, but a consultation with local lawyers suggested that the boy, having broken and entered, had no rights in the case. Ben had been not only locked up, he had been chained.

Still, it became clear to Wright that he could not keep Ben any longer; hunting trips kept him away from home for long periods, and the bear needed his authority or it would become unruly. So Wright finally sold it to a traveling circus, perhaps closing a circle even he did not notice. Just perhaps, somewhere out in the West along the route of that circus, Ben, lumbering about his cage, looked through the bars one day and saw a little boy watching him with an unaccountable gleam in his eye, and another dream was born.

Chapter Nine

Ben Lilly

*I*N early April 1913, when he was fifty-six, Ben Lilly was by some accounts working as a predatory animal control hunter in New Mexico and Arizona. His assignment was, apparently, to kill wolves, but he preferred to concentrate on mountain lions and bears.

Lilly was working in what is now the Gila National Forest, along the Blue River in eastern Arizona, when he came upon the trail of a big grizzly bear just out of its den. Tying a "slow-track dog" (one that does not race off and leave the hunter to keep up as best he can, and one that can hold to a trail even if it is only a few days old) to his waist by a long rope, he set out after the bear. He had no food with him, and was dressed in light clothing with only a sweater for added warmth. He had a rifle, some matches, and his large hand-made knife.

The country was high enough that the snow was still thick and often crusted. Sometimes the crust was so hard the bear did not even break through. If you've ever tried to cross country where the snow ranges from one foot to waist deep, and where it ranges from stubborn, jagged crust to rotten, sopping slush, and where those conditions change with the time of day, the wind, and other functions of natural whimsy, you must admire the man's determination. Each day, he plowed along behind his hound, hurrying when the trail was obvious, scanning the hard snow crust when the bear took flight across glazed-over drifts. Each night, he and the dog huddled near a small fire; no food, no blanket.

Three times Lilly caught up within sight of the grizzly, and each time he managed to put a bullet into its rear flank, never bringing it down but weakening it and slowly draining it of power and endurance.

An adult grizzly bear can go a long way in a hurry. I remember seeing a radiocollared sow grizzly at a dump just north of Yellowstone Park in the 1970s that, one night, suddenly lit out for the south, yearling in tow. Within a couple of days, she was tracked by her radio signal more than seventy miles away. And the males are far more likely to make long trips than the females.

Undated photograph of Lilly with dogs and pet lion. The picture accompanied an article on Lilly in *American* magazine in March 1919. (Photo courtesy of David Brown.)

So this bear Lilly was chasing was probably no stranger to travel. But it certainly must have been alarmed and surprised at his tireless pursuit. Bears just weren't in the habit of this sort of thing, being followed day after day by a single man on foot, much less having the guy catch up with them again and again and shoot at them.

I surmise that the bear had just recently emerged from its den, because on about the fourth day Lilly tracked it back to the den, a tunnel some sixteen feet deep, where the bear took a rest from the chase. Lilly found blood in the den, knew his quarry had not been vitally wounded, and took up the trail again, half dragged along by the dog on the other end of the rope.

Only a few hundred yards farther, Lilly spotted more fresh blood, and knew he was close now. The snow was almost up to the rope knotted around his waist, and all movements were slow and difficult; there would be no opportunity for flight or tree climbing in this confrontation. As the snowy trail led him and his dog into a thick brushy patch of evergreens, Lilly alertly swept his limited field of vision with his rifle, luckily looking in the right direction just as the bear emerged from the brush only five yards in front of him and floundered ponderously through the wet snow in a determined charge.

Lilly's first shot hit the bear full in the chest. The impact and shock of the bullet brought it to a halt for a second, but then it was up and leaning into a new charge. The second shot went into the head under one of the eyes, and the now mortally wounded animal came to rest against Lilly's side. Bogged there in waist-deep snow, Lilly was unable to even see the bear's head as it lay against him. But he could hear and feel its hoarse gasping, and, fearing it might rise yet again, he managed to get the muzzle of his rifle against its side and put a bullet into its chest. When that did not seem sure enough to quiet the bear, Lilly drew his knife and finished the bear with a stab to its heart.

Three days without food left the hunter feeling "weak," as he allowed when reporting this incident, but he and the dog continued on their way for a quick lion hunt before coming back, skinning the bear, and having a big feed of bear meat.[1]

"The Boones and the Crocketts skimmed the cream; Ben Lilly scooped up every drop of splattered milk from the cracks." So wrote

J. Frank Dobie, the great southwestern folklorist whose biography of Lilly, *The Ben Lilly Legend* (1950), remains the standard work on this strange man. Dobie was right; Lilly came too late to most of his hunting grounds to have the sort of fast sport available to the true pioneers, and he made up for lateness by an astonishing persistence in pursuing every animal that came his way. It was rarely easy; no ten-bear days for Ben Lilly. But if there was a bear to be got, Lilly got it.

I have to say that of all the hunters in this book, Ben Lilly is the one I find least easy to appreciate. In a recent letter to me, David Brown, author of the authoritative book *The Grizzly in the Southwest* (1985), spoke of Lilly's unusual attraction:

> There must have been something unique about Lilly; all who knew him—Musgrave, Hibben, Dobie, Burrige, etc. felt compelled to write about him. Yet, his historic record leaves me with the impression that he was single-minded and a bit addled. Obviously his personality was an important part of his charm.

That is about the best short summary I've read of Lilly, a man who has been written about almost to absurdity, most often by people who hadn't the least understanding of the historical or ecological realities of his world and work. Many of the articles written about him during his lifetime transform him into a superhuman game killer, something to be admired if only because it is so efficient at what it does. From the distance at which I see him, Lilly lacks whatever magic he had for those, like Dobie, who knew him. To me, at times, he seems to have been nothing but a goofy old coot who made a religion out of killing things. At times, he seems to have been nothing less than a fanatic (Theodore Roosevelt, who met him once in Louisiana when Lilly was invited to help out on a presidential hunt, privately described him as a "religious fanatic") whose oddness went far beyond anything that could safely be called eccentricity. It is clear that at times he loved to spin yarns, leading his citified audience on; they knew he was an outstanding woodsman, and were easily gulled by him.

All those things pile up against him in the historical record: his strange behavior, his quasireligious conviction that he should be out there killing animals, his unreliability as a reporter of information. And yet men as thoughtful as Dobie—who was neither a city slicker nor an abject worshiper of rough characters—went out of their way to glorify the man, and to defend him from criticism. They point to his singular skills as a hunter, his enormous practical knowledge of the habits and behavior of wild animals (and he really did know an amazing amount), his frequently significant reports to the federal government when he was employed to hunt predators or collect specimens, and his lofty religious principles. And they make quite a case. Ben Lilly was, without question, really something.

He was born in Alabama in December 1856. His father was a blacksmith and skilled knifemaker, his mother a teacher; both parents believed in education. But Ben had ideas of his own, and they didn't include schooling. The family moved to Kemper County, in eastern Mississippi, just before the Civil War, and there Ben grew and showed his independent nature. There is no record of him from the time of his early teens, when he ran away from a military academy his parents had sent him to, until he was a young man living in Memphis, Tennessee. There, his uncle Vernon one day saw the family name on a blacksmith shop, went in, and discovered his missing nephew hard at work at the family trade.

Vernon, a fairly prosperous planter, owned a few hundred acres in eastern Morehouse Parish, northern Louisiana. He had no heirs, and apparently was fond of young Ben, to whom he offered to will the land if the young man would return with him and settle on it. The boy agreed, and soon found himself in the sort of wilderness setting that he would prefer for the rest of his life, where, in the words of Dobie, there was time for "withdrawing into solitudes, hunting bears and panthers, observing wild life, keeping the Sabbath Day holy, preserving independence of body and mind, and cultivating eccentricities."

There, Ben Lilly found his way and made his first mark. It seemed that everyone who looked into those piercing blue eyes, or who heard his strong voice emerge from his flowing beard, remembered him and later had a story to tell about him.

Dobie was the foremost gatherer of Lilly stories. His book is a treasure just for its collections of legends and tales about this man. And though it seems to me that Dobie was a little too easy on some of the storytellers—he comes near to swallowing almost every piece of information he was given—and a little too willing to believe stories of Lilly's prowess—he recounts with a straight prose face that Lilly could outrun a horse, a simply preposterous notion—it also seems to me that Lilly was an extraordinary woodsman.

And no wonder. He spent most of his time, even before he came to live exclusively in the wild, in the woods. When he stepped out the door, his family (he was twice married, and had several children) did not know if he would be back in hours or months. He thought little of running through that miserable tangle of cane, grass, and swamp for twenty miles or more in a day's chase, and then doing it again the next day. Dobie collected many stories, some without question true, of Lilly's extraordinary athletic power. Lilly could jump amazing distances; he could jump out of a high barrel without touching the sides. A fairly reliable witness saw him jump, from a standstill, ten and a half feet. He was known at various times to carry packs of skins weighing 125 pounds without undue effort. For a man of not unusual size—well under six feet, perhaps 180 pounds—his strength was all the neighborhood needed to gear up the legend machine, and if his strength was not enough, there was always his wacky exuberance. One of his neighbors happened by the Lilly farm one day and saw Ben plowing a furrow behind his horses, all of them going across the field at a full gallop.

Though the stories of Lilly's sense of direction and place probably were exaggerated, he seemed to have the sort of unerring geographical instinct ascribed to the western mountain man Jim Bridger (another inspirer of mighty lies), about whom it was said that he could be plopped down anywhere in the Rockies and, whether he'd been there before or not, could easily find his way to a place he knew. Lilly was famous for this skill, one especially important to any hunter in the vast, seemingly unchanging canebrakes, jungles, and bayous of the Mississippi bottomlands. "It was his boast that he could enter a pathless swamp in the middle of the night," wrote Dobie, "stick his knife in any tree, come out, and the next night enter the swamp from any direction and go straight to the tree and reclaim the knife. He could backtrail himself like a range horse. His sense of direction was not based on a knowledge of the compass, on observations of landmarks, the stars, currents of air, or any other observable form of matter. It was inside of him; it was an instinct, like that of a bear or a pigeon—something more elemental than reason—something that civilized man has almost lost."

Well, I imagine there was a lot more to it than that. It's clear from his unpublished journals and reports, now in the Eugene C. Barker Texas History Center at the University of Texas at Austin, that Lilly was a keen observer, one who did not simply rely on some mystical sense of direction to get where he needed to go. We've learned a lot about wild animals' homing abilities since Dobie wrote, so we aren't as likely to ascribe all their knowledge of terrain to "instinct." The wild animal sees more, and senses different things, about its environment than we do, and the exceptional woodsman, like Lilly, is the same way. He sees things we don't, and knows how to read things we would miss completely. I'm sure that there was little brag in this statement he made in an undated manuscript about bears, probably written in the 1920s:

> . . . they have their traveling grounds selected from manye [sic] years experience and ones who have not the experience has the natural instinct—this [I] believe to be true from my association with bears tracking them up and studding [sic] their habits after following a bears track for a mile or so I have the ide [sic] of his trip reasoned out whether it is just prowling or in search of some certain food and I can look at the country ahead and can tell where that bear is likely to go knowing their nature and having the benefit of seeing what it did while I was tracking it . . .[2]

This was no idle boast. On several occasions, Lilly amazed companions by studying some tracks, looking at the country ahead, and pointing to some ridge or other landmark and saying the bear will come out *there*. It always did.

Lilly was also, by all accounts, a great shot. Though I doubt the stories Dobie collected that claimed Lilly could unerringly shoot the bill off a flying duck (Dobie at least refused to believe the tales of Lilly shooting mosquitoes with a .22), it's obvious that there was great skill behind this portion of the Lilly legend.

It's also obvious that there was an appalling lack of discrimination on Lilly's part about what he killed. He just loved to shoot things, from songbirds to squirrels. There seemed no end to his interest in killing wild animals, and I suppose that's what finally bothers me most about him. I know he wasn't unusual in his excesses in those days, but he was just too efficient at it to suit me.

Maybe I'm not bothered by Lilly's killing so much as by his reasons for killing. Rather like Wilburn Waters, Lilly "got religion" early in his life, and from then on his interest in hunting became a passion, almost like an ardent desire to subdue the earth. I haven't found any single instance of his clearly articulating just how he saw all this; he doesn't seem to have come out and said, "God told me to rid the earth of vermin," or anything like that. But, as Dobie was to realize, hunting was Lilly's big answer to life: "In Ben Lilly's mind, as we shall see, all panthers were dragons. Like many other men, he came to regard his own desire as a destiny imposed from on high. His deepest desire was to hunt. He hunted, and called hunting a patriotic duty."

It is unclear when Lilly first shot a bear. He seemed to have been hunting by the time he was twelve, but in the same manuscript that comments on his tracking ability, he says that, "I hunted bear since 1882." That would make him about twenty-six when he began.

If that is the case, it took Lilly practically no time at all to establish himself as one of the foremost hunters in the Mississippi Valley. Only five years later, he was already famous, and had largely abandoned house living in favor of extended expeditions to the wild country, at least for a time. In that year, 1887, we meet him in the pages of the sporting press, as a writer from Vicksburg reports on a hunt made the previous year with Lilly and Major Monroe Hamberlin, another prominent sportsman of the Old Southwest. The first impression of Lilly, then about thirty, was a strong one:

Our curiosity and interest were not a little aroused when
the man of the horn and dog came up. He introduced himself as Lilly, and from that night until this time Mr. L.
leads my list of men who love the free life in the forests
where game and fish are plentiful ... Since then I have
learned more of this "gone wild" man. He is a resident of
Louisiana, where he is in comfortable circumstances,
being the owner of three plantations. Being a widower
[Dobie said he left his first wife, and that she lived another
thirty years; perhaps Lilly was misrepresenting himself to
the writer, or perhaps Dobie was wrong] his children were
placed in school [Dobie said his only child died, which was
why he left his wife] and his plantations leased before he
took his leave for his long stay in the woods. Since last
April his home has been in the woods in the heart of a
game country with his dogs, his pony and a faithful negro
servant as his chief companion. He leaves his camp for an
occasional visit only to the plantations. He is not essentially a "backwoodsman," as one might expect, but
intelligent, using good language fairly free of slang, entirely free of oaths; he touches no tobacco, uses no strong
drink, not even coffee, and Sunday is said to be a hallowed
day with him; the wildest animal is free to hudge him in
camp on that day if it wants to, but is warned to leave no
tracks for Monday ... he has been known to sit all night
under one tree for a very old gobbler, and another night at
the root of another tree in the hollow trunk of which a bear
had taken refuge, each game being killed early the following morning. Such is Lilly, the most ardent hunter in the
Mississippi swamp.[3]

As the years passed, Lilly's "gone wild" traits became more pronounced. He slept on the ground whenever possible, avoiding
buildings, beds, and any other signs of comfort. Even in snow, he
preferred being outside to accepting an invitation to share a warm
cabin. If compelled by circumstances to sleep indoors, he would
throw his blanket on the floor. If it was raining too hard for him to

sleep on the ground, he'd sleep in a tree, no coat or covering over him. He thought nothing of going without food for three days or more while tracking an animal, or of eating enough for three men for two days at one sitting. He rarely changed clothes, but he was not filthy; he would bathe in snow if he had to, and he tried to keep his hair and beard groomed. He thought the rain and wind did a fair job of keeping his clothes clean most of the time.

Lilly was an odd mix of habits in other ways. Though he had abandoned civilized ways, his personal principles were a matter of great pride to him, at least when he wasn't joshing some greenhorn. He could quote extensively from the Bible. He wore his clothes to rags, and usually avoided coats, preferring adding an extra shirt or two. Late in life, he soled his boots with pieces of car tires. He refused under any conditions to work on Sunday, he loved children, and he could play a cruel practical joke. He was everything he needed to be in order to become a Mississippi legend, including a daring, even reckless, hunter.

His early career, hunting the local black bears and cougars, gave him experience of inestimable value for his later years, when he would move on to bigger game. But it was not easy hunting by any means. One large black bear, already responsible for the death of one of Lilly's prize dogs, led the young hunter into a near-fatal fight. Apparently a little too eager for the kill because of his desire to avenge the dead dog, Lilly peppered the huge old male until his .44 rifle was empty, then rushed in for the kill with his heavy steel knife. The bear stood its ground, and Lilly brashly took a quick chop across its nose with the big blade, bringing on an attack which not even Lilly could withstand. He turned and ran, later saying that only the relatively open country kept him free from the bear, which lumbered painfully after him; a dense brake would have been too small an arena for such a chase, and would have given Lilly no chance for escape. As it was, he was able to make it to some trees, hide momentarily while reloading his rifle, then kill the bear as it wandered off in another direction.[4]

Lilly's recklessness nearly killed him in another fight with a bear. He was hunting on the Sunflower River in Mississippi. He had shot a large male as it ate wild plums. Then, assuming the bear was disabled, he casually put aside his rifle and walked up to finish it off with the big knife. He was leaning over, knife raised, when the bear jumped up and with a quick swing of a forepaw sent the heavy knife flying from the shocked hunter's hand. Lilly fled, putting a tree between himself and the approaching bear, and the two of them played a deadly tag around the tree until, just as Lilly was about to collapse, the bear's wounds finally killed it.[5]

There was a recognized technique for stabbing a bear, one that appears in many of the accounts I've seen, in slightly different variations. It involved bringing the blade over one of the bear's shoulders from behind (which is to say the hunter had to stand more or less behind the bear). If the hunter, with the knife in his right hand, reached over the bear's right shoulder and stabbed it in the heart, his odds were thought to be best of escaping a bad clawing. The idea was that the bear, according to conventional wisdom, would think the pain came from somewhere in front of it, or off to one side, rather than from behind it.

It's an idea with some interesting basis in fact. I've seen several accounts of bear hunts, for example, where the hunter commented that when a bear was shot it would immediately attack the bear next to it, assuming its pain came from that source. I also wonder if some of the charges reported in the hunting literature were the result more of the bear rushing toward the direction of its pain rather than knowing it was rushing toward a particular hunter.

In any event, stabbing from over the back was a technique that, as one writer understated it, had to be "executed at close range," and it must have taken a good deal of gumption to belly up to the backside of a big raging black bear as it swung this way and that. It must have taken even more to reach over the shoulder and plant a big blade in its chest, hold on tight, and search around with the blade until you found the heart.

The trick almost killed Lilly once. He had wounded a black bear, but the bear managed to get hold of Red, his favorite hunting dog. Lilly made the prescribed stab from over the shoulder, burying the whole blade in the bear's chest, but instead of folding up quietly, the bear rose up in anger onto its back legs, spun, and gave Lilly a fearful clawing on the shoulder as it batted him away.

Had the bear not taken the wound, it would have killed him there, but before it could press its advantage on the dazed man, it fell over dead.[6]

In 1890, Lilly was showing no signs of leaving his wild life behind. He remarried, and managed to stay home once in a while, for over the next few years, he became the father of two daughters and a son. But having set up housekeeping for the family didn't slow him down; he was usually off on a hunt, and would start on one with no notice whatsoever. One minute he'd be busy at some routine task, then he'd simply announce he needed to go hunting and he'd be gone, maybe for weeks. His wife, Mary, put up with this for more than ten years; then, by one account tracked down by Dobie, she told him that the next time he took off like that he should just keep going forever. So, in 1901, he gave her his property, kissed her and the kids good-bye, and headed southeast to Tensas Parish, where there was still good bear hunting.

Tensas did not disappoint Lilly. He hunted there for a few years, killing waterfowl for the market, selling wild honey, and hunting not only bears but wild pigs. He started a long, loyal habit of sending money home whenever he could, and spent practically none himself. In 1904, through Ned Hollister of the Biological Survey (an ancestor of the U.S. Fish and Wildlife Service), Lilly was hired to send specimens of various animals into Washington, and here he proved repeatedly the wisdom of his observations and the utility of his hunting methods. He eventually was to send in specimens and information on animals in several western and southern states. No matter that his own writings never became well known or even published; his knowledge and work were not all for naught. But, as Dobie pointed out, getting to know biologists and conservationists did not affect Lilly's enthusiasm for killing things in the least; he still rarely met a lion he didn't immediately shoot at, and he showed no slackening of his rate of bear killing.

But a combination of restlessness, interest in new gamelands, and perhaps a decline in Louisiana game populations made Lilly move again. In 1906, he left Louisiana for Texas, and, except for a brief visit in 1907 during Roosevelt's bear hunt, Lilly was now a western hunter.

Ben Lilly in the Big Thicket in Texas about 1906. (Photo courtesy of the Arizona Historical Foundation.)

He moved, specifically, to the Big Thicket, a marvelous ecological jigsaw puzzle northwest of Beaumont, thousands of acres of wild, almost impenetrable country with a wealth of wild animals even at that late date. It would later be recognized, in a much reduced form, as a remarkable crossroads of environments, from swamps to evergreen forests, and would be set aside, in a dozen or so units totaling eighty thousand acres, as a national preserve. But in Lilly's day it was wide open, at least to those who knew how to deal with it.

And there were quite a few who did. Lilly moved into an established regional culture of bear hunters, men such as old "Uncle" Bud Brackin, who killed more than three hundred bears in a lifetime of hunting in the Thicket.[7] The Big Thicket was being chewed away at even in Lilly's day, but it was still a place of legend and danger, and Lilly had no trouble there finding others who loved bear hunting. He hunted mostly that year with Bud and Ben Hooks, Texan brothers now remembered for their many wilderness adventures in the Big Thicket, and celebrated in books such as Callie Wilson and Ellen Reinstra's *A Pride of Kin* (1985) and Francis Abernathy's *Tales from the Big Thicket* (1966).

What is noteworthy from our point of view about Lilly's brief stay in the Big Thicket is that, while there, he killed a specimen bear that he told a companion was the one hundred and eighteenth bear he'd ever killed. Piecing together his totals is not an entirely useful process, but I think it's interesting for what it shows us about the changing times. Two years earlier, he had told Ned Hollister that he had killed 105 bears to that time in his hunting in Louisiana and Mississippi, so the figure of 118 is probably a good one. Other observers of him reported higher numbers, but I suspect that these he gave are close to right.

Lilly was not a full-time bear hunter. He hunted other game, he farmed, he did other work, including cowboying and logging. After he left Texas and went farther west, he was probably even less a bear hunter and more a lion hunter. But he hunted a great deal, and he loved to hunt bear, and he was very good at it, so good that many considered him the best alive. Yet in the twenty-four years from 1882 to 1906, he killed less than five bears a year. The truth of

Dobie's remark about the Boones and Crocketts skimming the cream, quoted at the beginning of this chapter, is borne out in these numbers.

> Too many Crocketts had gone before him for him to make a Crockett record. Yet he was far superior to Crockett in hunting skills, and as an observer of wild life Crockett had absolutely nothing to report. In the West, Ben Lilly became more of a lion man than a bear man. What he saw in the animals he hunted is of more consequence than the numbers he slew. It is to be doubted if during his whole lifetime of hunting he killed more than a thousand bears and lions put together. Considering his time, this was an enormous toll.

Again, I think Dobie was being a little too protective of his favorite. It's clear to me, from what Crockett *did* tell us incidentally about bears in his short autobiography, that if some scientist had been around to ask him, he could have said a lot more about the habits of bears than he did. Crockett, as I suggested in Chapter One, left us more than "absolutely nothing," even if he didn't leave us as much as Lilly did. But most of what Lilly left us was incidental to his personal passion for killing bears; he found that scientists and institutions would actually *pay* for what he knew, and that the money could help him keep killing. I'm not sure he was at all altruistic about his search for knowledge about bears, which is the implication of Dobie's defense of him.

And I suspect that his lifetime total of bears, judging from the periods in which he reported his totals, was probably between three hundred and four hundred. J. Stokely Ligon, the man who hired Lilly for the Biological Survey work in New Mexico, wrote that in January 1928, when Lilly made a rare public speech at a stockmen's convention in El Paso, the old hunter claimed to have killed four hundred bears. But Ligon did not claim to have heard the statement personally, only secondhand through people who apparently did not approve of Lilly and thought he must be lying. There were lots of bears in the Southwest in those days, black and grizzly, and it's just possible Lilly added three hundred to his 1906 total of 118.

At the end of 1906, Lilly was on the move again, down the Gulf Coast to a wild area near Bay City. There he hunted for the market, staying in southern Texas until the summer of 1908. In that time he did a little bear hunting, killing at least one in a hand-to-hand (or claw-to-knife) fight described to Dobie in a letter from a San Antonio businessman, S.L. Carrico, who was at the time developing homesites in the area.

> He had set a heavy steel trap in a cornfield down near Boone Settlement. A bear had walked into it and then ripped out the stake to which the trap chain was fastened and made off a short distance into a dense thicket of rattan and wild peach. When Mr. Lilly got to the site, he found a group of Negroes raising bedlam and wondering what to do to get the bear. The Lilly hounds were so well trained that they did nothing without his command. He left them on the outside of the thicket, took his gun, and crawled in on hands and knees until he got within twenty feet of the bear. He then worked his body against the rattan vines on both sides to clear out enough space for free movement. When he had the vines worked back and down, he moved over as far to the right as he could get and purposely antagonized the bear with a shot that merely wounded him. The bear charged and when it was nearly on him, Mr. Lilly jumped to the left as far as the thicket would permit. As the bear rushed past, he grabbed him around the neck, jumped on his back, pulled his big knife, and stabbed him. Bear and man went down together. By the time the Negroes got to him, he had pulled himself free. Meanwhile his dogs had bayed mournfully but stayed behind him about fifty feet, precisely where he had told them to stay.

From the coast Lilly cut across country to Eagle Pass on the Texas/Mexico border and worked his way down into the Mexican highlands roughly between Monterey and the Big Bend of the Rio

Grande. Some parts of that wild borderland still had grizzly bears then (some people hold faint hopes that a few Mexican grizzly bears still survive today in the western mountains, but those hopes grow dimmer each year), and Lilly spent enough time there to add to his legend a few more bear stories of dubious reliability. There was one in which the hunter killed a female bear, skinned it out, and slept under the skin the same night (which hardly sounds like a good hunter, who wants to let the skin dry straight and properly). Anyway, as the story went, the bear's mate came sniffing up to the skin, waking Lilly, who shot the bear and kept its skin, too.

These were Lilly's first grizzly bears, and the rest of his hunting career he was often concerned with the bigger bear. He hunted here and there—for ranchers and the federal government and for his own reasons, through Arizona and New Mexico and as far north as Idaho, even going back into Mexico itself—from 1911 until the mid- to late-twenties. He might get a bounty for a grizzly scalp, or for a cougar, or he might get some money from the Biological Survey for a good study skin. He never could get clear around the notion that he shouldn't kill just *any* bear, and he wrangled with his federal employers, who insisted that he only kill bears that were taking stock. As far as Lilly was concerned, all bears were bad, and would eventually cause trouble. Why not take care of them when you see them, rather than wait until you have to track them down? he reasoned.

Perhaps the most remarkable hunt of this later period of Lilly's career was one in which he never got the bear, and indeed did not intend to. In 1921, as he approached his sixty-fifth birthday, Lilly was hired by a wealthy Oklahoman named McFadden as part of a team that would manage an extravaganza of a hunt throughout the West and all the way to Alaska. It was to be a hunt of many parts, with many events planned along the way. Lilly's assignment was to find a big grizzly for McFadden himself, who would come and go from the extended hunt as business and whim demanded.

Lilly found his bear near Taos, New Mexico, on June 29. He trailed it and reported in to McFadden, but the businessman was on a trip east just then, so Lilly went back to the trail. By August 6, the bear had crossed into Colorado. Lilly followed patiently, keeping far enough back and using only one dog tied to his waist, so that the bear would not sense it was being followed, cold-trailed, for weeks until it became convenient for a rich sport to find the time to shoot it.

Lilly checked in now and then with McFadden, usually getting encouragement or no news at all, then returned to the trail, doggedly tailing after the big grizzly bear as it wandered to hell and gone across the rugged Colorado Rockies and back into New Mexico, week after week. It was a new kind of hunting for the old man, but he seems not to have found it unpleasant.

The bear was never shot. As Lilly shivered in the first snowstorms of winter, and as the bear bedded down for the winter in some mountain den, McFadden was on his way to Europe. Lilly came down and occupied himself otherwise for the winter. The next summer, he was back in McFadden's service, guiding him and his friends on an Idaho trip for trout and bears.

By the mid-1920s, Lilly had hunted successfully over much of the West, and was gratefully received at some large ranches he had more or less wiped clean of grizzly bears and cougars. He became, in these later years, more famous as a lion hunter than as a bear hunter, and articles began to appear about him with greater frequency, if no greater reliability. An article by Rene Rivierre in *American* magazine in March 1919 said Lilly had hunted in the Yukon, Oregon, Canada, and even Africa.

But he was getting too old to keep it up. By 1928, the year he made his famous speech at the American National Livestock Association convention in El Paso (where Dobie met him), his hunting was nearly over, and he was getting more and more strange and quirky in his behavior. There is a sad tale of a hunt in 1931, where the seventy-five-year-old man tried to find a mountain lion for friends of a rancher he worked for. The two hunters had seen the lion in broad daylight, and even got a shot at it, but it got away. The following day, they took Lilly to the place they saw the lion, and watched as the old fellow once again roped a dog to his waist. He told them he would hunt it down alone, and was promptly dragged clumsily off behind the strong dog. He came back that night and announced to the surprised hunters that there were no mountain lions in that mountain range. He had lost the ability to live up to his legend, and soon needed care and protection, which were provided by one of the ranches he'd served so faithfully. In the end, his health was so poor that he was moved to a "county farm" near Silver City, New Mexico, where he died in December 1936. Dobie, with whom I have disagreed occasionally in this chapter, but whom I admire for many reasons including his careful and devoted study of Lilly, caught the sadness of Lilly's departure very well:

In 1947, some of Ben Lilly's friends erected this monument to him in the mountains of New Mexico. (Photo courtesy of David Brown.)

One morning he told Mrs. Hines [who ran the home] that he believed he would stay in bed. His mind seemed to lighten. He spoke about a small amount of money he had in a bank. Two hours before he breathed his last he said, "I'll be better off." He died December 17, 1936. A Methodist minister who had never seen him and had never heard of him until the day preceding conducted the funeral services. To his daughters, who came, he must have looked very strange in the coffin in Silver City, where he was buried. Somebody had shaved off his beard.

Chapter Ten

Holt Collier

*T*HE pack of bear hounds ran through the thick forest in long, stretching leaps, their motion a combination of frenetic excitement and smooth, conditioned ease. This was what they were bred for, and what they lived for. The leaf canopy was so dense that at times only a half-light, a sort of dusky murk, penetrated to the forest floor where the hounds ran. Their chorus of howls and yowls was all that kept them connected to the hunters who lagged far behind. Horses just couldn't move through this stuff as fast as dogs could.

Now the sound was muffled from the hunters as the dogs passed around a canebrake wall bordered by a dark bayou. Now the sound was clear as the hounds raced in a long, scattered string through an open glade. But always the sound was telling the hunters what was happening.

The houndsman, the only black man on the hunt, heard much more than the others. His friends and clients knew bear dogs and bear hunting, but this was his pack, and he knew each voice, each inflection, and he knew that, to the extent that the hounds called for any reason besides the exuberance of a hot trail, they called for him.

Then, off in the distance, the houndsman heard the hounds bark treed, as he'd heard this pack and others do a thousand or more times. But there was something different this time. The sound was

Collier and his hunting companions about 1907 on the Newstead Plantation, Metcalfe, Mississippi. From left: hunting dog with splint, Harley Metcalfe, Jr., Harley Metcalfe, Holt Collier, Clive Metcalfe, bear cub, Uncle "Jug" Metcalfe, Edmund K. Metcalfe (who died in 1987, at age eighty-five). (Photo courtesy of Harley Metcalfe III and Sandra Dahl Desmond.)

muffled and unfamiliar. Something was wrong up there with the dogs, and he rushed on anxiously to find out what.

The something was an enormous downed tree, hollow through its lower trunk. The bear had sought refuge in it, and as the houndsman and his friends pulled up in sight of it, the muffled squeals of the dogs, which had instantly followed the bear in, told the men that the pack was getting smaller every minute.

This pack was famous throughout the lower Mississippi Valley, almost as famous as its owner had become in the years since the Civil War, when he'd settled in to a life of bear and panther hunting. This was more than his pack; it was his life. Without hesitation, holding his long hunting knife in his mouth, the houndsman bent to the opening and, before his companions realized what he was doing, was almost out of sight in the tree. One man was quick enough to grab his ankle and let out a firm objection, but the foot slipped free from the boot and the houndsman was gone into the tight tunnel full of frantic dogs and furious bear.

The surviving account of this incident doesn't say how many dogs were in that trunk, or how many of them died. The man, as near as can be told, crawled on hands and knees to a point where he could work his way past the tangle of bleeding dogs.

Imagine him in there. Imagine the ripe smell of swamp-wet dogs, the acrid stench of overheated, enraged bear, the slippery warm blood of pack members already lost; the simply insufferable noise and confusion in that dank little hole. Imagine him grabbing the nearest dog by whatever he could get a grip on and yanking it past him as he moved toward the bear.

And imagine the bear, cornered in an unfamiliar lair, seeing the light of the only exit blocked by this larger attacker that did not howl or bark, but crawled silently toward him through the addled dogs.

It was apparently too much for the bear, which broke, and rushed at him, trying to squeeze past to reach the light and freedom. As it did so, it raked him with its claws, one of only two or three times in nearly three-quarters of a century that a bear would cut this man at all. And as it did, the man, holding his balance in the slimy trunk with his right hand, laid into the bear with the knife he held in his left, wounding it mortally and saving the rest of his pack to hunt again.[1]

I have saved my favorite for last. As much as I admire, or am intrigued by, other men in this book, none has so captured my interest lately as has Holt Collier.

It isn't a simple interest that Collier inspires, because he was a complex and remarkable character. Born a slave near Fayette, Mississippi, in Jefferson County, between 1846 and 1848, he led an advantaged life for a slave child. His father was plantation chef for Howell Hinds, a wealthy planter with about thirty-five hundred acres of land south of present Greenville, Mississippi. Young Holt not only went to school with his master's children, he traveled with the family around the country as Hinds's valet.

Hinds had trouble keeping young Holt in the classroom; the boy loved the woods too much to sit still in school. Recognizing (and sharing) the youngster's enthusiasm for outdoor life, Hinds let him go, and when the boy was ten he was given a twelve-gauge shotgun and instructed to sit on the front porch of the Hinds home and keep the blackbirds out of the chinaberry trees.

In those days, as we've already seen, wilderness began just beyond the doorstep of many plantation homes, so the youngster was soon ranging farther and farther away with shotgun and rifle. He learned to shoot from either shoulder, and became a skilled woodsman. By the time he was twelve, he had ridden behind his master on a hunt with the men, and had shot his first bear.

When the Civil War began, Hinds refused to let the boy go along. Barely in his teens, Collier stowed away on a riverboat headed north and rejoined Hinds in Memphis, at which point his master, now a colonel, relented and let the boy stay and help out in the Confederate cause.

It was a matter of great pride to Collier that he didn't serve as a camp aide or servant. He was a soldier. In one of the more reliable interviews, published in *The Saturday Evening Post* in March 1909, Collier told of his first battle. He was fourteen or so, and was with Confederate troops near Bowling Green, Kentucky, when Union forces were encountered near camp. These are supposedly Collier's own words, and though I think they were heavily filtered by the writer, they seem to reflect the wit and character of the man as he reminisced about being a boy.

> When the fight broke out that time they all went away and left me in camp by myself—and I was a mighty little darky. Somebody had left a musket an' a sack full of cartridges. So I jes' buckled on the cartridge belt, an' follered along 'til I got to where the shootin' was goin' on. All the

men was a-pluggin' away, so I got in a place where I could see real good, an' commenced a-shootin', too.

Twarn't long until I heerd some one bust out in a big laugh behine me, and there was Mr. Tom Hinds a-settin' up mighty straight on his hoss.

"Look here, boy, ain't you scared you'll get kilt?" Mr. Tom said, an' he looked so peculiar I couldn't help but laugh.

"Dunno, sir; ain't my chances mighty nigh as good as yours?"

He jes' laughed an' laughed, then rode off a-hollerin' at some men. Co'se he was my master, an' if *he* didn't say nothin' it warn't nobody else's business, so I kept on a-shootin'. When everybody said the fightin' was over with I come on back to camp with the rest of 'em, and the men all laughed at me and my big musket.

"Where you reckon that big gun is a-goin' wid that little bit o'nigger," one of 'em said.

"You let that nigger alone," another one assured'im, right brief. "That nigger's a soldier." I sholy did feel proud when he said that.

And a soldier he was, distinguishing himself throughout the war, the only black man serving in the Confederate Army from the state of Mississippi, according to the state's Department of Archives and History.[2] As a cavalryman and sharpshooter, he fought in many campaigns; his woodcraft was invaluable to his fellow troopers. In one of the few reliable published interviews, he described those times.

During that time I did a great deal of scout duty. The whole country was a wilderness and if our boys got lost I could always find the way out. I had been raised in this part of the country and had hunted in the woods all my life.

Holt Collier's adventures in the Civil War are beyond the scope of this book, but it must be said that he was a fine and daring enough soldier to come home a hero among both his white and black neighbors. Still just a teenager, he was a well-known man around Greenville by 1865, long before he became a regional legend as a bear hunter.

Studying the life of Collier has been as frustrating as it has been rewarding, because there are so many obstacles in the way of really getting to know him.

There is a shortage of firsthand information about him. As articulate as he was, and as prominent as he was, he was illiterate—legal documents show only his "mark," with his name written in by some other person. We rely almost entirely on secondhand information, and it is wildly variable in its quality. Thus, various sources give his birth date as January 1, 1846, or January 21, 1846, or some time in 1848. Many people who wrote about him did so with casual attention to details, having no idea that such information would matter to anyone fifty or more years later.

There is another obstacle, a racial one. This man fought for the Confederacy, a choice that would not endear him to some people even today, though he obviously fought out of loyalty to his master more than out of any concern for the political or social issues of the war. Still, it will always be part of the irony of Holt Collier's saga that he was a slave fighting on the side of proslavery forces.

I don't think that Collier's involvement in the war was really of much importance to those who produced the later portrayals of him, though. Many of those who wrote about Collier did so in the 1920s and 1930s, late in his life. The fashionable style then among many journalists was to turn any southern black into a stereotypical "darkie" who spouted remarks like "Yas, suh," and "Sho 'nough." More reliable sources, including local historians who took the trouble to interview him before his death in 1936, pointed out that a lifetime of contact with well-heeled, educated whites, and more educational opportunities than most blacks of his day, had made Collier an able speaker who could tell his story with clarity and strength.[3]

And it is an exciting picture. Following Collier's discharge from the Confederate Army, he returned to Greenville, a small town in Washington County along the Mississippi River, also sometime home of Wade Hampton. (There is evidence that Hampton and Collier hunted together at least once; I also am sure that it would not have been impossible in the 1870s or 1880s for Collier, Hampton, Lilly, and Bobo all to have been on the same hunt.) Whenever he made some extra money, from bear bounties for example, he traveled, once going to Texas to visit army friends, more often going to horse races and other sporting events. He took to the life of the hunter-guide, married and had children, and seemed to live about as happy a life as he could have wished.

Except for politics. Probably because of his service in the war, but also because of his friendships with various influential Mississippians and his own strong personality, Collier frequently ran afoul of the carpetbagger rulers of the state. More than once, his white planter friends stood by him in court and kept him from unjust imprisonment and even execution. On one occasion, Collier was the only black among several hundred white southerners who staged a protest march in Greenville against the carpetbaggers. He was not merely tolerated, he was welcome, and occupied an odd position of social prominence in a confused and struggling society.

I do regret that we do not have more stories of Collier's hunting experiences in print. But I think that he is like Hampton; he was well known, and the stories may still be out there, undiscovered, even yet.

We know that Collier hunted in many quail-shooting matches as representative of Colonel Hinds. He was said to have once won a thousand-dollar purse in a match against a famous Arkansas shooter.

He and the Colonel also hunted the now-extinct passenger pigeon, though it was more like harvesting than hunting. At night they would take pine knot torches into the woods and beat the pigeons from the trees by the buggyload with no stouter weapons than cane fishing poles.[4]

But mostly Collier seems to have hunted bigger game, especially deer, bear, and cougar. In what were something near his own words, published in April 1909 in *The Saturday Evening Post*, Collier reminisced about those years.

In the spring I'd go away and foller the races, same as I used to—St. Louis an' Saratoga an' New Orleans, an' way out in Texas takin' in the fairs. Then in the fall I'd come home, git my dogs together and hit the cane-brake again—I jes' nacherly loved a hoss and loved to hunt bears. Didn't do nothin' much 'cept hunt. I would kill on an average one hundred and twenty-five to one hundred and thirty and one hundred and forty bear in a season. I reckon I have kilt more bear than any man in the whole entire world. I kept count of 'em up to twenty-one hundred, an' the book what the tallies was in got burnt up in my house twenty years ago. When the Valley Railroad was being built through here I kept the commissary supplied constant with bear meat—they bought it reg'lar instead o' beef. Out o' seventy-six bear I shot fifty-four of 'em in the head; made over nine hundred dollars that season sellin' bear meat . . .

Since that time I never did know what 'twas to kill less'n fifty to seventy-five bear in a season; but now the bear is got so scarce I won't go to the trouble to train the hounds like I used to. My dogs would fight a bear three or four days an' nights until they 'most starved to death, waitin' for me to come. I often found 'em the third or fourth day treein' or fightin'. Me an' them both has lived off o' raw meat an' not cared whether 'twere cooked or not.

After the death of his old master, Collier came to be good friends with the Metcalfe family of Greenville, and for most of the rest of his life, Clive and Harley Metcalfe cared for the man with the solicitousness of older brothers (this touching friendship alone would merit substantial attention in any complete biography of him). They hunted with him, saw to it that he had what he needed if he ran short of money, and involved him in their family life.

All of this sounds like a full enough existence for any man who loved the outdoors, who had strong loyalties to his friends, and who was lucky enough to have friends who deserved such loyalties. But we would know much less of Collier than we do if his existence had gone only this far. Collier's war adventures may have set him apart from most men, and his career as a hunter may have made him rare in the annals of sport, but we would probably have almost no record of him at all today were it not for a single hunt he guided in 1902. It was a hunt, ironically enough, in which the main client didn't even get a shot at a bear. But it was a hunt that made Collier famous and gave him a peculiar and enduring place not only in sporting history but in American political history as well. It was the infamous Mississippi bear hunt of Theodore Roosevelt.

Pencil portrait of Holt Collier done near the end of his life by a Chicago artist. Original of drawing now owned by James Robertshaw, Greenville, Mississippi. (Copy courtesy of Harley Metcalfe III and Sandra Dahl Desmond.)

I introduced the hunt briefly in Chapter Seven. The results of it are well known: an embarrassed President, an amused press, and a

disappointing shortage of bears. The hunt itself is surprisingly rich
in lore, however, as well as in conflicting details. It seems that for
every participant, as well as for every journalist who reported on it,
there is a different version of exactly what happened. Donald Finn,
a history buff who has spent years gathering information about it, is
certain that *none* of the published accounts is totally accurate.[5]

My own reading of the accounts, assisted by the extensive readings and research of Sandra Dahl Desmond, shows me that the
accounts are troublesome in that way. Some disagree in this detail,
or that sequence of events, or this alleged quotation, or that reported participant. I would need a hundred pages, rather than a
chapter, to simply list and analyze the variant versions of the story,
so instead I will concentrate on Collier's role in the hunt and give a
generalized account of the affair based on a careful reading of the
surviving accounts.

Roosevelt had been interested in southern bears for many years,
and had read a good bit about the hunting of them. Shortly after he
took office, in 1902, Roosevelt received an invitation from Mississippi Governor Longino to join him and a couple dozen or so other
prominent southerners in a bear hunt. Roosevelt wanted a bear
hunt, but knew that the crowd would make hunting impossible, so
he declined with regret. Then, Stuyvesant Fish of the Illinois Central Railroad, whose line ran right through the bear country, made a
similar invitation and offered to keep the party small. The President
perked up, took notice, and decided to go. Lindsay Denison, one of
the three professional journalists eventually allowed to join the
party, wrote up the hunt in *Outing* in February 1903, and described
the filling out of the guest list:

> Mr. Fish wrote to Mr. John M. Parker, of New Orleans,
> a cotton factor, whom he knew had hunted in the delta.
> Mr. Parker wrote to E.C. Mangum of Sharkey County,
> who owns and manages four cotton plantations on the
> edge of the bear cane brakes. Mr. Mangum wrote to Holt
> Collier, the negro guide, former Confederate scout and a
> marked character through all the delta; to Major George
> Helm, to Hugh Foote, and to Leroy Percy, all crack shots

and all familiar with jungle hunting, as every planter and Mississippi gentleman must be. Mr. Fish wrote to Judge Dickinson, the general solicitor of the railroad. Mr. Roosevelt, asked to invite a guest, sent for John McIlhenny, a young man of New Orleans, who had been under his command in Cuba. It was, of course, understood that the Secretary to the President, Mr. Cortelyou, and the President's surgeon, Dr. Lung, should accompany him. It will be seen, therefore, that with the sincerest desire in the world to keep down the membership of the party, there were already ten white men in it.

Ten was, of course, too many, what with the addition of camp helpers, assistants, aides, and so on. (Gentlemen like these can hardly be expected to cook their own meals and saddle their own horses, can they?)

Collier seemed the logical choice for houndsman, but the organizers of the hunt took no chances with their arrangements. They also invited, as mentioned in Chapter Six, Robert Bobo, who could not attend.

Anyway, Collier learned of the hunt about a month in advance, and was sent out to find a good bear ground. He investigated the brakes along the Little Sunflower River near the plantation of Smedes, Mississippi, scouting for bear sign and assuring himself and the others that there were lots of bears around. He found the prints of nine different bears at one water hole near the chosen campsite. It looked promising. It should have been a good hunt.

It wasn't. Roosevelt had a lot to learn about hunting while at the same time serving as President. There were simply too many people. Collier remembered that Roosevelt showed up with "a carload of guards." Most of the party were left behind or stationed here and there on the borders of the hunting area, but the party was still too big.

Still, three bears were taken, an admirable catch in the southern tradition of bear hunting. So Roosevelt's hosts were a bit puzzled by the President's disappointment. Being on a hunt where three bears were taken was just about as good as having shot the bears yourself, to their way of thinking. The President got three bears, didn't he? What was he upset about? As one writer put it, "It was something of a blow to the sense of southern hospitality—which is no stronger anywhere than in Sharkey County—to find that the President had a vigorous desire to kill a bear himself."

Actually, the failure of Roosevelt to get a bear may have been more his own fault than he admitted. According to Theodore Roosevelt scholar Gregory C. Wilson, former curator of the Theodore Roosevelt Collection at Harvard and author of the most authoritative of the modern accounts of the hunt, Roosevelt missed a perfect chance on the first day of the hunt.[6]

Someone, either Collier or one of the others, stationed Roosevelt and a companion or two near a spot they were sure the bear would pass during the chase. They were reluctant to risk the presidential person on a wild-running horse in that country, so to the embarrassment of the President he was left afoot at this hopeful junction of trails. After a few hours of waiting in the drizzly November woods, the President and his friend impatiently returned to camp. Not long after they had deserted their post, Collier and his hounds drove the day's bear within a few yards of it. If the President had stayed parked where he was supposed to, it all would have worked out fine.

But to his everlasting chagrin, as things turned out, Roosevelt had not seen the last of that bear. About a mile past the spot where he should have stayed, the bear was run into a pond, exhausted. What happened next has found a small place in American history. A president was about to get a mascot.

Let's back up a moment first, to set the stage before Collier walks out on it. According to some of the better accounts, the night before the hunt Roosevelt and the rest had been talking as they sat around the campfire. The conversation turned inevitably to Collier's life and skills. Someone wondered if Collier could rope a bear alive. One of Collier's friends asserted, as the black man sat in respectful silence, that Collier could catch a bear *without* a rope if he wanted to, and that with a rope it would be easy.

This may be why, as he watched the fatigued bear flounder in the water with his equally worn-out dogs, Collier took his rope and waded in. He was impressed, above all else, with making sure "the

Colonel" got a chance at a bear, and here was one that couldn't get away. His own reminiscence, taken down by a historian years later, does the moment justice.

> I followed the bear into the lake with my Texas rope on my arm. I slicked up the rope with the blue mud from the bottom. I had one dog in the water with me; he tangled with the bear and they went under. I kicked the bear and he stuck his head up. While he was shaking the water from his eyes, I dropped the rope over his head, moved back about ten feet or so, and tied it to a tree. The bear was old, but he was fat; he had gray hair on his paws and head, and he had two big black teeth. That bear killed several fine dogs for me.[7]

Later reports would place the bear's weight as high as six hundred pounds, but the most reliable estimates were less than two-fifty. (They had scales in camp, and some news reports gave a weight of 235 pounds.) It appears that at least one dog was killed, bitten through the neck, while the bear was in the water. Some stories say that Collier broke his rifle over the bear's head while trying to protect the dogs; but his own remembrances sometimes leave that out. In any case, somehow Collier and one or two others who caught up with him tied the bear to a tree, leaving the animal entangled in the rope and wallowing in exhaustion in the shallow water. Someone went to get Roosevelt.

When the President arrived, he unhesitatingly refused to shoot the bear. Some accounts say that Collier quietly approached him and advised him that it was poor form to shoot a tied bear, but without question Roosevelt would have known this anyway. There does seem to have been a high and immediate sense of understanding and appreciation between the President and Collier, so such an exchange between them seems possible. Roosevelt laughed at the idea of shooting a roped animal and told his companions to put the bear out of its misery, then left.

This caused a good deal of confusion, as I say, because the others had a different idea of what one did on a bear hunt. As one put it, "If

The most famous version of the Clifford Berryman cartoon showing Roosevelt refusing to shoot the bear.

I'd had the slightest idea he was going to feel that way about it, sir, I'd 'a' had those ropes cut off that bear long before he came in sight."

But the press loved it. *Washington Post* cartoonist Clifford Berryman quickly produced a cartoon showing Roosevelt refusing to shoot a tiny bear cub with big sad eyes and a rope around its neck. The cartoon, of which there were eventually at least three variants published, was entitled, "Drawing the Line in Mississippi." It was apparently a caption of multiple meanings, including some boundary dispute Roosevelt was involved in settling between Mississippi and Louisiana, Roosevelt's position on racial issues (the color line, so to speak), and his drawing a line between sporting and unsporting conduct.

Interestingly, the man depicted holding the rope was white.

Within a few weeks, other political cartoonists began to feature small bears in Roosevelt cartoons. An informal political symbol was born. A brisk business sprang up in related items, such as postcards and buttons. A Brooklyn merchant named Morris Michtom created a small toy bear and called it "Teddy's Bear." Almost overnight, the teddy bear became associated with Roosevelt, who, as we've seen, didn't even like the name Teddy. (Michtom, incidentally, eventually expanded his Teddy Bear business into the gigantic Ideal Toy Corporation.) And all because Holt Collier's friends wondered if he could really rope a bear.

The rest of the hunt went just as poorly. Roosevelt left without a trophy but with a determination that he would try these southern bears again someday.

It took five years, but Roosevelt came back, in October 1907. This time it all went well.

This next is a well-documented hunt, and perhaps the best account of them all is Roosevelt's "In the Louisiana Canebrakes," published in *Scribner's* magazine in January 1908.[8]

Again the President's host was John Parker, and again John McIlhenny was along. Again Collier was the houndsman. A few others were involved, the most extraordinary of whom was Ben Lilly, then on a brief visit to Mississippi from Texas. Roosevelt was struck by Lilly's appearance and behavior:

> The morning after we reached camp we were joined by Ben Lilley [sic], the hunter, a spare, full-bearded man, with wild, gentle, blue eyes and a frame of steel and whipcord. I never met any other man so indifferent to fatigue

and hardship. He equalled Cooper's Deerslayer in woodcraft, in hardihood, in simplicity—and also in loquacity.
The morning he joined us in camp, he had come on foot
through the thick woods, followed by his two dogs, and
had neither eaten nor drunk for twenty-four hours; for he
did not like to drink the swamp water. It had rained hard
throughout the night and he had no shelter, no rubber
coat, nothing but the clothes he was wearing, and the
ground was too wet for him to lie on; so he perched in a
crooked tree in the beating rain, much as if he had been a
wild turkey. But he was not in the least tired when he
struck camp; and, though he slept an hour after breakfast,
it was chiefly because he had nothing else to do, inasmuch
as it was Sunday, on which day he never hunted nor la-
bored. He could run through the woods like a buck, was
far more enduring, and quite as indifferent to weather,
though he was over fifty years old. He had trapped and
hunted throughout almost all the half century of his life,
and on trail of game he was as sure as his own hounds. His
observations on wild creatures were singularly close and
accurate. He was particularly fond of the chase of the
bear, which he followed by himself, with one or two dogs,
lying down to sleep wherever night overtook him; and he
had killed over a hundred and twenty bears.

It's worth including that entire quote just for the pleasure of
Roosevelt's gifts at succinct summary. But the passage is also revealing because that is about all he had to say about Lilly. The
eccentric old woodsman seems to have taken no real part in the hunt,
and to have been mostly just a curiosity in camp. This was primarily
Collier's show.

The hunt took place in northeastern Louisiana, very near Lilly's
own properties. The first camp was on Tensas Bayou, a few miles
west of Tallulah. It was a hunting ground as historic as any in Mississippi; George Lowery, in his *Mammals of Louisiana and Its
Adjacent Waters* (1974), reports on bear hunting expeditions in
Mississippi River canebrakes as early as 1750, and I've seen a num-

ber of accounts from before the Civil War, including those in *A Sporting Family of the Old South* (1936), a book edited by Harry Worcester Smith that contains several hunting adventures written by Frederick Gustavus Skinner. Skinner hunted the Tensas River in the years before 1860, and left vivid descriptions of the wild state of the land at that time.

It was still wild, if being chopped down fast, when Roosevelt arrived:

> Beyond the end of cultivation towers the great forest. Wherever the water stands in pools, and by the edges of the lakes and bayous, the giant cypress loom aloft, rivalled in size by some of the red gums and white oaks. In stature, in towering majesty, they are unsurpassed by any trees of our eastern forests; lordlier kings of the green-leaved world are not to be found until we reach the sequoias and redwoods of the Sierras . . . The canebrakes stretch along the slight rises of ground, often extending for miles, forming one of the most striking and interesting features of the country. They choke out other growths, the feathery, graceful canes standing in ranks, tall, slender, serried, each but a few inches from his brother, and springing to a height of fifteen or twenty feet. They look like bamboos; they are well-nigh impenetrable to a man on horseback; even on foot they make difficult walking unless free use is made of the heavy bush-knife. It is impossible to see through them for more than fifteen or twenty paces, and often for not half that distance. Bears make their lairs in them, and they are the refuge for hunted things.

One more observation from Roosevelt concludes discussion of the arrangements for this hunt:

> Late in the evening of the same day we were joined by two gentlemen, to whom we owed the success of our hunt. They were Messrs. Clive and Harley Metcalf [sic], planters from Mississippi, men in the prime of life, thorough woodsmen and hunters, skilled marksmen, and utterly

fearless horsemen. For a quarter of a century they had hunted bear and deer with horse and hound, and were masters of the art. They brought with them their pack of bear hounds, only one, however, being a thoroughly staunch and seasoned veteran. The pack was under the immediate control of a negro hunter, Holt Collier, in his own way as remarkable a character as Ben Lilley [sic]. He was a man of sixty and could neither read nor write, but he had all the dignity of an African chief, and for half a century he had been a bear hunter, having killed or assisted in killing over three thousand bears . . . After the war he continued to stay with his master until the latter died, and had then been adopted by the Metcalfs; and he felt that he had brought them up, and treated them with that mixture of affection and grumbling respect which an old nurse shows toward the lad who has ceased being a child. The two Metcalfs and Holt understood one another thoroughly, and understood their hounds and the game their hounds followed almost as thoroughly.

But there were no bears to be found right then on the Bayou, so after a few days, camp was moved to Bear Lake, a long, winding body of water once part of a river but now still water. The hunters were joined by Ichabod and Tom Osborn, planters whose ancestors had settled in the area a century before, and who contributed a few dogs of their own to the pack. A small yearling bear was killed; then, after a couple days, the pack crossed the trail of an adult female. While Collier managed the dogs, the white men split up, each aiming to head the bear off when it would "break cover."

The descriptions of the hunt don't make it clear just where anyone was when Roosevelt got the bear. Clive Metcalfe led the President to a likely spot, then another, listening all the while to the sound of the pack as it drifted here and there in the heavy growth, trying to estimate where it was headed, and ultimately doing a good job of guessing its course. Furious riding was alternated with brief, puffing interludes of listening. The bear would approach a clearing, the pack and Collier hard on its heels, but then it would turn and leave the disappointed hunters waiting in vain. They would mount up and tear through the cane to a new spot.

This, according to one probably trustworthy account, was the arrangement settled upon by Collier. According to this version, Collier had told Roosevelt that if the hunt was turned over to him, completely, the bear would be found. Collier directed the hunters on their movements, and gave the following instructions to Clive:

> Now, Mr. Clive, you take the Cunnel and bum around with him in the woods like you an' me always does, an' don' put him on no stand. He ain't no baby. He kin go anywhere you kin go; jest keep him as near to the dogs as you kin. Mr. Harley an' me'll follow the hounds an' when we strike a trail you and the Cunnel come a-runnin'.[9]

If that speech was made, I can imagine Roosevelt's face disappearing behind his great smile when he heard he "ain't no baby," to know that at least one man present wasn't going to overpamper him. And whether just those words were said or not, that's just how it worked out. Clive and Roosevelt at last heard the shouts of the others and the wild baying cry of the lead dogs, unable to bring the bear to a full bay but easily able now to keep it in sight. Clive, with the unerring judgment of a man who'd learned his sport from one of the world's premier bear men, and following the advice that man had given him earlier in the day, led the President to what he thought was the right place.

Roosevelt crouched next to his host in the heavy cane and brought his rifle up as he peered this way and that through the tangle, looking for the bear. It came then, badgered and distracted by Collier's lead dogs, Rowdy and Queen. At twenty yards, it stood sideways to the hunters, and Roosevelt had what was the closest he could come to a clear shot. The bullet from his .45-70 bulled undeflected through the dense cane and passed through the bear behind the shoulder, a shot sure to prove fatal but not necessarily to cause instant death. In order to prevent damage to the dogs in the bear's dying moments, Metcalfe and Roosevelt rushed to within a few paces of the

Holt Collier about the time of the second Roosevelt hunt. (Photo courtesy of Harley Metcalfe III.)

struggling bear, where Roosevelt finished it with a second shot as the dogs came up and jumped on the carcass. Roosevelt, after a five-year wait, finally had his canebrake bear, shot in "true hunter fashion" over the dogs of Holt Collier.

The bear, which weighed 202 pounds, was the last bear Roosevelt shot in his long, colorful hunting career.

Collier's life was never the same after these hunts. From then on, for the next thirty years, no matter what he did as a hunter, he was known as the man who guided Roosevelt in the canebrakes. The President sent him a Winchester 30-30 Model 1894, a near-duplicate of the rifle used to kill the bear, and Collier kept the gun wrapped and carefully stored, a treasured memento of the historic hunts.

But, as near as I can tell, Collier didn't hunt as much after that. Ben Lilly was right when he left Mississippi a few years before: the bears were getting thinned out, and the wilderness was sadly reduced. By the early 1920s, much of the old hunting grounds were gone. Old "Uncle Holt" became a fixture, even something of an institution, around Greenville, spending a goodly amount of time telling tales of the old days and being interviewed by the regular stream of journalists who came to take down, one more time, the story of the big hunts. Locals were regaled with other stories, of bears, panthers, and other game killed where now there were houses and farms. Collier outlived the wild country he loved; he saw the habitat destroyed, a surer end to the bears than all the bullets he'd fired in his long and deadly career as a hunter and guide.

According to *The Black Bear in Modern North America* (1977), there were fifteen to twenty-five black bears in Mississippi in 1977. A more recent report, in *Audubon* in 1984, gave the even sadder news that, "for all practical purposes the species is extinct." Neighboring Louisiana is doing only a little better than that, and a movement is afoot to restore that state's bear population. I'm sure some will blame Collier and his contemporaries for this sad state of bearlessness, but I'm equally sure that's not an entirely fair charge to make. The old Mississippi wilderness provided generations of bear hunters with many bears without running short; it was only after the canebrakes were cut down and the settlements came and grew that there seemed to be an end to the bear. Even in his last days, Collier seemed to understand this, and he lamented the loss of the wild country even more than he lamented the loss of any particular wild animal. To hunters, it might seem a shame that a life like Collier's could not be led today, but we have to keep in mind that even in his day it was extraordinarily rare. No bear population, even one as obviously robust as the southern one, could withstand the withering assaults of very many Colliers, Bobos, and Lillys. The reason these men could kill so many bears year after year is that there were so few of them doing it.

It was a different world, and it gave a different sport. Who today would even *want* to kill several dozen bears in one year? The way of life and system of values that could support and justify that kind of hunting vanished with the wilderness that made it possible.

We should keep Holt Collier—and William Pickett, and Wilburn Waters, and John Adams, and the rest of them—in our memory not so much for their magnificent efficiency at killing bears as for the vicarious excitement they bring us. We can imagine Collier riding hard after his hounds, or following them into some hollow tree, or sitting and jostling them as he jokes and laughs at the campfire with his most famous client. We can appreciate the world he knew, in all its richness and diversity, by hearing of his hunts, and we can provide ourselves with a benchmark for measuring the health of our own world by recalling the productivity and ecological robustness of his.

But it is on a less lofty level that Collier and his spiritual kin are probably most satisfying: on the personal level of the hunters out doing what hunters do, and doing it with a sense of satisfaction and goodwill that have so much to do with honest sport. It is in this realm, of personal fulfillment, that we may find Collier most meaningful to us.

I find that when I think of Collier, one moment comes to mind, a fraternal vignette during the first Roosevelt hunt, described by Denison, who obviously sensed the greater value in all of this excitement over bears:

> There was the instructive picture of Holt Collier and some of the white men, too, dipping their horns into the water hole where the first bear had died, and drinking their fill of a puree of bear and dog and mud, all held in solution in water that had been standing for at least eight months.

It was, indeed, a different world, and for all its faults and mistakes, it wouldn't hurt us to mourn its passing.

Notes

I have used notes in this book in order to give those interested in learning more the information they need to pursue various subjects. Where possible, for example in citing various stories in periodicals, I have given enough information in the text and so do not include those references again here.

Introduction

1. William Faulkner, *Go Down, Moses* (New York: Random House, 1942). "The Bear" is one part of this novel, and first appeared in magazine story form a few years earlier than the book was published.
2. A good introduction to the history of the Plott hounds is Curtis Wooten, "Johannes Plott's Famous Hunting Dogs," *Wildlife in North Carolina*, October, 1983, p. 5.
3. Bear Howard is profiled briefly in David Brown, *The Grizzly in the Southwest* (Norman: University of Oklahoma Press, 1985), p. 188.
4. Henry W. Shoemaker, *The Black Bear of Pennsylvania* (Altoona: Times Tribune Company, 1921), p. 25.
5. Tracy I. Storer and Lloyd P. Tevis, *California Grizzly* (Berkeley: University of California Press, 1955), p. 138.

1 David Crockett

1. Francis Lee Utley, "Pride and Humility: The Cultural Roots of Ike McCaslin," in *Bear, Man, and God: Eight Approaches to William Faulkner's "The Bear,"* eds. Francis Lee Utley, Lynn Z. Bloom, and Arthur F. Kinney (New York: Random House, 1971), p. 170.
2. Thorpe's story is readily available to modern readers in Utley, Bloom, and Kinney, *Bear, Man, and God.*
3. James Atkins Shackford, ed. John B. Shackford, *David Crockett, the Man and the Legend* (Chapel Hill: University of North Carolina Press, 1956).
4. Mathew St. Clair Clarke, *Life and Adventures of Colonel David Crockett of West Tennessee* (Cincinnati: "For the Proprietor," 1833).
5. And we must keep in mind that, in the words of one of his many biographers, "Crockett became famous as a hunter, but he was also a farmer" (Constance

Rourke, *Davy Crockett* (New York: Harcourt, Brace and Company, 1934). I'm sure part of his appeal to the common man was that he was himself so practiced in the crafts and skills of homesteading and farming.

6. Richard Boyd Hauck, *Crockett, A Bio-Bibliography* (Westport: Greenwood Press, 1982), p. xviii. This book is, along with Shackford's biography, essential first reading if you are interested in pursuing the Crockett story.

7. Hauck, *Crockett,* p. 18.

8. Texas Jim Cooper, "A Study of Some David Crockett Firearms," *The East Tennessee Historical Society's Publications* 38 (1966), p. 62. This weapon has survived, as reported in the following paragraph from Cooper's article:

   "While journeying through northern Texas, Crockett traded a long-stemmed rifle to a traveling companion from Tennessee named Andy Thomas, receiving in return a short-barreled flintlock. The Crockett weapon was more than five feet in length, weighed 27 pounds, was of definite quality, and was adorned by an eight-point star carved in the butt by the Colonel himself. Carved before Crockett left Tennessee, it was to symbolize Texas' anticipated rise to greatness. In Nashville Crockett had had a silversmith inlay the star with silver. Andy Thomas was a woodsman and marksman of note and used Crockett's rifle in hunting and in defending himself, family, and home. The prized weapon was kept in the Thomas family for many years until donated to the Alamo where it is presently on view."

9. See, for example, James Shackford and Stanley Folmsbee's comments in their edition of *A Narrative of the Life of David Crockett of the State of Tennessee* (Knoxville: University of Tennessee Press, 1973), pp. 154, 193.

10. Thomas C. Eagle and Michael R. Pelton, "Seasonal Nutrition of Black Bears in The Great Smoky Mountains National Park," in *Bears—Their Biology and Management,* ed. Charles Meslow (West Glacier: International Association for Bear Research and Management, 1983), p. 94. The period just following emergence from the den is often a lean time as the bears spend a week or several adjusting to resumed feeding. During this period, according to several observers, bears may lose weight. I cite Eagle and Pelton because their study is closest geographically to the area Crockett hunted.

   What's more important here, in defense of Crockett, is that other knowledgeable bear hunters and students agreed with him. For example, J.A. McGuire, for many years editor of *Outdoor Life,* once wrote an article on "Some Sidelights on Bruin's Annual Sleep," in which he made the following statement:

   "Contrary to the general opinion entertained by some classes of even our sportsman friends, Bruin doesn't come out of his long sleep in the spring the emaciated being that he is so often pictured. He is usually in pretty good condition physically, and sometimes even fat. His sectional habitat may have some influence on him in this respect, but I now speak of the bears of the Rockies that are found between the Canadian boundary and the northern line of Arizona and New Mexico. These bears, both grizzly and black, are usually in good order when they wake up during April and May and go out to look for their long-deferred breakfast."

Crockett's beliefs about bear weight loss were also held by many other observers.

It would seem likely, moreover, that for bears living in southern habitats, where the winters are not as long and the denning period is shorter (in some areas almost nonexistent), weight loss could in some years be negligible.

11. Shackford and Folmsbee, *A Narrative*, p. 190.

2   *John Adams*

1. Storer and Tevis, *California Grizzly*, p. 164.
2. P.T. Barnum, *Humbugs of the World* (London: J.C. Hotten, 1866), p. 29.
3. Richard H. Dillon, *Grizzly Adams: A Memorable Mountain Man* (Davis: University of California Library Keepsake Number 1, 1966), p. 4.
4. Storer and Tevis, *California Grizzly*, p. 234, give a review of many articles and pamphlets in which Adams was involved.
5. Francis Farquhar, *The Grizzly Bear Hunter of California, A Bibliographical Essay* (San Francisco: The Grabhorn Press, 1947). Farquhar's essay was originally published as part of a book, *Essays for Henry Wagner*, issued by the same publisher in 1947. This essay is one of the most important sources on the Adams record, and establishes with reasonable certainty, I think, that his true name was John Adams.
6. See, for example, G.M. Burghardt and L.S. Burghardt, "Notes on the Behavioral Development of Two Black Bear Cubs: The First Eight Months," in *Bears—Their Biology and Management*, eds. Michael R. Pelton, Jack W. Lentfer, and G. Edgar Folk (Morges: International Union for the Conservation of Nature, 1972), p. 207. The best discussion of bear behavior for a general audience, especially as bear facial and other communicative features relate to aggression, is found in various chapters in Stephen Herrero's book, *Bear Attacks: Their Causes and Avoidance* (New York: Nick Lyons Books/ Winchester Press, 1985).
7. Arthur Pearson, *The Northern Grizzly Bear Ursus arctos L.* (Ottawa: Canadian Wildlife Service Report Series Number 34, 1975), p. 18, reviews some of the technical literature on cementum aging that has appeared since 1950.
8. Farquhar, *The Grizzly Bear Hunter*, p. 10.
9. Herrero, *Bear Attacks*, p. 24, recommends playing dead if attacked by a grizzly bear. The rules may differ with black bears.
10. Rambler was a female that had nursed Ben and his sibling when they were cubs; must have been some interesting bonding going on there.
11. Barnum, *Humbugs*, p. 23.
12. Storer and Tevis, *California Grizzly*, p. 216.

3   *Wilburn Waters*

1. Dale Burk, ed., *The Black Bear in Modern North America* (New York: The

Boone and Crockett Club and the Camp Fire Club of America, 1979), is a nice review of the current status of the black bear in most states.

2. Charles B. Coale, *The Life and Adventures of Wilburn Waters, The Famous Hunter and Trapper of White Top Mountain; Embracing Early History of Southwestern Virginia, Sufferings of the Pioneers, Etc., Etc.* (Richmond: G.W. Gary & Company, 1878). The book's history is explained in the author's preface.

3. Theodore Roosevelt, *The Wilderness Hunter* (New York: G.P. Putnam's Sons, 1893).

4. The story of Waters was reprinted in 1929 in a volume entitled *Annals of Southwest Virginia,* edited by Louis P. Summers and published in Abington. In 1960, those portions of Coale's book having to do with Waters were again reprinted, by Rev. M.H. Hart of West Jefferson, North Carolina. Rev. Hart provided some commentary on the death of Waters, and described his successful efforts to raise a monument to the hunter. One chapter of the Coale book was reprinted in Clarence Gohdes, ed., *Hunting in the Old South, Original Narratives of the Hunters* (Baton Rouge: Louisiana State University Press, 1967). Brief mentions of Waters also appear in John Preston Arthur, *Western North Carolina: A History (1730–1913)* (Raleigh: Edward & Broughton Printing Company, 1914), p. 331, and Arthur L. Fletcher, *Ashe County, A History* (Jefferson, North Carolina: Ashe County Research Association, no date). Waters's story is also retold in an account of the David Clark portrait of him: Lillian Stuart Butt, "The Wilburn Waters Portrait," in *The Historical Society of Washington County, Virginia, Publication Series II, No. 15, August, 1978,* p. 20. The story of the Waters Memorial, erected by Hart and his friends, is also told in Dallas Mallison, "Ashe Pioneer Was A Rugged Man," *Mount Airy News,* clipping dated 1959, in the North Carolina Clipping File through 1975, U.N.C. Library, Chapel Hill.

4   Wade Hampton III

1. Thorpe's article was one of many later reprinted in William Porter, ed., *Instructions to Young Sportsman in all that Relates to Guns and Shooting,* by P. Hawker (Philadelphia: Lea and Blanchard, 1846), the first American edition of this British classic on hunting.

2. Henry T. Ireys, "The Mound," in William D. McCain and Charlotte Capers, eds., *Memoirs of Henry Tillinghurst Ireys: Papers of the Washington County Historical Society, 1910–1915* (Jackson: Mississippi Department of Archives and History and Mississippi Historical Society, 1954), p. 394.

3. McCain and Capers, *Memoirs of Henry Tillinghurst Ireys,* p. 398.

4. Among the biographies of Hampton are Edward Wells, *Hampton and Reconstruction* (Columbia: The State Company, 1907); Manly Wade Wellman, *Giant in Grey, A Biography of Wade Hampton of South Carolina* (New York: Charles Scribner's Sons, 1949); and Virginia Meynard, *The Venturers, the Hampton, Harrison, and Earle Families of Virginia, South Carolina, and*

Texas (Easley, South Carolina: Southern Historical Press, 1981). Of course, there are huge numbers of articles and other short works as well.

5. Harry Hampton may have gotten his "eighty bears" misinformation not from Roosevelt but from Wellman, *Giant in Grey*, p. 44, where the figure is used. I have not found it anywhere in Roosevelt's writings; I quote the only numbers Roosevelt used when referring to Hampton.

6. Unless otherwise noted, these quotations are from Charles E. Cauthen, *Family Letters of the Three Wade Hamptons, 1782–1901* (Columbia: University of South Carolina Press, 1953).

5 William Pickett

1. George Bird Grinnell, ed., *Hunting at High Altitudes* (New York: Harper & Brothers, Publishers, 1913), p. 7.

2. Background on Pickett's life is found in Grinnell, *Hunting at High Altitudes,* p. 11.

3. Bob Edgar and Jack Turnell, *Brand of a Legend* (Cody: Stockade Publishing, 1978).

4. John K. Rollinson, "Brands of the Eighties and Nineties Used in Big Horn Basin, Wyoming Territory," *Annals of Wyoming* Vol. 19, No. 4 (July 1947), p. 67.

5. Dave Wasden, *From Beaver to Oil* (Cheyenne: Pioneer Printing & Stationery Co., 1973), p. 57. A short biography of Pickett with discussion of his political ambitions appeared in the *Cheyenne Sun,* January 14, 1890. He occasionally corresponded with the *Confederate Veteran,* a publication still in existence, and his writings therein can be located in that publication's index.

6. Larry Roop, "The Yellowstone Grizzly Bear: A Review of Past and Present Population Estimates," in *Yellowstone Grizzly Bear Investigations, Annual Report of the Interagency Study Team, 1978–1979* (Helena: Montana Department of Fish, Wildlife and Parks, 1980), p. 61.

7. Wasden, *From Beaver to Oil,* p. 301.

8. I later returned to a book I had not read for ten years or so, A.A. Anderson's autobiography, *Experiences and Impressions* (New York: The Macmillan Company, 1933). Anderson told about his feud with Pickett at some length, portraying Pickett pretty much the way Seton did. Anderson's autobiography is consistently self-congratulatory and self-serving, so I have no more faith in his account than I do in Seton's, which, as near as I can tell, was simply Anderson's viewpoint put in fiction.

6 Robert Eager Bobo

1. Robert Bobo, Sr., "From Cross Keys, South Carolina to Cross Keys, Mississippi," unpublished typescript, Carnegie Public Library, Clarksdale, Mississippi, 1971. There is also a substantial amount of information in

Linton Weeks, *Clarksdale & Coahoma County, A History* (Clarksdale: Carnegie Public Library, 1982), p. 67. Also useful is Stella Martin, "Pioneer Family Gave Its Name to Bobo, Small Farm Village," *The Clarksdale Press Register,* March 19, 1959, and a lengthy unattributed newspaper clipping dated March 18, 1928, "When Coahoma County Had 3 Families and a Hand-Mill," Carnegie Public Library, Clarksdale, Mississippi.

2. Unattributed newspaper clipping dated December 17, 1902, "Bob Bobo is Dead Today," Carnegie Public Library, Clarksdale, Mississippi. This is an extended obituary, with many biographical details.

3. Lamar Satchfield, "Those Famous Bobo Bear Hunts," *Delta Scene* magazine, Spring, 1974.

4. Ibid.

5. "Coahoma," "Bruin in the Canebrake," *Forest and Stream,* March 24, 1887, p. 179.

6. Clipping, "Bob Bobo is Dead Today."

7. Weeks, *Clarksdale & Coahoma County,* p. 69.

8. Martin, "Pioneer Family."

9. Kit Dalton, *Quantrell, Under the Black Flag* (Memphis: Lockard Publishing Company, n.d.), p. 184.

7   Theodore Roosevelt

1. Roosevelt's outdoor books included the following titles: *Hunting Trips of a Ranchman* (New York: G.P. Putnam's Sons, 1885); *Ranch Life and the Hunting Trail* (New York: Century, 1888); *The Wilderness Hunter* (New York: G.P. Putnam's Sons, 1893); *Some American Game* (New York: G.P. Putnam's Sons, 1897); *Outdoor Pastimes of an American Hunter* (New York: Charles Scribner's Sons, 1905); *Good Hunting* (New York: Harper & Brothers, 1907); *African Game Trails* (New York: Charles Scribner's Sons, 1910); *Through the Brazilian Wilderness* (New York: Charles Scribner's Sons, 1914); *A Book-Lover's Holiday in the Open* (New York: Charles Scribner's Sons, 1916); and several books he either cowrote or coedited, including three classic volumes from the Boone and Crockett Club, coedited with George Bird Grinnell.

2. Two volumes that serve to introduce the scholarship of Theodore Roosevelt are Aloysius Norton, *Theodore Roosevelt* (Boston: Twayne, 1980); and Gilbert J. Black, *Theodore Roosevelt, 1858–1919, Chronology, Documents, Bibliographical Aids* (Dobbs Ferry, New York: Oceana Publications, Inc., 1969). Norton makes a wonderful comment about Roosevelt scholarship on page 162:

"If there really are more stars in the heavens than there are grains of sand on all the beaches of the world, then their number can be rivaled by the seemingly infinite number of allusions to Roosevelt in the memoirs, autobiographies, biographies, and letters of his time."

I have found this to be true even in my own limited studies of Roosevelt's outdoor adventures. If he even knew the names of, much less hunted with, all the people who later would claim to have hunted with him, or guided him, his mind would have been too full for such minor pastimes as the presidency. He was a little like bears, in that way: everyone wants to have had some kind of experience with them to tell people about.

3. Elting Morison, ed. *The Letters of Theodore Roosevelt* (Cambridge: Harvard University Press, 1951–1954), Vol. 1, p. 82. Later references to his letters in this chapter are from this set.

4. I review these weights and their meaning in my book *The Bears of Yellowstone* (Boulder: Roberts Rinehart, 1986).

8   *William Wright*

1. McGuire, though he wrote many articles about bears early in this century, seems never to have written a book. That surprises me, because he was interested in bears for so long and obviously could have written a good one. He is one of the many bear writers who could stand further study.

2. Burk, *The Black Bear in Modern North America*, Harold McCracken, *The Beast that Walks Like Man* (Garden City: Hanover House, 1955), and Andy Russell, *Grizzly Country* (New York: Alfred Knopf, 1967), all discuss the demise of bears in North America.

9   *Ben Lilly*

1. This story is a perfect example of the trouble of tracking down a Ben Lilly story. It has several versions. In his transcribed journals at the Eugene C. Barker Texas History Center, The University of Texas at Austin, entitled "Ben V. Lilly on Bears and Lions," he tells this story (manuscript pages 70–71) as if there was only one dog with him. When telling it to his friend M.E. Musgrave, who wrote it in "Ben Lilly—Last of the Mountain Men," *American Forests*, August 1938, p. 349, there were several dogs, and right when the bear charged, the dog tied to Lilly lunged and pulled the old man over in the snow, making his situation even worse. A cleaned-up version of the unpublished diary is quoted without reference to source by Dobie in *The Ben Lilly Legend* (Boston: Little, Brown and Company, 1950); Dobie says it's in Lilly's words. In this version, there was one dog tied to him, but others were also along, though their role is not explained.

2. Lilly, "Ben V. Lilly on Lions and Bears," p. 75. This manuscript material, along with Dobie's biography, are the chief sources of this chapter. Dobie's biography contains an extended bibliographical essay, which I have explored at some length. Generally, his synthesis of information from all of his sources is reliable. I point out a few places in the text where I disagree with him.

3. W.L.P., "With the Bears in Coon Bayou," *Forest and Stream*, February 10, 1887, p. 47.

4. *Ibid.*

5. Dobie, *The Ben Lilly Legend,* p. 34.
6. Musgrave, *Ben Lilly—Last of the Mountain Men,* p. 379.
7. Brackin is discussed in Francis Abernethy, ed., *Tales from the Big Thicket* (Austin: University of Texas Press, 1966), p. 97.

10 *Holt Collier*

1. This is, I believe, an accurate dramatization of an adventure Holt Collier reported to an interviewer late in his life. The details of the interview were published in one of the most accurate and helpful accounts about Collier, in George P. Rawick, ed., *The American Slave: A Composite Autobiography, Supplement, Series 1, Volume 7, Mississippi Narratives Part 2* (Westport, Connecticut: Greenwood Press, 1978), p. 457. This is the source of much of the information about the sporting career of Collier in this chapter. A pair of stories by Harris Dickson in *The Saturday Evening Post*—"The Bearslayer," March 13, 1909, and "Bear Stories," April 10, 1909—also give a great deal of biographical information on Holt Collier, supposedly as direct quotes from him. Of less reliability is Orland Kay Armstrong, "He Tracked Bear for Roosevelt," *New York Herald Tribune,* January 3, 1932. The obituary, "Holt Collier, Colored Soldier of the South, Dies," the *Daily Democrat Times* (Greenville), August 3, 1936, is a brief review of basic facts of his life.
2. Laura D.S. Harrell, Research Assistant, State of Mississippi Department of Archives and History, letter to Major Robert Greene, U.S. Army, Washington, D.C., March 20, 1970. The letter says, in part:
   "The only Negro for whom we have evidence of service in the Confederate States Army is Holt Collier. Enclosed are a letter attesting to that fact and a copy of his pension application. Although we do not have an official record of his service, there seems to be no doubt of it."
3. Sandra Dahl Desmond has accumulated a wealth of material on Collier that does not relate to this book, but that will one day make an exciting book of its own. I cannot resist including in these footnotes at least a few hints of his other adventures.
   During the war, for example, he was once called upon to swim to an island in the Mississippi and ingratiate himself with a group of river pirates who would have instantly killed him had they realized he was a spy. He succeeded in doing so, then sneaked away and returned at night, leading a group of soldiers in a boat with muffled oars on a raid that captured the whole band.
   In 1881, according to an article in the *Greenville Times* for July 9, Collier was asked by the local constable to stop a suspected murderer from crossing the Bogue Phalia River at Washburn's Ferry. Collier, who was on his way to a bear hunt, hurried to the Ferry, found the man, and attempted to detain him. The man resisted, and a fight ensued. Collier eventually shot the man, who was white, dead in self-defense, with no more stir from the local courts than if any *white* man had shot any other white man.
   Collier became a noted and respected citizen, not only for his skills as a hunter but for his high sense of honor and his consistent friendship to nu-

merous powerful men, who, for their part, could not have been more grateful to have such a man as a friend. I have the impression that by 1900, he was as important in the Greenville area as a man without much money or any political power could be. His is a story of loyalty, even love, and of almost unrelieved adventures in war and wilderness hunting. It is also the story of a truly extraordinary American character, an unusual and forgotten hero.

4. Rawick, *The American Slave*, p. 458. There are stories that Collier traveled as far away as Alaska to hunt bear, but so far no evidence has surfaced to support or reject the stories. He obviously traveled a lot, at least in the South, and claimed also to have met Frank James in Texas. The stories of Texas are almost certainly true; Collier seemed to have none of Lilly's sense of sport about telling tall tales.

I do suspect that Collier got his own story a little mixed up over the years, though. As I mention in the text, the different tellings of the Roosevelt hunt stories that are attributed to Collier do not always agree in details (even allowing always for the errors of the interviewers, I still think he told the story differently). And, in a peculiarly revealing episode, he changed his telling of the time he ran away to join his Colonel Hinds during the Civil War. When telling the story to *The Saturday Evening Post*, as quoted in my text, he says that Hinds expressed concern about his safety during a battle, and that Collier responded by saying, "Ain't my chances mighty nigh as good as yours?" But later in his life, when interviewed for Rawick's *The American Slave*, Collier had the exchange take place when Hinds first discovered that he had stowed away on the steamboat. In this exchange, Hinds expressed concern that if he and his son Thomas "both go to the devil that boy will have to go along," to which young Collier responded, "I got as good a chance as you." It seems unlikely that both conversations took place. I just assume that over time Collier confused his details, having told the stories so often to so many people.

5. The most respected version of the 1902 hunt is Gregory C. Wilson, "How Teddy Bear Got His Name," *Washington Post Potomac*, November 30, 1969, p. 33. The story has been told countless times. Some of the chief sources, besides Wilson, are: Lindsay Denison, "President Roosevelt's Mississippi Bear Hunt," *Outing*, February 1903, p. 603 (probably the best of the firsthand versions); Anon., "Teddy Left Too Quick," *The Commercial Appeal* (Memphis), November 15, 1902; Jacob Dickinson, "Theodore Roosevelt's Mississippi Bear Hunt," *Outdoor America*, April 1924, p. 5; Anon., "Fruitless Day for 'The Colonel,'" *The Commercial Appeal* (Memphis), November 18, 1902; Anon., "Bears Run from Teddy," *The Commercial Appeal* (Memphis), November 19, 1902, and the various references to Holt Collier already given.

6. Wilson, "How Teddy Bear Got His Name."

7. Rawick, *The American Slave*, p. 455.

8. This hunt, too, has been widely written about. A nice summary of the event, though I wish I knew its sources, is Douglas Wynn, "Remarks at Dedication of Theodore Roosevelt Monument, Bear Lake, Madison Parish, Louisiana,

October 14, 1960," unpublished typescript. A short article with beautiful color photographs of the Tensas area is Maurice Cockerham, "Teddy's Tensas," *Louisiana Conservationist,* September/October 1983, p. 12.

9.   Wynn, "Remarks at Dedication."

Bear Books:
A Bibliography, of Sorts

This is a specialized sort of bibliography, restricted to books about bears and bear hunting. There are countless books that contain material about bears, but for practical reasons I have chosen to limit this list to those that are more or less *only* about bears; exceptions to that rule, such as Hittell's biography of John Adams, are included for obvious reasons.

I have provided this list, rather than another, because books are the place most people start when they want to learn about something. From this list one can move on to technical publications, to other books not listed (such as those from Europe or Asia, for example), and to the vast assortment of nontechnical periodical material out there waiting to be enjoyed.

As I suggest at various places in the text, books are only the beginning for the enthusiastic reader. There have been thousands of bear-related stories and articles in sporting periodicals, as well as in general-interest magazines. Relatively few of these items are included in the huge bibliographies for black and brown bears compiled by the Alaska Cooperative Park Studies Unit, in Fairbanks (see Tracy in the following list); these two bibliographies each contain more than four thousand titles, including the vast majority of all technical papers, journal articles, unpublished reports and interim draft reports, and books that relate to bears. The bibliographies would go from huge to immense if they also included all the obscure, repetitive, brief little tales, as well as longer stories, that have appeared in *Forest and Stream, American Field, Outdoor Life, Field and Stream,* and the dozens of other sporting periodicals that have at various times celebrated, misrepresented, studied, and slandered bears.

For the bear student who wants to move beyond sporting history, there are a series of volumes listed below that are the best place to start. Popular books, no matter how well written, are no substitute for solid scientific reporting. I recommend first the published proceedings, each titled *Bears—Their Biology and Management,* listed below under their editors' names (Herrero, Martinka, Meslow, Pelton). These volumes not only contain dozens of fascinating research articles, but are rich in references to hundreds of other similar works. Some of the popularly written books below also have substantial bibliographies (Craighead, Herrero, McNamee, Schullery, Shepard, and Sanders).

For the sake of variety, and for further enticement to the interested, I have included a few technical volumes, though some are more correctly called monographs or reports than books, just to suggest the breadth of material available. Some of the most productive modern bear scientists—Gary Alt, Lynn Rogers, Charles Jonkel, Michael Pelton, Richard Knight, and others—have published many reports and technical papers, but no books, so they are not listed here in proportion to their output.

I have also included a few juvenile titles. There is no end to those, either. With one or two exceptions where the story relates directly to hunting or to bear natural history, I have not included fiction; bears have figured in great numbers of fictional works.

Here and there through the list below, I have commented on some titles—on their historical significance, their unusual features, or my opinion of their value.

Bauer, Erwin. *Erwin Bauer's Bears in Their World.* New York: Outdoor Life Books, 1985.
Erwin Bauer is among the most famous of the outdoor photographers, and this book is in good part a collection of his best work. There are many marvelous, striking pictures of bears (black, brown, grizzly, and polar), and Bauer's stories of his own experiences with photographing bears and of other bear lore and natural history. There is misinformation here and there, and he gets embarrassingly over his head in trying to discuss bear management in the Lower Forty-Eight (this is the book's least accurate part), but the pictures are very nicely printed, and in fact may be the best one-volume collection of bear photographs I've seen.

Bialosky, Peggy and Alan. *The Teddy Bear Catalog.* New York: Workman Publishing Company, 1980.
I guess the fascination with the teddy bear is like a lot of other things: either it gets you or doesn't. It's never gotten me, at least not to this extent, but if you're interested, you might try this, or the book by Peter Bull listed below.

Beebe, B.F., and J.R. Johnson. *American Bears.* New York: David McKay, 1965.

Bledsoe, Thomas. *Brown Bear Summer, Life Among Alaska's Giants.* New York: Truman Talley Books/E.P. Dutton, 1987. The bears of McNeil Falls, Alaska, were the subject of studies conducted by the author and others in the 1970s and 1980s. This is written in a modestly technical manner but is no less engaging for that, and the photographs are wonderful. It falls into perhaps my favorite category of bear books, those written by the authorities themselves.

Bray, O.E., and V.G. Barnes. *A Literature Review on Black Bear Populations and Activities.* National Park Service and Colorado Cooperative Wildlife Research Unit, 1967. Now dated, this is still an excellent bibliography for black bears, especially for older works in technical journals.

Brown, David. *The Grizzly in the Southwest.* Norman: The University of Oklahoma Press, 1985.

A very fine study of the natural history, lore, and extinction of the grizzly bear in the southwestern United States and northern Mexico. Modeled after Storer and Tevis's classic, *California Grizzly,* Brown's book is similarly authoritative as a reference. He makes an intelligent plea for the restoration of grizzly bears in the region.

Brown, David, and John Murray, eds. *The Last Grizzly and Other Southwest Bear Stories.* Flagstaff: University of Arizona Press, in press.

Bull, Peter. *The Teddy Bear Book.* New York: Random House, 1970.

Burk, Dale, ed. *The Black Bear in Modern North America.* New York: The Boone and Crockett Club and the Camp Fire Club of America, 1979.

This is based on the proceedings of a 1977 symposium in Montana, and is an important reference for its reports on the status of bears in many states and provinces, as well as its many discussions of management objectives and techniques.

Callaway, C.C. *Bears of the Great Smokies.* Maryville, Tennessee: Big Brazos Press, circa 1951.

A small tourist booklet, modestly distinguished by the inclusion of a bear story by Ernie Pyle.

Caras, Roger. *Monarch of Deadman Bay.* New York: Little, Brown and Company, 1969.

A well-told fictional account of an Alaskan bear.

Cardoza, James. *The History and Status of the Black Bear in Massachusetts and Adjacent New England States.* Westborough: Massachusetts Division of Fisheries & Wildlife Research Bulletin 18, 1976.

I wish more states had books like this. It is a wonderful historical review of the presence and status of black bears in the state, with extensive discussions of surrounding states.

Carey, Alan. *In the Path of the Grizzly.* Flagstaff: Northland Press, 1986.

Primarily a color picture-book, with light narrative by the author/ photographer, this is a great collection of grizzly bear photography.

Cherr, Pat. *The Bear in Fact and Fiction.* New York: Harlin Quist, 1967.

I think this is a children's book. At least it reads as if directed at a juvenile audience. It is something of a miscellany, with more errors than a book with such a confident title ought to have.

Clark, Marvin. *Pinnell and Talifson: Last of the Great Brown Bear Men.* Spokane: Great Northwest Publishing and Distributing Company.

Tales of two famous Alaskan bear guides.

Contreras, Glen, and Keith Evans, compilers. *Proceedings—Grizzly Bear Habitat Symposium.* Ogden: Intermountain Research Station, 1986.

The key issue for grizzly bear survival is giving the bears enough room, and this symposium addressed that issue from many directions, including the latest habitat mapping technology, applying habitat research findings to reducing human-bear encounters, evaluating the effects of various types of encroachment on habitat, and measuring the carrying capacity of habitat.

Craighead, Frank. *Track of the Grizzly.* San Francisco: Sierra Club Books, 1979.
The Craighead brothers, John and Frank, studied Yellowstone's grizzly bears for twelve years, 1959–1970, and this is Frank's story of their adventures and experiences. Most of the book is devoted to their field work, and is a lively mix of their activities and their discoveries during this pioneering study. The last chapter is Frank Craighead's angry account of the great grizzly bear controversy of roughly 1967–1973, when he and his brother were at odds with the National Park Service over just how the bears should best be managed. I recommend the book for its exciting story of the study, and recommend caution in taking the author's account of the controversy at face value. As one Wyoming biologist put it, listening only to the Craighead side of the controversy is like listening to one side of a divorce case.

Craighead, John, and Frank Craighead. *Grizzly Bear Prehibernation and Denning Activities as Determined by Radiotracking.* Washington: The Wildlife Society, Wildlife Monograph 32, 1972.
One of the many technical reports to come out of the Craighead study, it is based on their important work in radiotelemetry.

Craighead, John, J. Sumner, and G. Scaggs. *A Definitive System for Analysis of Grizzly Bear Habitat and Other Wilderness Resources.* Missoula: Wildlife-Wildlands Institute Monograph Number 1, 1982.
Based mostly on John Craighead's work in habitat research after leaving Yellowstone, this is an analysis of LANDSAT satellite habitat-mapping.

Cramond, Mike. *Killer Bears.* New York: Outdoor Life Books/Charles Scribner's Sons, 1981.
This book doesn't do much for me. I recommend instead a much more authoritative, professionally analytical, and readable book, Dr. Stephen Herrero's *Bear Attacks,* listed below. Cramond, a veteran outdoor writer, interviewed many victims of attacks, and gathered a lot of information, but Herrero, one of the world's foremost experts on bear-human interactions, is far better able to relate attacks to bear science and environment.

Davids, Richard. *Lords of the Artic: A Journey Among the Polar Bears.* New York: Macmillan Publishing Company, 1982.
Spectacular color photographs of the polar bear, with a thoughtful text about bear natural history and conservation.

Day, Beth. *Grizzlies in Their Back Yard.* New York: Julian Messner, 1956.

Dillon, Richard. *The Legend of Grizzly Adams: California's Greatest Mountain Man.* New York: Coward, McCann and Geohegan, 1966.

DeHart, Don. *All About Bears.* Boulder: Johnson Publishing Company, 1971.

Dufresne, Frank. *No Room for Bears.* London: George Allen and Unwin, Ltd., 1966.
Frank Dufresne, onetime director of the Alaska Game Commission, wrote this very nice little plea for bear conservation.

East, Ben. *Bears.* New York: Outdoor Life Book Club/Crown, 1978. Not a book I admire, though I'm a little hard-pressed to say exactly why. It's generally pretty accurate, and it doesn't all that often degenerate into the sensationalism that characterizes too much outdoor writing, but the thinking is sometimes a little casual, and the writing style gets on my nerves. George Laycock's book *The Wild Bears* is more recent and therefore more up to date, and is also more carefully written and more comprehensive.

Eddy, J.W. *Hunting the Alaska Brown Bear, the Story of a Sportsman's Adventure in an Unknown Valley after the Largest Carnivorous Animal in the World.* New York: G.P. Putnam's Sons, 1930.

Erickson, Albert, John Nellor, and George Petrides. *The Black Bear in Michigan.* Ann Arbor: Michigan State University Agricultural Experiment Station, Research Bulleton 4, 1964. An early state study, including research findings on breeding biology, movements, population structure, and hunting harvest.

Fish, Chet, ed. *The Outdoor Life Bear Book.* Harrisburg: Outdoor Life Books/Stackpole Books, 1983.
For enthusiasts of the famous *Outdoor Life* cover stories about bear hunting, maulings, and other adventures, here is the perfect book—a large collection of tales, gathered by a veteran editor of outdoor books.

Flowers, Ralph. *The Education of a Bear Hunter.* New York: Winchester Press, 1974.
Flowers was a government hunter in the Pacific Northwest, and killed many black bears as part of programs to protect commercial forests from bear depredations.

Ford, Barbara. *The Black Bear: The Spirit of the Wilderness.* New York: Houghton Mifflin, 1981.

Graham, Ada and Frank. *Bears in the Wild.* New York: Delacorte Press, 1981.

Grinnell, George Bird, ed. *Hunting At High Altitudes.* New York: Harper & Brothers, 1913.
I include this for its first 294 pages, devoted to the life and memoirs of William Pickett, with detailed commentary in notes by George Bird Grinnell.

Hanna, Warren. *The Grizzlies of Glacier.* Missoula: Mountain Press, 1978.
Mostly a collection of mauling and attack stories, redeemed in part by an appended reprint of one of Clifford Martinka's research reports on grizzly bears in Glacier National Park.

Haynes, Bessie, and Edgar Haynes. *The Grizzly Bear: Portraits from Life.* Norman: University of Oklahoma Press, 1966.
This is still the best collection of bear literature under one cover, though there

are many others. Haynes and Haynes give a sampling of the most interesting, exciting, and colorful of writings by hunters, naturalists, and explorers.

Herrero, Stephen, ed. *Bears—Their Biology and Management.* Morges, Switzerland: International Union for the Conservation of Nature, 1972.

_____. *Bear Attacks, Their Causes and Avoidance.* New York: Nick Lyons Books/Winchester Press, 1985.

One of the best, most generally useful of bear books published since Andy Russell's *Grizzly Country.* Herrero has studied bear-human encounters for many years, and provides not only evaluation of such encounters, but also relation of bear attacks to bear environment and human behavior, excellent surveys of bear habitat, philosophical meditations on bear behavior and bear management, and much more. I could not recommend this too highly. It is all too rare that the scientific authorities find the time and skill needed to relate their findings to the general public.

Hibben, Frank. *Hunting American Bears.* Philadelphia: J.B. Lippincott Company, 1950.

Hinshaw, Dorothy. *Bears of the World.* New York: Holiday House, 1980.

Hittell, Theodore. *The Adventures of James Capen Adams, Mountaineer and Grizzly Bear Hunter of California.* San Francisco: Towne and Bacon, 1860.

Hoshino, Michio, *Grizzly.* San Francisco: Chronicle Books, 1987.

Holzworth, John. *The Wild Grizzlies of Alaska.* New York: G.P. Putnam's Sons, 1930.

A generously proportioned book, mostly about the grizzly bears of Admiralty Island, and the extraordinary Alan Hasselborg, who lived with them. There is material on other wildlife, but the bear stories and photographs make this a classic (a neglected one) of bear literature.

Householder, Bob. *The Grizzly Bear in Arizona.* Phoenix: the author, 1966.

A small but important booklet on early encounters with a now-extinct grizzly bear population.

Hubbard, W.P., and Seale Harris. *Notorious Grizzly Bears.* Chicago: The Swallow Press, 1960.

Stories of famous stock killers and "renegades" and how they were hunted. Not accurate ("...the average weight of adult grizzlies in our western states would be about eight hundred and fifty pounds," says Mr. Hubbard), but it was written before modern bear research, so we should be a little tolerant, I suppose.

Jonkel, Charles, and Ian McTaggart Cowan. *The Black Bear in the Spruce-Fir Forest.* Washington: The Wildlife Society, Wildlife Monograph 27, 1971.

Charles Jonkel is now one of the leading figures in bear science, having studied grizzly, black, and polar bears over the years. This, one of his early publications, is about black bears in northern Montana.

Kaniut, Larry. *Alaska Bear Tales.* Anchorage: Alaska Northwest Publishing Company, 1983.

A book along the lines of Hubbard and Seale, above, but more reliably gathered. This is not a book for the faint of heart and stomach; the accounts of maulings are specific and often detailed. But it is a reasonably thorough collection of such accounts.

Kelley, Allen. *Bears I Have Met—and Others.* Philadelphia: Drexel Biddle, 1904.
Not regarded as especially reliable, this volume was written by a newspaper reporter who admitted he added some fanciful touches to his stories, and also said that Joaquin Miller's book was pretty shoddily produced as well.

Krott, Peter. *Bears in the Family.* New York: Dutton, 1964.

Kurten, Bjorn. *The Cave Bear Story: Life and Death of a Vanished Animal.* New York: Columbia University Press, 1976.
Kurten, who is also a fine novelist, is one of the world's foremost scientific writers on prehistoric animals. This is a uniformly fascinating book that relates prehistoric bears to modern ones in intriguing ways.

Larsen, Thor. *The World of the Polar Bear.* New York: Hamlyn, 1978.

Laycock, George. *The Wild Bears.* Harrisburg: Outdoor Life Book Club/ Stackpole Books, 1986.
Probably the best modern, popularly-written book that introduces the wild bears of North America. Laycock is a veteran nature and outdoor writer, and he covers a lot of territory: biology, lore, history, management. There are many well-printed color and black and white illustrations, including some excellent historical paintings and superb photographs.

Leslie, Robert Franklin. *The Bears and I: Raising Three Cubs in the North Woods.* New York: E.P. Dutton, 1968.
An entertaining tale of a man's adoption of three black bear cubs in the British Columbia wilderness.

Martin, Martha. *Home on the Bear's Domain.* New York: MacMillan and Company, 1954.

Martinka, Clifford, and Katherine L. McArthur. *Bears—Their Biology and Management.* Washington: U.S. Government Printing Office and the Bear Biology Association, 1980.

Matson, J.R. *The Adaptable Black Bear.* Philadelphia: Dorrance and Company, 1967.

McCracken, Harold. *The Beast that Walks Like Man: The Story of the Grizzly Bear.* Garden City: Hanover House, 1955. McCracken wrote a lot about bears, and this is his best book. Prior to the publication of Andy Russell's *Grizzly Country*, this was probably the best all-around book on the grizzly bear in North America.

_____. *The Biggest Bear on Earth.* Philadelphia: Stokes, 1943.

_____. *Alaska Bear Trails.* Garden City: Doubleday, Doran and Company, 1931.

McNamee, Thomas. *The Grizzly Bear.* New York: Alfred Knopf, 1984.
Thomas McNamee has written one of the best modern bear books, a careful examination of the management, biology, and political issues of grizzly bears

in the Lower Forty-Eight states. There are several populations, including the famous ones in Yellowstone and Glacier National Parks and less-well-known ones, mostly in Montana.

McGee, Senator Dale. *Senate Hearing Before the Committee on Appropriations, Proposed Critical Habitat Area for Grizzly Bears.* Washington: U.S. Government Printing Office, 1977.

Meslow, E. Charles, ed. *Bears—Their Biology and Management.* West Glacier: International Association for Bear Research and Management, 1983.

Meyer, Jerry. *Bear Hunting.* Harrisburg: Stackpole Books, 1983.
An introduction to all parts of the sport, including bow hunting and black powder.

Miller, Joaquin. *True Bear Stories.* Chicago: Rand, McNally & Company, 1900.
Though it has a complimentary foreword by that eminent scientist David Starr Jordan, the opinions in this book would give most bear students the willies.

Mills, Enos. *The Grizzly, Our Greatest Wild Animal.* Boston: Houghton Mifflin Company, 1919.
Mills was a popular and influential Colorado nature writer, author of numerous books on the outdoors and a moving force in the creation of Rocky Mountain National Park. I know one bear biologist who found this book so unbelievable that he couldn't even finish it. There are problems, but it's still exciting, with some great stories of Mills's experiences with grizzly bears.

Milne, A.A. *Winnie-the-Pooh.* New York: E.P. Dutton, 1926.

Morey, Walt. *Gentle Ben.* New York: E.P. Dutton, 1965.

Morrison, Ellen Earnhardt. *Guardian of the Forest, A History of the Smokey Bear Program.* New York: Vantage Press, 1976.
Smokey ranks with Winnie, Teddy, and Yogi among the bear-people created by modern culture. This is a nice history of the development of his image.

Mundy, K.R.D., and D.R. Flook. *Background for Managing Grizzly Bears in the National Parks of Canada.* Ottawa: Canadian Wildlife Service Report Series, Number 22, 1973.

Murie, Adolph. *The Grizzlies of Mount McKinley.* Washington: United States Department of the Interior, National Park Service Scientific Monograph Series 14, 1981.
Published posthumously, this is the kind of old-fashioned natural history that is too seldom written these days. Murie reports in this book on his many years of personal observations of bears in Alaska. I accept the enormous value of modern scientific techniques—radiotracking, computer population modeling, and all of those wonderful things—but I find this kind of informal narrative very satisfying and consistently educational.

Nero, Robert. *The Great White Bears.* Winnipeg: Winnipeg Department of Mines, Resources and Environmental Management, 1971.

Olsen, Jack. *Night of the Grizzlies.* New York: G.P. Putnam's Sons, 1969.
The story of the famous pair of bear-caused mortalities in Glacier National Park in 1967.

Ormond, Claude. *Bear!* Harrisburg: Stackpole Books, 1961.
A thorough hunting manual for black, brown, grizzly, and polar bears.

Palmer, J. Frederick. *Kodiak Bear Hunt.* New York: Doubleday, 1958.

Pearson, Albert. *The Northern Interior Grizzly Bear, Ursus Arctos L.* Ottowa: Canadian Wildlife Service Report Series Number 34, 1975.
Pearson's report covers his research into the ecology of a southwestern Yukon Territory population of bears in the years 1963–1972, a study almost as long and productive as the more famous Craighead study.

Pelton, Michael, Jack Lentfer, and G. Edgar Folk, eds. *Bears—Their Biology and Management.* Morges, Switzerland: International Union for the Conservation of Nature and Natural Resources, 1976.

Perry, R. *The World of the Polar Bear.* Seattle: University of Washington Press, 1966.

——. *Bears.* London: Arthur Barker, 1970.

Poelker, Richard, and Harry Hartwell. *Black Bear of Washington: Its Biology, Natural History and Relationship to Forest Regeneration.* Olympia: Washington State Game Department Biological Bulletin Number 14, 1973.
Black bears have at times done considerable damage in commercial forests in Washington state. This report was the result of a study initiated in good part to determine what could be done about the damage. It contains much information, necessarily, on bear ecology and hunting harvest.

Prodgers, Jeanette. *The Only Good Bear is a Dead Bear.* Helena: Falcon Press, 1986.
A collection of early bear-related accounts suggesting the extent to which Americans have thought little of bears.

Rennicke, Jeff. *Bears of Alaska in Life & Legend.* Boulder: Roberts Rinehart in cooperation with the Alaska Natural History Association, 1987.
A handsomely produced little book that introduces the lore and natural history of Alaska's various bears.

Richardson, A.G. *King of the Grizzlies.* Chicago: Rand McNally, 1925.
A juvenile book.

Roosevelt, Theodore. *American Bears: Selections from the Writings of Theodore Roosevelt.* ed. Paul Schullery. Boulder: Colorado Associated University Press and the Outdoor Life Book Club, 1983.

Russell, Andy. *Grizzly Country.* New York: Alfred Knopf, 1967.
If there is a favorite of all grizzly-bear books, I suppose this is it. Russell, a longtime guide-turned-photographer and writer, produced one of the classics, a well-written and stirring personal account of a life spent in bear country.

Samson, Jack. *The Bear Book.* Clinton: Amwell Press/National Sporting Fraternity, 1979.
Another collection of hunting stories by various writers.

Schaller, George, Hu Jinchu, Pan Wenshi, and Zhu Jing. *The Giant Pandas of Wolong.* Chicago: University of Chicago Press, 1985.

The panda is, these days, not considered a true bear, but I thought I ought to include one title with a good bibliography for those wanting to read more about the "panda bear." This is the best, most current information on the panda, by a distinguished international team of scientists who conducted panda studies in the early 1980s in China.

Schneider, Bill. *Where the Grizzly Walks.* Missoula: Mountain Press Publishing Company, 1977.

A book that reviews the status of the grizzly bear in the Lower Forty-Eight; largely replaced by Thomas McNamee's book, which is much more thorough.

Schoonmaker, W.J. *The World of the Grizzly Bear.* Philadelphia: J.B. Lippincott Company, 1968.

Schullery, Paul. *The Bears of Yellowstone.* Yellowstone Park: The Yellowstone Library and Museum Association, 1980, revised edition; Boulder: Roberts Rinehart, 1986.

Seton, Ernest Thompson. *The Biography of a Grizzly.* New York: Grosset & Dunlap, 1900.

————. *Monarch the Big Bear of Tallac.* New York: Charles Scribner's Sons, 1904.

Shepard, Paul, and Barry Sanders. *The Sacred Paw: The Bear in Nature, Myth, and Literature.* New York: Viking, 1985.

Shoemaker, Henry. *The Black Bear of Pennsylvania.* Altoona: Times Tribune Company, 1921.

Early in the 1900s, Henry Shoemaker was an energetic collector of information on many aspects of early-Pennsylvania history. He published dozens of small books on various subjects, many on wildlife, and this is his gathering of stories (many from old newspapers) about the bears and bear hunters of Pennsylvania.

Skinner, Milton P. *Bears in the Yellowstone.* Chicago: A.C. McClurg & Company, 1925.

Spencer, Howard, Jr. *The Black Bear and Its Status in Maine.* Augusta: State of Maine Department of Inland Fisheries and Game, 1961.

Stehsel, Donald L. *Hunting the California Black Bear.* Arcadia: the author, 1965.

Stevens, Montague. *Meet Mr. Grizzly: A Saga on the Passing of the Grizzly.* Albuquerque: University of New Mexico Press, 1943.

Like McCracken's *The Beast that Walks Like Man,* this is a small milestone of grizzly-bear literature, and, like that book and Russell's, and Wright's, it is mostly a personal view.

Storer, Tracy, and Lloyd Tevis. *California Grizzly.* Berkeley: University of California Press, 1955.

From the viewpoint of the historian, as well as from the viewpoint of the naturalist, this is one of the classics. It is the reconstruction, through the use of a vast array of incidental historical evidence, of the ecology and world of the now-extinct California grizzly bear. Exhaustively documented, it is nevertheless hospitable in tone and consistently entertaining. It is available in paperback from the University of Nebraska Press.

Tracy, Diane, Frederick Dean, Candy Anderson, and Teresa Jordan. *Brown Bear Bibliography*. Fairbanks: Alaska Cooperative Park Studies Unit, 1982.

Underwood, William Lyman. *Wild Brother, Strangest of True Stories from the North Woods*. Boston: Atlantic Monthly Press, 1921.
This is a remarkable little story. William Underwood found, early in this century, a rural Maine family that had adopted a black bear cub. The mother was nursing the cub along with her human baby (Underwood includes a photograph of the nursing in the book), and the baby bear was a happy part of the family. Underwood took to the cub and raised it.

Utley, Francis Lee, Lynn Z. Bloom, and Arthur F. Kinney, eds. *Bear, Man, and God: Eight Approaches to William Faulkner's "The Bear"*. New York: Random House, 1964.
This volume contains some excellent examples of early bear stories, including the text of Faulkner's story and the text of Thorpe's "Big Bear of Arkansas," the story mentioned in Chapter One as a prototype of later American bear stories.

Van Wormer, Joe. *The World of the Black Bear*. Philadelphia: J.B. Lippincott Company, 1966.
Joe Van Wormer did a fine job in gathering what was known of black bears more than twenty years ago and combining it with his many outstanding black and white photographs. Still a good introductory book.

Wentworth, Jim. *The Kodiak Bear*. Harrisburg: Stackpole Books, 1958.

Willey, Charles. *The Vermont Black Bear*. Montpelier: Vermont Fish and Game Department, 1978.
The results of a ten-year study of Vermont's hunter harvest of black bears.

Wright, William H. *The Grizzly Bear: The Narrative of a Hunter-Naturalist*. New York: Charles Scribner's Sons, 1909.

———. *Ben, the Black Bear*. New York: Charles Scribner's Sons, 1910.

Young, F. M., and Coralie Buyers. *Man Meets Grizzly, Encounters in the Wild from Lewis and Clark to Modern Times*. Boston: Houghton Mifflin Company, 1980.

Young, Ralph. *Grizzlies Don't Come Easy*. Tulsa: Winchester Press, 1981.

Index